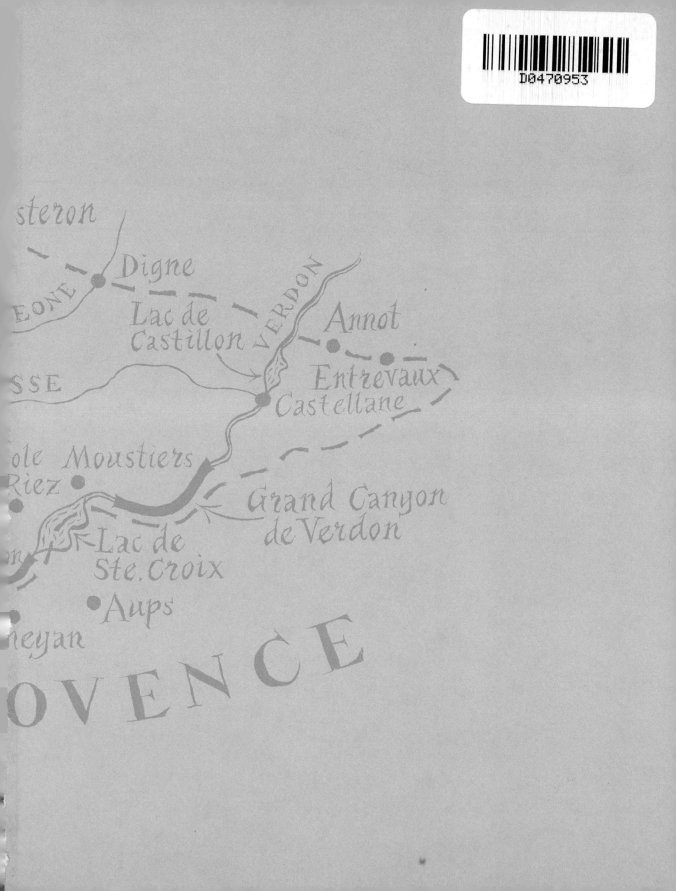

D0470953

The Food and Flavors of Haute Provence

The Food and Flavors of Haute Provence

BY GEORGEANNE BRENNAN

FOREWORD BY PATRICIA WELLS

Illustrations by Jeffrey Fisher

CHRONICLE BOOKS
SAN FRANCISCO

Text copyright © 1997 by Georgeanne Brennan.
Foreword copyright © 1997 by Patricia Wells.
Illustrations copyright © 1997 by Jeffrey Fisher.
All rights reserved. No part of this book may be reproduced
in any form without written permission from the publisher.

Library of Congress Cataloging-in-Publication Data:
Brennan, Georgeanne, 1943–
      The food and flavors of Haute Provence/by Georgeanne Brennan;
      illustrations by Jeffrey Fisher.
            p. cm.
      Includes bibliographical references (p.) and index.
      ISBN 0-8118-1235-9
      1. Cookery, French. 2. Cookery—France—Alpes de Haute-Provence. 3. Menus.
        ·4. Alpes de Haute-Provence (France)—Social life and customs.
      TX719.B749 1997
      641.5944'95—dc21
                                                    97-11389
                                                    CIP

Printed in the United States of America.
Book and cover design by Gretchen Scoble.

Distributed in Canada by Raincoast Books
8680 Cambie Street
Vancouver, British Columbia V6P 6M9

10 9 8 7 6 5 4 3 2 1

Chronicle Books
85 Second Street
San Francisco, California 94105

Web Site: www.chronbooks.com

For Ethel and Oliver, with love

ACKNOWLEDGMENTS

I wish first to thank Donald Brennan, with whom I began this odyssey and who is so much a part of it. I wish to thank my friends, old and new, throughout Haute Provence, who have taught me and shared so much with me and who have enriched my and my family's lives immeasurably: Georgina and Denys Fine, Marie and Marcel Palazoli, Adèle and Pascal Degremont, Joanne Kaufman, M. and Mme. Lamy, Mlle. Lamy, M. Ricci, M. and Mme. Caplan, Anne and Jacques Deregnaucourt, M. Blanc, M. de Geeter, Mark and Nina Haag, M. and Mme. Cruvelier, M. and Mme. Chabot, M. Richi, Luc and Nelly Chaffard, and all the myriad villagers who over the years have taken time to answer my questions and to tell me tales of life in Haute Provence.

A special thank you to Sharon Silva for her careful and thoughtful editing, to Gretchen Scoble for her design, and to Jeffrey Fisher for his evocative illustrations.

I also want to thank Charlotte Kimball, in California, for her enthusiastic assistance with research and recipe testing and for her support of this project, and also Tom Olson and his family. Thank you to my agent, Susan Lesher, my editors, Bill LeBlond and Leslie Jonath, who believed in this book from the very beginning, and to their wonderful assistant Sarah Putman. Thank you to my children, Ethel, Oliver, Tom, and Dan, and to my dear husband, who first listened to my stories of the food and people and life of Haute Provence, then read and reread every word of the book.

Contents

Spring

Summer

MENU 1
Tart of Leeks and Dried Morels
Thyme-Stuffed Roast Chicken
Fresh Tomato Platter
Green Bean and Potato Ragout
Canteloupe Halves Filled with Vin de Noix

MENU 2
Fennel-Flavored Cream of Summer Squash Soup
Cherry Tomato Pasta with Fresh Goat Cheese
Green Salad
Peach and Nectarine Gratin

MENU 3
Tapenade, *Roasted Red Peppers, and Goat Cheese Sandwiches*
Pork Medallions and Green Olive Sauté
Squash Blossom Rice
Tomatoes Provençale
Melon Sorbet

MENU 4
Melon Slices Wrapped with Jambon Cru
Polenta Terrine with Roasted Garlic and Black Olive Sauce
Green Beans in Vinaigrette
Peach Beignets

Fall

MENU 1

Green Olive and Almond Tapenade
Escarole and Chestnut Salad with Lardons
Pumpkin-Filled Ravioli with Walnut Sauce
Tarte Tatin *of Brandied Pears*

MENU 2

Poor Man's Foie Gras
Baked Pasta with Chanterelles
Braised Greens and Black Olives
Warm Fig and Goat Cheese Dessert

MENU 3

Sanguins *Grilled with Garlic and Parsley*
Honey-and-Lavender-Glazed Chicken
Roasted New Potatoes with Rosemary and Sage
Crêpe Packets of Nuts and Dried Fruits with Rum

MENU 4

Pear, Grape, and Dried Goat Cheese Salad
Trout with Toasted Almonds
Gratin of Forest Mushrooms
Vanilla Ice Cream with Brandied Cherries

Winter

Menu 1

Warm Potato and Truffle Salad

Beef Daube with Dried Cèpes

Boiled Potatoes with Parsley and Butter

Green Salad

Rosemary-Orange Sorbet

Menu 2

Fennel, Black Pepper, and Dried Goat Cheese Salad with Lemon Vinaigrette

Chicken Ragout with Black Olives

Pumpkin Gratin

Dried-Apricot and Fresh-Apple Pastry

Menu 3

Belgian Endive and Mâche Salad

Snails Provençale

Roast Pork Loin with Red Wine Glaze

Apple-Quince Cakes

Fresh Apple Compote

Menu 4

Cabbage Salad with Jambon Cru

Salt Cod and Potato Terrine

Green Salad

Pain Perdu *with Honey Crust*

Foreword

WITH A VOICE OF WISDOM and experience, Georgeanne Brennan brings us into her own private world of Provence, a world that is at once romantic, rustic, earthy, and as the French like to say, *"sans façon,"* without fanfare or ceremony.

Her private world is not the Provence of sunny beaches or ultra-trendy perched villages but a dwindling universe of skillful, worldly-wise French farmers, peasants, shepherds, beekeepers, poachers, cheese makers, hunters, housewives, and retirees who live according to the rhythm of the seasons as they and their ancestors have for centuries.

This is the dry and mountainous Provence beyond the Mediterranean, a sweet land scented with lavender and its vibrant rolling hills of purple, a world dotted with gnarled olive trees, carpeted with fields of fragrant wild thyme, and forested with sturdy stands of oak and of pine. Sometimes called "lost" or "hidden" Provence, this remote and largely agricultural land is still unspoiled by the glitz and glamour of neighboring Cannes and Nice.

Even the names of the villages that dot the land have a lilting, joyous, solid sound—Manosque, Sisteron, Sault, Moustiers, Digne, and Forcalquier. Some of them still look as though they could have been plucked from the pages of a fairy tale: fountains, undulating wrought-iron balconies, sky-blue-shuttered shops, and a church tower with fantastical decorative campaniles set the scene. Tiny open-air markets are crammed into village squares where, under the shade of aging chestnut trees, farm wives sell creamy disks of alabaster goat cheese crowned with a sprinkling of fresh *sarriette,* or summer savory.

Roadside stands sell all manner of lavender treats, from sachets to honey produced by bees that transform the fragrant nectar from the herb's purple blossoms. Bread shops lure us in with intricate local ladder breads known as *fougasse,* looking much like spider web's, tasting remarkably like a crispy baguette. Elswhere in the region, *fougasse* might resemble a pizza with holes, topped with capers and anchovies, or appear as a dessert, filled with almonds, orange-flower water, and grains of fennel. In fact, markets might even be rated by the number of "pizza trucks" parked under the giant, shade-providing plane trees. I once counted six parked bumper to bumper along Forcalquier's Place du Bourguet.

Throughout the seasons, Haute Provence provides a kaleidoscope of color and fragrance, beginning with the wildflowers in early spring and deep purple irises in May. Honey-scented golden Scotch broom paint the hillsides a vibrant ochre in June, and come July all senses are invaded with the power of the brilliant, shocking blue fields of lavender. By late October, the vineyards have given their all and put on a whimsical exhibition of warming oranges and gold as leaves fall from gnarled black trunks.

In Haute Provence, one learns to appreciate the local wines (the pleasantly acidic whites and the light and fruity red *vin de pays)* and to gather sometimes useful facts (in the winter months, the blue-skied region welcomes 1,037 hours of sunshine, while Paris gets by with a meager 539!).

But most of all, what is striking about the people of this region is their easy acceptance of daily life, their ability to derive pleasure from the simplest acts. One morning I studied a slender young woman as she chose a melon at the Forcalquier market. Slowly, she lifted melon after melon to her nostrils, inhaling, concentrating on selecting the sweet, ripest, most perfect of fruit.

Time was not the question, excellence was. Even before that melon made it home from the market, the shopper had already derived pleasure from a simple fresh fruit.

As Georgeanne Brennan points out, nothing in this dry but mystical land goes to waste: That mildly peppery, slightly crunchy herb that grows wild everywhere—we call it purslane, they call it *pourpier*—is there to add new dimension to simple mixed salads. And zucchini blossoms, which in other worlds might wither on the vine, are elevated to luxury status as they are deep-fried and stuffed, layered in gratins, or cut into chiffonade and tossed in a salad.

Georgeanne has packed *The Food and Flavors of Haute Provence* with an abundance of authentic recipes, but more than that, she brings us out into the woods to gather mushrooms, to the edge of the rolling fields of lavender where the bees make their honey, out to the edge of the road to gather tiny snails known as *petits gris*. We revel in the thought of her American-born children making their own snail-hunting baskets or receiving a gift of a fishing pole.

Almost like a modern-day archeologist, she chronicles a way of life that is slowly being lost to the modern age. And her picture of modern life in the Haute Provence is both complete and unfiltered, unglossed. As a longtime resident of this rustic region north of Nice, Georgeanne lives the life that many only dream of. Raising goats, making her own fresh goat's milk cheese, adding to the family a sow named Lucretia. By her side, we watch Georgeanne tentatively sauté her first blood sausage (from a freshly killed goat, no less), or to try (unsuccessfully) to capture the elusive black truffle by eyeing the tiny flies that swarm above the fragrant mushroom. Wandering in and out of farmers' houses, farmers' fields, and farmers' kitchens, she shares with us her every experience.

And, of course, this author of the modern classic *Potager* brings us back to her first love, the vegetable garden. Taking us by the hand, through the seasons, she creates a fresh and vibrant green *barigoule* of artichokes and plump, nutty fava beans flecked with thyme, forming fresh ravioli stuffed with garlic and spinach, or inventive gratins of summer squash, new potatoes, and sweet bell peppers.

France

Nyons

JABRON Noyers · Sisteron

Montagne
de Lure

DURANCE

Digne

BLEONE

VERDON

Lac de
Castillon

Annot

Sault Redortiers

ASSE

Entrevaux
Castellane

Plateau
d'Albion

Banon

Forcalquier

Plateau
de Valensole · Moustiers

Manosque

Riez

Grand Canyon
de Verdon

Valensole
Esparron
Quinson

Lac de
Ste. Croix

Gorges
de Verdon

Aups

Montmeyan

HAUTE PROVENCE

Nice

Marseille
Toulon

Mer Méditerranée

locally produced lavender honey, fresh goat cheese, or wild mushrooms or herbs. Even in the few larger cities of Sisteron, Digne, and Manosque, regional products are proudly displayed: olives and olive oil, conserves made from quinces and figs, pâtés and sausages of wild game, honey nougat, locally grown vegetables and fruits.

Geographically, Haute Provence may be said to encompass areas of four different departments, the northernmost reaches of the Var, the lower regions of the Alpes-de-Haute-Provence, where the climate allows the cultivation of olives, a finger of the Vaucluse, and an easterly bit of the Drôme. Upon asking for a precise delineation of the region, replies will be opinionated and authoritative—and different. Some will not allow for the inclusion of any bit of the Var, others exclude the Drôme or the Vaucluse. Some say that properly it is only the *départment* of Alpes-de-Haute-Provence, minus its alpine regions, others that it begins with the Gorges du Verdon, or where the rosemary ceases to bloom wild. Haute Provence is as much a point of view, a place defined by its spirit and attitude, by a shared view of the regional culture and landscape, as it is a specific entity. To ask someone for a definition is like asking for a true recipe for beef daube. There are dozens of versions of the truth, with certain elements agreed upon.

Haute Provence is the land of lavender and wild herbs. Its altitude is higher than that of the bordering valley of the Rhône River and of those valleys and rolling hills that lie behind the Mediterranean, and its climate is harsher, but far milder than that of the bordering Alps, where butter, not olive oil, flavors the food. The lower Durance and Verdon rivers cut through Haute Provence. The valley of the Durance is rich, akin to the lush lands that benefit from the largesse of the Rhône River, but on either side of the valley rise the lavender-covered plateaus that have become a symbol for the region. The Verdon cuts through a rocky, forbidding canyon so deep and so long that it is referred to as the Grand Canyon of Europe, and from there it flows into a lake and more gorges to join the Durance, and with it, eventually, the Rhône.

Sisteron sits nearly top and center in Haute Provence, astride a narrow gorge of the Durance River, and is not surprisingly called the Gateway to

Provence (or to the Alps, depending upon which direction one is headed). Sisteron lies slightly northeast of Aix-en-Provence, about an hour-and-a-half drive from there, and northwest of Nice, a drive of two and a half hours. Grenoble, to the north, is easily reached by car in less than an hour. From Sisteron one can head west through the Valley of Jabron and cross the passes of the Lure Mountains to arrive on the windswept reaches of the Plateau d'Albion, now planted to lavender, and the hills of Contadour and Redortières, so vividly depicted in the novels of Jean Giono, who wrote of the life and the places of Haute Provence until his death in 1962. Or one can keep heading west, through the mountains and small valleys to reach the farthest outpost of Haute Provence, Nyons, an olive capital (and some would not include it at all, saying that it draws its influence from the north, from the Alps and from Lyons, not from the south).

Turn southeast from Sisteron to reach Digne-les-Bains and continue south from there to cross the lavender-studded Plateau de Valensole, dropping down from it to the ancient Roman town of Riez, situated at its base. From Riez, a climb to the opposite side of the plateau, traversing its eastern edge, will bring one, after a brief descent, to Quinson on the border of the *département* of the Alpes-de-Haute-Provence, only twelve miles from Montmeyan, just over the border in the Var. Or turn northeast from Riez, and make the short climb to reach Moustiers-Ste.-Marie, and only a mile or two more to reach the shore of Le Lac de Ste.-Croix, the largest manmade lake in Europe, stretching for nearly twenty miles, created by the damming of the Verdon River. From Moustiers, heading south, lies Aups, in the Var, only a scant fifteen miles distant. But leave heading east, and instead take either the right or the left *corniche* of the Grand Canyon du Verdon, to drive at dizzying heights above the thin silver thread of the river, deep in the gorge below, on narrow roads carved into the rock, to reach the easternmost borders of Haute Provence, through Castellane and Annot to Entrevaux on the edge of the *département* of the Alpes-Maritimes. From there, the land drops rapidly away to the south, to Nice, only eighty-five miles away. Once in Nice, though, it seems like Haute Provence is centuries away.

In 1970, fleeing from the turmoil of life in the United States during the Vietnam era, my husband and I bought a house in Haute Provence, returning us to a part of the world we loved and where we felt we could make a quiet, sensible life for ourselves and our two-year-old daughter. We had envisioned a small but cozy farmhouse in the lush countryside around Aix-en-Provence, where we had friends and where I had briefly gone to school. The prices, although not expensive by the standards of Southern California, where we had been living, were still far beyond our modest means, and a kindly real estate agent, recognizing the probable size of our nest egg, steered us an hour and a half northeast from his office in Peyrolles-en-Provence, along very narrow, twisting roads, to a farmhouse near Quinson.

The farther we drove from Peyrolles, the more empty and more wild the country became. Following the little map the agent had drawn for us, we turned up a dirt road and ventured back to what we thought would be the house he had marked with an *X* on the map. Knocking, and explaining why we were there, we were warmly welcomed by the farmer and his family. We were the first Americans since World War II to visit the remote area, and they thanked us effusively, as if we were emissaries for America's assistance during the war.

We followed the owner, M. Moret, to visit the farmhouse of his deceased mother-in-law, which he and his wife were selling for the equivalent of five thousand dollars. The wind was howling, the vines were bare, and the houses lining the streets of the tiny villages through which we passed were shuttered against the cold. No tall beautiful cypress trees here, or *allées* lined with elms and cafés full of stylish people, familiar sights in Aix and its environs. Abandoned for a number of years, the farmhouse had no plumbing, a huge crack down one of its outside stone walls, and patches of falling plaster inside, but it did have a well and prewar electricity, with a light bulb in every room. We bought it, with another couple, and moved there the following November. The adventure in shared living lasted only a few months, and we soon moved, first renting, then buying another place of similar vintage, though without electricity. My imagination and passion had been captured by the stark simplicity and beauty of the life and the land, where in a short time I had begun to feel profoundly at home.

We kept a herd of goats and made goat cheese that I sold in the markets, and we raised pigs. Our son was born the following year. It was a difficult life but intensely rewarding. I had the privilege to live in Haute Provence when life there was still dominated by the seasons, by undertaking the tasks necessary to fill the pantry and to earn a simple living. It was a time when few people had telephones or televisions, water came from deep wells, and the outlying farms were on the route of traveling bakers, fishmongers, butchers, and grocers. Driving to Nice or Marseille on a regular basis—the only places where supermarkets existed—was unthinkable to the farmers and artisans, who, along with the schoolteacher, the odd artist or two, and a few owners of great estates, made up most of the population.

My life was like that of my neighbors. Of necessity, the majority of our food was determined by what could be grown, gathered, raised, and hunted within the region, supplemented by pasta, rice, polenta, and bread. Honey came from the beehives kept in the lavender fields that covered the nearby Plateau de Valensole. Cheese was made from the milk of local goats, like ours, and from the sheep that grazed on hillsides covered with wild thyme, rosemary, and juniper. Olives and olive oil, wine, seasonal vegetables from the *potager,* the kitchen garden, and fruits from small orchards or single trees were the daily foods, augmented by occasional trout from the small streams, and wild hare, boars, pheasants, birds, mushrooms, and truffles from the forest. From the flocks that overwintered in the area came an occasional lamb or mutton, and every family raised a baby pig to slaughter size to provision the household with pâté, *jambon cru,* and a host of other delectable charcuterie.

Rituals, small and large, accompanied the growing, gathering, and preparing of food. In late October, the first successful collecting of meaty *sanguin* mushrooms meant that dinner's first course would be whole mushroom caps sprinkled with olive oil and garlic, then grilled in the fireplace or over an outdoor *braise*. Spring's earliest fava beans were sure to be set out raw along with a little dish of salt to accompany an aperitif of licorice-flavored pastis. On the day the pig was slaughtered, a traditional midday meal of *boudin noir*—black sausage made with the fresh blood, onions, garlic, and herbs—chunky cooked apples, and mashed potatoes was served to everyone who had participated in the morning's activities. Today it remains one of my favorite meals, not just for the taste, but because it carrries me back to those cold, mist-laden mornings of camaraderie when the itinerant butcher came, first to drink a glass of eau-de-vie and talk over the local gossip and weather, then to sharpen his knives and test to see if the scalding water in the big oil drum was adequately hot.

Although freezers, swimming pools, and satellite televisions are as common in the area now as well-drawn water and two-burner stoves used to be, the village and its surrounding countryside, like much of Haute Provence, maintain their distinct character. Regional holidays and occasions continue to be celebrated in traditional ways, and the game of *boules* has yet to be usurped by golf, although a golf course has been proposed where a sheep farm once stood. At the miniscule *épicerie,* or grocery store, one can buy pots of locally made lavender honey, creamy country goat cheeses topped with sprigs of wild winter savory like the ones I used to make, and, if ordered in advance, liters of the local unfiltered olive oil, deep green and so rich that the particles solidify when the bottle is left in a cool place.

Certainly the heavy food that fueled a day's labor in the fields is no longer typical, but the ingredients remain indelibly a part of the food and flavor of Haute Provence. Now the fare is different, lighter, and more quickly prepared than it was even thirty years ago and certainly half a century ago.

In 1973, after our son was born, we returned to make our life in California, but we kept our little piece of Haute Provence, and over the years spent summers there, and later other seasons as well. Initially it was difficult to return to the United States, to be without so many of the flavors and rituals that I had come to love, that had represented a certain connection with the land and with the life around me. We planted a *potager* and an herb garden in our suburban front yard, bought pigs from outlying farms, and made our own pâté and sausages, and even once or twice tracked down goat's milk to make cheese. Now I can buy several varieties of goat cheese at the local supermarket in my small town, and although I still have a *potager* and an herb garden, and fruit, nut, and olive trees, I, like many people in the United States today, can go to a nearby farmers' market and buy local seasonal fruits, vegetables, and other regional products. The custom of preparing simple foods in simple ways with fresh local ingredients is as applicable today in the United States as it is ingrained in Haute Provence.

In telling the stories of the people and places of Haute Provence in these pages, I have kept to the truth as I experienced it, but I have changed the names of people to protect their privacy. The recipes themselves are a combination of traditional ones, told to me by friends and neighbors in their kitchens where I have sat, listening, or more often, working alongside them, cutting herbs, mincing onions, stuffing sausages, and rolling out dough. Other recipes are not traditional at all, but use the regional ingredients, those of the *terroir*—wild herbs and lavender; olives and olive oil; wild mushrooms and truffles; cheeses; vegetables; sheep, goats, and pigs; wild game and fish; nuts; and honey and fruits. The importance of these defining ingredients of the *terroir* of Haute Provence is reflected in how this book is organized. Each chapter includes instructions on making some of the basic elements of the Provençal pantry. Drying herbs and making *herbes de Provence;* curing, brining, and seasoning olives; seasoning fresh cheeses; drying and pickling mushrooms; desalting and poaching salt cod; and preserving fruits in alcohol are among them.

These ingredients overlap, however, so I have placed recipes in specific chapters according to the ingredient that seems to give each dish its particular character. Sometimes this is evident, such as the Salad of Wild Greens in the Wild Herbs and Lavender chapter, or Pâté Maison in the Sheep, Goats, and Pigs chapter. But Pork and Green Olive Sauté is not in the chapter that includes pigs. It is instead in the Olives and Olive Oil chapter, as it is the olives that make this dish distinctive.

In the Game and Fish chapter, I have restricted the fish to freshwater varieties—trout, pike, crayfish, carp—and salted fish—salt cod, anchovies—because for many years, Haute Provence was too isolated to have the fresh fish of the Mediterranean that so distinguishes much of Provençal cooking. Although fresh fish and seafood from the Mediterranean are now available at the local markets, I have chosen to focus on the region's indigenous ingredients.

I know that few readers will be able to make their own *boudin noir,* but I nevertheless included a recipe for it in the Sheep, Goats, and Pigs chapter, along with the other dishes typically made on slaughter day in Haute Provence. Each of them represents an extraordinary process, and if the ingredients are at hand, the recipes are both relatively easy and extremely satisfying to make.

There are only a few beef recipes. Cattle are not traditional in Haute Provence, so it has always been necessary to purchase beef from a butcher, and it is traditionally expensive. In some of the more distant rural areas, the butcher shop did not appear until the mid-1920s, and then was open for only one hour a day. Even today, many people in the more remote villages rely on the once-a-week visit of the traveling butcher, who stops at the central square on a designated day to sell beef, lamb, pork, innards, and charcuterie from a van. The cost of beef is still higher than that of the other meats, although a *grillade* of beef is always welcome, if not common, on the daily table.

The cooks of Haute Provence, especially those in the last century, have taken the ingredients of their *terroir* and created hundreds of flavorful dishes. Gratins, *fricots,* ragouts, daubes, soups, salads, pastas, tarts, and *grillades* form much of the repertoire of *la bonne cuisine du terroir,* many of them vegetable based, all of them varying with the seasons. A gratin of zucchini in summer, of pumpkins in fall, of potatoes and turnips in winter, or of asparagus in spring reflects the rhythm of the season, just as a *fricot,* sauté, ragout, daube, soup, or salad does. Pastas are combined with sweet fresh peas in spring, tomatoes in summer, fresh mushrooms in fall. Tarts, savory and sweet, are often made from puff pastry, which is sold fresh in even small grocery stores in France, and although the butter-rich dough is not typical of the traditions of Haute Provence, it is so pervasive in cooking today that I have included recipes calling for it, suggesting that we, like the French, buy it already prepared. The toppings for the tarts, like so much else, reflect the shifting seasons. The seasonings always include herbs, and more often than not garlic and onions, with *jambon cru,* lardons, and olives playing supporting roles. Olive oil perfumes the dishes, but butter is used, too, although more frequently today than in the past. Local wine is poured with a free hand in cooking.

Above all, I want the recipes in this book to convey the sense and the ease of cooking seasonally with local and regional ingredients that is the essence of life in Haute Provence.

Wild Herbs & Lavender

RECIPES

Salad of Wild Greens

Dandelion Salad with Lardons and Hard-Cooked Eggs

Chickpea Salad with Basil

Parsley Salad with Lemon Vinaigrette

Galettes of Wild Greens

Fennel-Flavored Cream of Summer Squash Soup

Wild Greens with Grilled Quail

Leg of Lamb in a Crust of Herbes de Provence

Grilled Butterflied Leg of Lamb with Herbes de Provence

Sage-Roasted Rabbit and Potatoes

Sage-Grilled Pork Chops

Pork Chops Grilled with Lavender, Thyme, and Rosemary

Thyme-Stuffed Roasted Chicken

Honey-and-Lavender-Glazed Chicken

Rosemary-Orange Sorbet

Figs Baked with Honey and Lavender

THE SCENT AND TASTE OF wild herbs, both woody and green, and of lavender permeate the countryside, kitchens, and pantries everywhere in Haute Provence and help define its identity. In the countryside, the scrubby *garrigue* is populated primarily with woody, resinous herbs such as rosemary, thyme, juniper, sage, and winter savory. When one walks through the brush, stepping and pressing through the thickets, the air fills with the scent of their powerful presence. Exploring the hillsides of the higher elevations will elicit the sharp scent of the wild marjoram that prospers there, and visits to spring-water courses reveal sweet bay laurel trees. The lavender fields of Haute Provence, in the lavender triangle that reaches from Castellane in the east, across the plateau of Valensole and Albion in the center, and west and north to the eastern edge of the Vaucluse and the Drôme, are legendary. When they are in full bloom in July, their deep fragrance carries on the wind for miles. Woody herbs all, these perennials find a comfortable home throughout the year in the poor, rocky soil of the region. Walking into a kitchen in Haute Provence you will be greeted by the mingled fragrances of the same herbs encountered on a walk across the hills, for they season everything on the tables here, from omelets to daubes.

Wild green herbs, used both for seasoning and as a main ingredient, are abundant in the countryside from fall through spring, the times of year when their water needs are met by rain and snowmelt. The most common of them are fennel, chicory, dandelion, purslane, parsley, borage, perennial lettuce, mâche, pimpernel, and mauve, plus garlic and leeks. Although the green herbs may lack the intense fragrance of the resinous woody herbs, they have pronounced flavors that are a signifying element in the food and culture of the region. During winter it is a regional imperative to prepare at least one *salade sauvage* of freshly gathered wild greens such as dandelion, purslane, roquette, parsley, bitter chicory, and the first shoots of the red poppies and of fennel. The wild leeks that appear in the vineyards and along roadsides in late winter and spring are pulled to make a savory omelet or to dress with a simple warm vinaigrette. Pieces of summer's flowering fennel stalks, *batons,* are stuffed into the cavity of fish, to infuse the flesh with a light licorice taste, and wild garlic greens are minced into soups and salads from late fall through winter.

These herbs are stronger and more intensely flavored when growing wild than they are when cultivated, and consequently, when cooking with wild herbs rather than cultivated herbs, lesser amounts are needed. The amounts of herbs used throughout this book refer to cultivated herbs grown at home or purchased.

The herbs of Haute Provence are as pervasive in the urban landscape as they are in the countryside, because cooking with them is as necessary to daily life as is a fresh baguette. Nearly every home or apartment has a pot or two of lavender growing, and perhaps also one of parsley or basil. Bay laurel, planted either in large terra-cotta containers or growing in the garden soil near the kitchen door, is kept clipped as a shrub. Sage and rosemary, if not potted, are planted on the border of the *potager* or, where space permits, are incorporated into ornamental plantings.

When it is not possible to have fresh herbs growing under one's care, they can be found at the open markets held once or twice a week, even in small villages. In the markets, vendors display foot-long pieces of fresh, bright green bay laurel, clutches of soft gray sage, sheafs of rosemary and thyme, all tied with twine. When in flower—winter for the rosemary and late spring for the sage and thyme—the bundled herbs look like gathered wildflowers.

Bunches of parsley and basil are also available at the markets, and one can also purchase small seedlings to take home and plant. These transplants are sold singly, each one uprooted and wrapped in newspaper for the buyer.

Basil is one of the common green herbs of the region, but it doesn't occur in the wild because it is sensitive to frost. Instead, each year it is seeded or transplanted into gardens or pots. From early summer until the first frost, the leaves are snipped as needed. Chervil, another cultivated green herb, is often found in mixed plantings of salad greens. In his little greenhouse every winter and spring, my neighbor, Maurice, tends a wonderful mixture of sweet and bitter greens that includes chervil because he came to Haute Provence from Nice, where the traditional salad mix *mesclun* always included chervil. Also from his greenhouse, or in summer from his garden, comes *céleri à couper,* the powerful, cutting celery that is used for flavoring, rather than as a vegetable.

Of all the herbs typically used in Haute Provence, it is the wild thyme, or *serpolet,* that is the keystone of the kitchen. Its gnarled and twisted grayish stems and branches resemble those of a carefully tended bonsai tree, and the grayish green leaves seem miniaturized as well. Wild thyme can be found in spotty patches here and there on the edges of cultivated fields, on open hillsides, and along the borders of the forest, and it grows in great carpets throughout open spaces. In May, when the thyme blooms, these spaces take on a soft purple hue and the flowers swarm with bees. The faithful still make thyme liqueur, *la farigoule,* by steeping freshly gathered blossoms in eau-de-vie and sugar to create a slightly dun-colored drink with the taste of honey-thyme. Everyone picks a bunch or two to hang and dry, and I, as my neighbors taught me, cut only the first six or eight inches, leaving a full one-quarter of the plant untouched and in good health to put forth more shoots. Long ago I was warned never to uproot a wild thyme plant, nor to clip it too close to the ground, but to clip only the uppermost stems in order to ensure its continuity in the wild.

Next to thyme, *sarriette,* or winter savory, is the herb most particular to the region. Sprigs of it are often pressed into the locally made goat cheeses, and it is considered to be indispensable for cooking with fava beans in spring, and with shelling beans later in the year. Also known by its Provençal name, *pebre-d'ai,* which means "donkey's pepper," wild winter savory is indeed peppery, tasting a little like thyme, but with a sharper and more pronounced flavor. It grows in an undistinguished spreading tangle, and to the amateur eye resembles just another trailing grayish-green plant. When I am trying to gather winter savory, I am continually tricked by an imposter, but long habit ensures that my neighbors are never misled. Winter savory, like thyme, grows in my back-door California herb garden, where it goes dormant in winter. Come March, new green shoots are peeping out at the base, soon to become two-foot-long stems, flowering in July and August.

Rosemary is one of the most popular of herbs throughout Provence and is used for landscaping as well as in the kitchen. The thick, sturdy upright stems are densely covered with needle-shaped leaves, and the plants grow quickly to create impenetrable and fragrant hedges to surround swimming pools or private patios and terraces. The prostrate rosemary drapes its curvy stems over retaining walls, hanging down like a thick curtain of deep green water. In the kitchen, the aromatic leaves are frequently used to season meat, especially lamb, but it can find its way into almost any dish, including poached fruits and breads. Its branches, stripped of foliage and soaked in water, are used for skewers.

Juniper is a spice rather than an herb because the berry is used, not the vegetative growth. The bushes are found in forested areas, and their purplish blue berries have a sharp and resinous taste that evokes the woods. Juniper is a frequent seasoning for game birds, pâtés, and daubes. When I am walking in the woods in fall it is easy to pick a few large pocketfuls of berries that will last me throughout the year.

Botanically speaking, wild *marjolaine* presents a problem in nomenclature. Although *marjolaine* translates as "marjoram," the wild version of marjoram, *Origanum vulgare,* is also called oregano or *origan.* Sweet or cultivated marjoram is *O. marjorana.* In Provence, *marjolaine* typically refers to the strong, intensely flavored wild plant. However, oregano and marjoram are closely related, the main difference being that marjoram has smaller leaves and a milder flavor. Throughout the book I have indicated either sweet marjoram or oregano in recipes.

At home in California I cultivate both sweet marjoram and oregano and use them both fresh and dried throughout the year rather than the wild *marjolaine* I use in France.

Wild *marjolaine* is easily found on the hillsides around Esparron-de-Verdon, St. Martin-de-Brome, and near Moustiers-Ste-Marie than in the lower regions around Aups. Its purplish pink flowers are followed by soft, green fuzzy balls. This is the ideal moment to pick it for drying. It is infrequently used fresh in Haute Provence, but I suspect this has to do with tradition rather than flavor. Unbound by custom, I use it fresh in many dishes, and find that it goes well with anything that includes tomatoes; that it can flavor soups, especially spicy ones; and that it is a necessity for sprinkling over pizzas hot from the oven. Although, I use it more sparingly than I do sweet marjoram.

Wild sage is so powerful that many people prefer to use cultivated sage, which is still potent, though less so. One day, as Victorine, one of my neighbors, balanced her long-handled grill already laden with pork chops, she told me that sage and pork are an ideal combination. She was on the way to her garden to pick sage to be tucked under the chops, then off to cook them in the fireplace. Sage, like rosemary, complements vegetables such as potatoes and winter squash, as well as chicken, lamb, and beef. While many different varieties are available, I find that common gray sage meets all my culinary needs. In late spring when it blooms, it sends up long flower stalks whose buds eventually burst into an inflorescence of brilliant purple. The blossoms can be deep-fried to make a delicious crispy garnish.

Lavender is more typically thought of as a flower than an herb, and not all traditional Haute Provence cooks use it. Some, however, employ it to flavor sweets such as ice cream and puddings and to impart a fragrance to meats and vegetables, especially roasted or grilled, and to goat cheeses. It is also increasingly being used in innovative restaurants of the region. Although fields of long rows of lavender are common today, it grows wild as well, and did not become a cultivated crop until after World War I. Even then, the gathering of wild lavender remained commercially viable until the late 1940s, as it had been since the 1800s.

Wild lavender, which has long been extensively used in the production of perfume, was harvested on a first-come, first-serve basis by the local people and purchased by manufactures and brokers. As the perfume industry grew, so did the importance of the lavender, and by the early part of the twentieth century, the gathering of wild lavender had an opening date and a closing date. Small, portable distilleries were set up throughout the countryside and lavender distilling became a family enterprise.

Gatherers had noticed over the years that there seemed to be two kinds of wild lavender, one they called *la lavande fine* or *la lavande vrai (Lavandula angustifolia)* and the other *la lavande aspic (L. latifolia)*. A third type occasionally appeared as well, called *lavendin*. The stems of the *lavande aspic* were longer, with larger and more numerous flowers that rendered more essential oil, but the blossoms were less fragrant and not as intensely blue as those of *L. angustifolia*. Laboratory analysis ascertained in 1927 that *lavendin,* or *grosse* lavender, was a hybrid of *L. angustifolia* and *L. latifolia*. It had to be propagated vegetatively by cuttings, as it did not grow true from seed. Hybridizing experiments were conducted, and by 1975, almost all the commercial plantings were of one of three *lavendin* hybrids. The gathering of wild lavender from the hillsides disappeared along with many of the small family distilleries. By far the greatest portion of the crop today goes for making perfume, pharmaceuticals, and soaps. The remainder ends up in the floral market for drying. *La lavande fine,* which is cultivated at the higher altitudes, is making a comeback, however, because of the high quality of its fragrance and oil.

In the open markets, supermarkets, and tourist shops of the area, bunched dried lavender and the woody herbs are sold individually as well as combined and in a near-pulverized form. The mixtures, called *herbes de Provence,* are comprised of rosemary, thyme, bay leaf, winter savory, marjoram, oregano, sage, and sometimes lavender, all important seasonings for *grillades* of beef, lamb, and especially chicken.

Unless you can be sure that the packaged herbs are not past their prime, it is better to dry and mix the herbs yourself. The essential oils of dried herbs can diminish after several months, and thus contribute little flavor to a dish, perhaps adding only a dusty staleness. Drying one's own herbs is effortless, particularly in the summer, when there is an abundance of both herbs and warm weather. Most kitchens or pantries in Haute Provence have several bunches of thyme, bay laurel, and oregano suspended from hooks or nails. They look rustic and homey and speak volumes about the food that is prepared and eaten in that home.

DRYING HERBS

The woody herbs are best cut for drying when they have just started to flower, although I cut and dry them as the need arises and find it quite satisfactory. To dry thyme, rosemary, bay, sage, oregano, marjoram, and winter savory either singly or mixed into loose bunches, tie them at the base with kitchen string or twine and hang the bunches upside down in a dry location. If kept in the dark, the leaves will retain more of their color. The warmer the temperature, the faster they will dry. Lavender should be stripped of its lower leaves before drying. You may instead simply spread out the stems on newspaper or racks to dry, but turn them each day. Once dried, they may be kept hanging in bunches and used as needed, or the leaves can be removed and the stems either discarded or saved to toss onto a wood or charcoal fire as a grilling flavor.

MAKING HERBES DE PROVENCE

Although there are various combinations of dried *herbes de Provence,* with pronounced advocates of one or the other, I like a mixture of one-half thyme leaves, one-quarter winter savory, one-eighth rosemary, and one-eighth sage, plus a pinch of lavender blossoms and a small crumble of bay. A teaspoon of this dried mixture is enough to season a roast chicken. Another mixture might replace the rosemary with marjoram or oregano.

Cooking with Herbs

The essential oils, which are what give herbs their flavor, are intensified in those herbs that retain their character when dried. Not all do. Rosemary, sweet bay, sage, oregano, marjoram, and thyme are good candidates for drying, but if added with a heavy hand to any dish, they can overwhelm it. On the other hand, fresh herbs added too gingerly will fail to distinguish a dish.

Dried herbs release their flavor over time, and thus are appropriate for slow-cooked dishes, marinades, or sauces and salad dressings, where there is ample time for them to come to full flavor.

Fresh herbs, especially the green ones, release their flavor immediately, and can be sprinkled onto cooked or raw vegetables and used in stir-fries, grills, sautés, pancakes and scones, and other quick-cooked dishes. Fresh green herbs can also be used by the handful in salads, while fresh woody ones can be used in quantity to flavor roasted dishes. Using fresh herbs in slow-cooked dishes, which is quite common, contributes a layer of flavoring when a second portion of fresh herbs is added shortly before serving.

Small clippings of herbs are referred to as sprigs, but larger, longer lengths are called branches.

Salad of Wild Greens

SERVES 4 TO 6

A classic salad of wild greens should be balanced between greens with a strong, assertive, bitter flavor and those whose flavors are mild, even bland. Dandelion, chicory, borage, and watercress fall into the former category, while mâche, purslane, and parsley fall into the latter.

The salad can still have a wild flavor using a balance of cultivated greens, including lettuce, spinach, purslane, chervil, mâche, and nasturtium for the mild component, and cultivated frisée, escarole, radicchio (all members of the chicory family), roquette (arugula), sorrel, and dandelion for the bitter component.

Whether made from wild or cultivated greens, the salad should be powerful and full flavored. Any mixture of the suggested greens may be used, depending upon your tastes.

The salad should be well seasoned with salt and pepper.

4 cups mixed young, tender greens (see recipe introduction),
   tough stems removed
¼ cup extra-virgin olive oil
2 tablespoons minced shallot
¼ cup red wine vinegar
1 teaspoon salt
1 teaspoon freshly ground black pepper

♦ Rinse and clean all the greens carefully, discarding any old or bruised leaves. Tear any large leaves into bite-sized pieces. Dry the greens well in a salad spinner or with a towel and set aside.

♦ Put the olive oil in the bottom of a large salad bowl. Add the shallot, vinegar, salt, and pepper and stir with a spoon or fork to mix it.

♦ Put the greens in the salad bowl and gently turn with two large spoons until the leaves are well coated with the dressing. Let the salad stand for about 10 minutes to soften the taste of the greens and to blend the flavors, then serve.

WILD HERBS & LAVENDER

Dandelion Salad with Lardons and Hard-Cooked Eggs

SERVES 4

From late fall through early spring, the saw-toothed leaves of dandelions start poking up around the edges of vineyards, orchards, roadsides, and creeks. They are at their mildest when harvested before the appearance of the characteristic yellow flower. Walking in the countryside and collecting dandelions for lunch or dinner is a fine way to spend a morning or afternoon.

> 4 cups wild dandelion greens and their roots or cultivated
>   dandelion greens mixed with baby spinach
> 1 teaspoon crushed garlic, minced
> ½ cup extra-virgin olive oil
> 3 tablespoons red wine vinegar
> ½ teaspoon salt
> 1 teaspoon freshly cracked black pepper
> 2 ounces *roulade* (pancetta) or thick-cut bacon, cut into pieces
>   1 inch long and ¼ inch wide (about ¼ cup lardons)
> 2 hard-cooked eggs, finely chopped
> 2 tablespoons minced red onion

◆ Rinse and clean the greens carefully, discarding any old or bruised leaves. If using wild dandelion greens, trim and use the root as well. Dry the greens well in a salad spinner or with a towel and set aside.

◆ In a small bowl, stir the garlic into the olive oil, and then stir in the vinegar, salt, and pepper to form a vinaigrette. In a small skillet, cook the *roulade* or bacon over medium heat until just crisp, 3 to 5 minutes. Using a slotted spoon, remove to paper towels to drain.

◆ Put the vinaigrette in a large bowl. Add the greens, turning them gently with two spoons until well coated. Top with the chopped eggs, bacon, and onion. Serve at once.

Chickpea Salad with Basil

SERVES 6 TO 8

Aromatic sweet basil heightens the nutty flavor of the chickpeas to make a simple bean salad, which can be dressed with a vinaigrette or with a fresh tomato sauce and served as a first course or as an accompaniment to meats or other vegetables.

    2 cups dried chickpeas
    2 quarts water
    2 fresh bay leaves, or 1 dried
    1 fresh thyme branch
    1 ½ teaspoon salt
    1 ½ teaspoon freshly ground black pepper
    ¼ cup chopped fresh basil, plus 1 basil sprig for garnish
    2 tablespoons minced red onion
    ¼ cup extra-virgin olive oil
    2 tablespoons red wine vinegar

◆ Pick over the chickpeas, discarding any tiny stones or other impurities. If the chickpeas are not recently harvested, soak them overnight in water to cover generously. When ready to cook, drain them, rinse well, and place in a saucepan with the water. Add the bay, thyme, and 1 teaspoon each salt and pepper and bring to a boil. Reduce the heat to a simmer, half-cover with a lid, and cook until the chickpeas no longer resist when bitten, 2 to 3 hours.

◆ Drain the chickpeas and let cool to room temperature. Place them in a serving bowl, stir in the chopped basil and onion, the olive oil, vinegar, and remaining salt, and pepper. Garnish with the basil sprig.

Parsley Salad with Lemon Vinaigrette

SERVES 4

Although parsley is usually thought of as a seasoning ingredient, it is excellent on its own, treated as a vegetable. Its clean flavor and crisp texture make it an ideal salad green alone or in combination with other greens. Parsley and young spinach, parsley and frisée or escarole, or parsley with young lettuces are suitable combinations.

6 tablespoons extra-virgin olive oil
2 tablespoons fresh lemon juice
1 teaspoon salt
1 teaspoon freshly ground black pepper
1 shallot, coarsely chopped
4 cups fresh flat-leaf parsley leaves, coarsely chopped

◆ Combine the olive oil, lemon juice, salt, pepper, and shallot in the bottom of a salad bowl, and mix well with a spoon or a fork. Add the parsley and turn it gently with 2 large spoons until well coated.

◆ Let stand for about 10 minutes to allow the flavors to develop, then serve.

Galettes of Wild Greens

Thin pancakes, with their slightly bitter taste tamed with a topping of brousse (the fresh curd of sheep cheese) or fresh goat cheese and a sprinkling of marjoram, make an excellent first course or appetizer. Served plain, spread with a little butter, they can accompany roasted meats or stews.

1 ½ cups all-purpose flour
1 ¾ cups milk
3 eggs
¾ teaspoon salt
½ teaspoon freshly ground black pepper
½ cup minced mixed fresh green herbs such as dandelion
    and parsley or basil and parsley, in equal amounts
¼ cup minced green onion or baby leek
1 to 2 tablespoons unsalted butter
4 ounces *brousse,* fresh goat cheese, or ricotta cheese (optional)
¼ cup minced fresh marjoram

◆ In a bowl, mix the flour a little at a time into the milk, whisking until the mixture is smooth. Beat in the eggs, salt, pepper, herbs, and green onion or leek.

◆ Heat 1 teaspoon of the butter in a skillet over medium heat. When it foams and the pan is hot, spoon in the batter to form a pancake about 6 inches in diameter. Cook until slightly golden, about 4 minutes. Turn over the pancakes and cook on the second side until golden as well, about 3 minutes longer. Remove to a platter and spread with about 1 tablespoon of the cheese, if desired. Keep warm. Repeat with the remaining batter, adding the butter as needed.

◆ Garnish with the marjoram and serve.

Fennel-Flavored Cream of Squash Soup

SERVES 4

The light anise flavor of the fennel leaves adds sprightliness to the subtlety of the summer squash. Zucchini, yellow crooknecks, pattypans, or a combination can be used. Remember, wild fennel is more potent than cultivated.

  2 tablespoons unsalted butter
  ½ yellow onion, chopped
  4 cups chopped summer squash (see recipe introduction)
  2 cups vegetable or chicken broth
  ¼ cup minced cultivated fennel leaves or 2 tablespoons wild
  1 teaspoon salt
  1 teaspoon freshly ground black pepper
  ½ cup heavy cream

◆ In a saucepan, melt the butter over medium heat. When it foams, add the onion and sauté until translucent, about 5 minutes. Add the squash, broth, half of the fennel leaves, the salt, and the pepper. Bring to a boil, reduce the heat to low, cover, and simmer until the squash is tender, about 10 minutes.

◆ Remove from the heat and let cool slightly, then purée in a blender or food processor. Return to the saucepan and stir in the cream. Heat to just below a boil. Ladle into warmed bowls and garnish with the remaining fennel leaves.

Wild Greens with Grilled Quail

SERVES 4 AS A FIRST COURSE

In Haute Provence, grives *(thrushes) are pursued and savored by nearly every hunter. Here, flavorful quail make a fine substitute. The greens, a mixture of mild and bitter, form a complementary background for the birds, juices and meat. For a main course, serve 2 birds to each diner. Accompany the quail with toasted baguette slices rubbed with garlic and drizzled with olive oil.*

4 cups mixed greens, dandelion, roquette, watercress, and baby spinach, in any combination, small leaves left whole, larger ones torn into bite-sized pieces
¼ cup extra-virgin olive oil
¼ cup balsamic vinegar
1 ½ teaspoons salt
1 ½ teaspoons freshly ground black pepper
4 quail, about 6 ounces each
6 fresh sage sprigs
3 fresh rosemary sprigs
5 slices baguette, each 1 inch thick, lightly sprinkled with water

♦ Prepare a charcoal or wood fire.

♦ Rinse and clean the greens carefully, discarding any old or bruised leaves. Dry the greens well in a salad spinner or with a towel.

♦ Place the olive oil in the bottom of a salad bowl and stir with a fork or spoon. Add the vinegar, and ½ teaspoon each of the salt and pepper. Add the greens to the salad bowl, but do not toss. Set aside.

continued

♦ Rub the quail first with the sage and rosemary, and then with the remaining 1 teaspoon each salt and pepper. Thread a baguette slice onto a long sturdy skewer. Thread a quail lengthwise through its body cavity onto the skewer, pressing it against the bread. Thread a second baguette slice onto the skewer and then another bird. Repeat with the remaining quail, ending with the last piece of bread. (The bread holds the birds in place during the frequent turning on the grill and soaks up some of the juices. Quartered onions would also serve this purpose.)

♦ When the coals are medium-hot, place the skewer on the grill. Cook, turning every 3 or 4 minutes, until a thigh can be readily moved and the juices run clear or slightly pink when the thickest part of a thigh is pierced, about 15 minutes.

♦ Just before serving, using 2 large spoons, turn the greens in the salad bowl until well coated. Divide the greens equally among 4 plates. Remove the birds and the bread from the skewer. Discard the bread, and place 1 quail atop each mound of greens. Using poultry shears, cut each bird in half, allowing the juices to run over the greens. Serve at once.

Leg of Lamb in a Crust of *Herbes de Provence*

The famous lamb of Sisteron is notable for its flavor because the animals graze on the wild herbs and grasses of the region. Rubbing a leg of lamb, whether from Sisteron or not, with sprigs and branches of thyme, rosemary, winter savory, and lavender, and then pressing the leaves into the flesh, re-creates the pungency and aroma of the garigue of Haute Provence, as if one could bite into a place.

Stripping the leaves from the thyme, rosemary, marjoram, and winter savory sprigs and the blossoms from the lavender and letting them dry out a bit overnight will remove some of their moisture. This will help them to adhere better when packed onto the meat, but they will still carry the full flavor of fresh herbs.

> 1 leg of lamb, 5 to 6 pounds
> Stems reserved from preparing herb mixture, plus several lavender
> stems
> 6 cloves garlic, cut into slivers
> 1 teaspoon salt
> 1 tablespoon freshly ground black pepper
> ½ cup semidry mixed fresh thyme, winter savory, rosemary, and
> marjoram in about equal amounts, plus a few lavender blossoms

◆ Preheat an oven to 450 degrees F.

◆ Dry the leg of lamb by rubbing it all over with the stripped herb stems. Using a sharp knife, make 20 to 25 slits 1 inch deep all over the leg. Insert the garlic slivers deep into the slits. Rub the meat thoroughly with the salt and pepper. Pack the entire surface of the leg with the mixed herbs by pressing them onto the skin and flesh with your hand.

continued

◆ Place the prepared lamb in a shallow roasting pan just large enough to hold it. Roast for 20 minutes. Reduce the heat to 350 degrees F and roast for about 1 hour longer, or until an instant-read thermometer inserted into the thickest part of the leg registers 135 degrees F for medium-rare, or 145 degrees F for medium.

◆ Remove the lamb to a cutting board or plate, cover loosely with aluminum foil, and let stand for 15 minutes, then carve into thin slices. Arrange the slices on a warmed serving platter and drizzle with the roasting juices from the pan.

N O T E : *French lamb is sold younger than American lamb and will take less time to cook.*

Grilled Butterflied Leg of Lamb with *Herbes de Provence*

SERVES 8 TO 10

An alternative to cooking the whole lamb leg in the oven is to ask the butcher to butterfly the leg, removing the bone and leaving the meat in a single piece that will lay flat. Studded with garlic and seasoned with salt, pepper, and herbs, the lamb cooks over a medium-hot fire in about half an hour. The thickness of the butterflied lamb varies from about 1 inch to 2 or 2 ½ inches, so a single leg can be well done, medium, or rare to suit a variety of tastes.

1 leg of lamb, 6 to 7 pounds, boned and butterflied
Stems reserved from preparing herb mixture, plus several lavender
   stems
6 cloves garlic, cut into slivers
1 teaspoon salt
2 teaspoons freshly ground black pepper
½ cup semi-dry mixed fresh thyme, winter savory, rosemary, and
   marjoram, in about equal amounts, plus a few lavender blossoms

◆ Prepare a charcoal or a wood fire in a grill.

◆ Dry the leg of lamb by rubbing it all over with the stripped herb stems. Using a sharp knife, make 20 to 25 slits about 1 inch deep (depth depends upon thickness of meat) all over the meat. Insert the garlic slivers into the slits. Rub the meat on both sides with the salt and pepper, then sprinkle with the herbs, pressing them into the flesh with the palm of your hand.

◆ When the coals are medium-hot, place the lamb on the grill rack about 8 inches above the fire and cook for about 10 minutes. Watch carefully so the meat does not burn. Turn the meat over and cook for another 20 minutes, or until an instant-read thermometer inserted into the thickest part of the leg registers 135 degrees F for medium rare or 145 degrees F for medium.

◆ Remove the lamb to a cutting board or platter, cover loosely with aluminum foil, let stand for 10 minutes, then carve into thin slices.

Sage-Roasted Rabbit and Potatoes

Serves 4 to 6

As this dish cooks, the sage leaves become crunchy and pick up the flavor of the bacon that wraps and bastes each tender rabbit morsel. Rabbit is common fare in Haute Provence, both in homes and in restaurants, where it is prepared in numerous ways.

> 1 young rabbit, 2½ pounds
> 2 baking potatoes
> 12 to 16 fresh sage sprigs (about 1 cup)
> 1 teaspoon freshly ground black pepper
> 10 slices bacon

◆ Preheat an oven to 350 degrees F.

◆ Cut the rabbit into serving-sized pieces, or ask the butcher to do it. In country homes, rabbit is generally cut into 10 pieces: 4 legs, 2 thighs, the rib section, the meaty saddle in 2 pieces, and the head left whole. The rib section and the small forelegs do not have as much meat as the thighs and saddle, however, so take into account the size of the pieces and of the appetites you are feeding.

◆ Peel the potatoes and cut them into ¼-inch-thick slices. Rub the rabbit pieces with 3 or 4 of the sage sprigs, and then with a little pepper. Wrap each piece with a slice of the bacon, and place in a shallow roasting pan just large enough to accommodate them. Slip the remaining sage sprigs and the potato slices between the rabbit pieces.

◆ Roast in the oven for 35 minutes. Remove from the oven and pour off the accumulated fat. Now place the potatoes beneath the rabbit pieces, turning over the rabbit pieces as you do so in order for the underside of the bacon to brown a little. Cook until the rabbit and the potatoes are tender when pierced with the tines of a fork, another 25 to 30 minutes. Remove from the oven and serve hot.

Sage-Grilled Pork Chops

SERVES 6

This simple grillade *is one of the most pleasing.*

    1 cup fresh sage leaves
    6 medium thick or 12 thin pork chops, preferably rib
    1 tablespoon freshly ground black pepper
    1 teaspoon salt

◆ Layer half of the sage leaves in a shallow baking dish. Rub the chops on both sides with the pepper and place them on the sage, then cover with another layer of sage leaves. Let stand for 1 hour.

◆ Prepare a charcoal or a wood fire.

◆ When the coals are medium-hot, place the chops (reserve the sage) on the grill rack, about 8 inches from the fire. Cook for 3 or 4 minutes, then turn the chops over and cook until the juices run clear when the chops are pierced with the tip of a sharp knife, another 3 or 4 minutes. Cook slightly less for thinner chops. Top with the reserved sage, turn, and grill for just a few seconds to crisp, but not burn, the sage. (The sage should adhere fairly well but do not worry if some of the leaves fall away.)

◆ Remove to a platter and serve along with the sage leaves. Sprinkle with the salt.

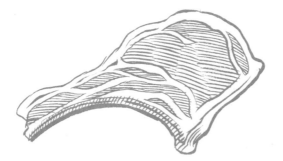

Pork Chops Grilled with Lavender, Thyme, and Rosemary

SERVES 4

Patting and pressing the fresh herbs into the chops and letting them stand an hour or two before grilling helps the flavors to penetrate the meat, which cooks quickly. The sparingly used lavender lends a mysterious, faintly smoky background to the more familiar thyme and rosemary.

Many homes in Haute Provence have a fireplace in the kitchen, dining room, or living room that is used for cooking grillades of pork, lamb, beef, or fish, which are then carried directly from the hearth to the table. There is the double pleasure of smelling the aroma of the herbs during cooking and then tasting the flavors.

    1 teaspoon salt
    ½ teaspoon freshly ground black pepper
    4 pork chops, each ½ inch thick
    ½ teaspoon minced fresh lavender flowers or ⅛ teaspoon dried
    2 teaspoons minced fresh thyme leaves
    1 teaspoon minced rosemary leaves

◆ Rub the salt and pepper on both sides of the chops. Combine the minced flowers and herbs, then rub each chop on both sides with an equal amount of the mixture, firmly pressing it into the flesh. Cover loosely with waxed paper or plastic wrap, and let stand for an hour or two at room temperature.

◆ Prepare a charcoal or wood fire in a grill or fireplace. When the coals are medium-hot, place the chops on the grill rack. Cook for 4 to 5 minutes, then turn the chops over and cook until the juices run clear when the chops are pierced with the tip of a sharp knife, another 3 to 4 minutes. Serve at once.

Thyme-Stuffed Roasted Chicken

SERVES 4

I make this dish frequently, first rubbing the chicken all over with thyme, then stuffing the cavity brimful with the aromatic herb. As the chicken roasts, it fills the kitchen with the intoxicating fragrance of fresh thyme.

> 1 chicken, about 3 pounds
> 1½ cups fresh thyme sprigs
> 1 teaspoon salt
> 1 teaspoon freshly ground black pepper

◆ Preheat an oven to 350 degrees F.

◆ Cut away any excess fat around the cavity opening of the chicken. Rub the outside of the chicken with the thyme, then rub the inside and the outside with the salt and pepper. Pack the thyme sprigs into the cavity, and place the chicken in a shallow roasting pan.

◆ Roast, basting occasionally, until the juices run clear when a thigh is pierced with a knife at its thickest point, 1¼ to 1½ hours. Remove from the oven and let stand for 5 to 10 minutes before carving.

Honey-and-Lavender-Glazed Chicken

SERVES 4

The powerful flavors and fragrance of the herbs create a tremendous woodsy tang mingled with sweetness. The skin of the chicken turns a glistening dark mahogany, while the meat beneath remains tender and fragrant. This is my version of a dish I had at Les Santons Restaurant in Moustiers-Ste.-Marie.

4 teaspoons lavender flowers, crushed
2 teaspoons minced dried lavender stems
1 tablespoon fresh thyme leaves
2 teaspoons dried winter savory leaves
12 black peppercorns
1 teaspoon salt
4 chicken breast halves
¼ cup strong-flavored honey, preferably lavender or acacia

◆ Preheat an oven to 450 degrees F.

◆ In a mortar, grind together 2 teaspoons of the lavender flowers, the stems, thyme, winter savory, peppercorns, and salt. Rub each chicken breast half with about 1 teaspoon of the mixture. Place the chicken breasts, skin side up, on a baking sheet. Roast for 10 minutes. Remove from the oven and baste the chicken skin thoroughly with the honey. Sprinkle all but 2 teaspoons of the remaining herb mixture evenly over the chicken breasts. Return to the oven, reduce the heat to 350 degrees F, and roast, basting frequently with the pan juices, until the juices run clear when a chicken breast is pierced with the tip of a knife, about 20 minutes longer. Frequent basting is important as the honey, once warm, pours off the chicken into the pan and regular basting ensures the honey flavor of the finished dish.

◆ Remove from the oven and serve immediately, sprinkled with the remaining 2 teaspoons crushed lavender flowers.

Rosemary-Orange Sorbet

MAKES ABOUT 1½ PINTS

The sharp flavor of rosemary provides a subtle background for a sweet orange sorbet. Serve with chocolates for dessert.

   1 cup sugar
   1 cup water
   2 rosemary branches, 4 inches long
   2 cups strained fresh orange juice
   1 tablespoon fresh lemon juice
   ½ teaspoon minced fresh rosemary, plus 4 sprigs for garnish
   3 tablespoons minced orange zest, plus 4 zest twists for garnish

◆ Place the sugar, water, and rosemary branch in a small saucepan over medium heat and bring to a boil, stirring to dissolve the sugar. Reduce the heat to medium-low and simmer, stirring often, for 5 minutes, to make a thin syrup. Remove from the heat and let cool for 10 minutes, then remove the rosemary branch and discard it. Stir in the orange juice and lemon juice, cover, and refrigerate until well chilled, at least 6 hours, or as long as overnight.

◆ Stir in the minced rosemary leaves and the minced orange zest. Transfer to an ice cream maker and freeze according to the manufacturer's directions. Serve in bowls or glasses. Garnish each serving with a sprig of rosemary and a twist of orange zest.

Figs Baked with Honey and Lavender

SERVES 6

The lavender creates a haunting undertone for this elegant rendition of figs.
A scoop of vanilla ice cream can replace the cream.

12 large, soft, ripe figs, any kind
¼ cup honey
1 teaspoon minced fresh lavender flowers, or ¼ teaspoon dried
⅔ cup water
¾ cup heavy cream

◆ Preheat an oven to 300 degrees F.

◆ Prick the figs all over with a fork. Place them upright in a shallow baking dish just large enough to hold them snugly. Drizzle or paint them with the honey and sprinkle the lavender over them. Pour the water into the bottom of the baking dish. Bake until the figs become shiny and plumped up, 25 to 35 minutes; the timing will depend upon the size and ripeness of the fruits. Remove from the oven and let cool for about 10 minutes. Serve the figs warm, spooning the juices from the dish over them and topping each one with 1 tablespoon of the cream.

RECIPES

Peppered Citrus Olives

Spicy Black Olives

Black Olive Tapenade

Green Olive and Almond Tapenade

Poor Man's Foie Gras

Classic Vinaigrette

Rice, Tomato, and Olive Salad

Olive and Lentil Salad

Olives, Roasted Red Peppers, and Eggplant Salad

Tapenade, *Roasted Red Pepper, and Goat Cheese Sandwiches*

Braised Greens and Black Olives

Rosemary Pasta with Black Olives and Carrots

Chicken Breast Stuffed with Tapenade

Chicken Ragout with Black Olives

Rabbit Sauté and Green Olives

Black Olive Bread

The northernmost boundaries of Haute Provence are determined by the extent of olive cultivation. Throughout the region, olive trees stand along roadsides, in front of houses, in the middle of vineyards, and on the borders of driveways. Olive groves are planted on the sloping edges of the small valleys, in terraces edged by stone walls, and across plateaus. Most are tidy and well kept, the trees pruned and healthy, the ground plowed, and the terrace walls intact. Some are vestiges of bygone centuries, or may have been last tended when World War I took the men away. These groves can be spotted perched high up a hill or stumbled upon, overgrown, in a forest clearing. Climbing north past Sisteron, the olive trees become fewer and fewer and pastures of milk cows more prevalent. The red-tile roofs of Haute Provence cease, replaced by layers of gray slate, and the Alps come closer, filling the eye with their ragged peaks.

In Haute Provence, the farthest reach of Provence's Mediterranean climate, the food is perfumed in all its forms by olive oil, in spite of the proximity of the Alps, where butter is abundant. Olive oil glistens on salads of wild greens, on warm potatoes and truffles, on *carrotes râpés,* and on slices of fennel. Trout, pulled fresh from the streams, are rubbed with olive oil before being grilled over a fire of grapevine prunings. Wild boar is sautéed in olive oil to initiate its long, slow cooking, and fava beans, artichokes, green beans, eggplant, chard, and cabbage—all the vegetables of the seasonal *potager*—are served as a *fricot* cooked in olive oil with onions, garlic, and herbs. Aioli, the highly prized garlic-infused mayonnaise that accompanies snails, salt cod, steamed vegetables, and their various combinations, is at its most potent when made with olive oil.

Olives from the trees are cured and invariably served at aperitif time to nibble while sipping a glass of *vin de noix,* rosé, or pastis. They appear with a first course of charcuterie, such as *jambon cru,* pâté, and *saucisson. Tapenade,* made from either black or green olives crushed into a paste with capers, anchovies, and olive oil, is spread onto grilled toasts or served alongside vegetables or meats. Olives are used as the main ingredient in salads, and as a flavoring element in cooked dishes to which they are added unpitted. Their flavors are complex for several reasons. Each variety has its particular characteristics, but since the bitterness must be removed from every olive for it to be edible, the leaching process adds another dimension of flavor. Within this dimension, further variations and nuances can occur, depending upon how the leaching was done and how much of the bitterness was attenuated during the process, which can be a matter of personal preference. Once the olives are cured, they are stored in various brines or preserved in oil, which is yet another factor that contributes to taste. Finally, further flavorings and seasoning can be added to the olives, with lemon and fennel, hot chilies and garlic, coriander and dill, anchovies, and small onions among the more common. These might be added to the original brine, to a new brine, or the olives may be removed from the brine and stored instead in olive oil, with or without additional seasonings.

Thus, the final flavor of a *tapenade* or other preparation using olives depends upon many factors. Green olives seasoned with fennel and lemon bring a very different flavor to a pork stew than do shriveled, salt-cured, oil-packed black olives. Because of their complexity, olives are a source of great versatility in the kitchen, and Haute Provence cooks make adept us of them, just as they are adept at curing their own olives.

Most homes, in the countryside and villages alike, have a *cave,* a cellar, a garage—somewhere to keep wine, olives, and roots at cool temperatures. At the beginning of the century, olives were still stored in big terra-cotta jars with interior glazes, but now widemouthed *bonbonnes* of plastic or wicker-wrapped glass, five to ten liters in size, are used. Generally, a wooden olive scoop rests nearby. It has a long handle and a deep round bowl pierced with holes, so that when it is plunged into the vat of olives, it scoops them up and drains the brine.

I've always liked going with my neighbor Françoise into her *cave,* especially before she moved to her new house. At the old house, the *cave* had an earthen floor and a high vaulted ceiling. One small dangling bulb, the fixture unchanged since its original installation in the 1930s, provided a dim light. The *cave* itself dated from the early 1600s, with walls six feet thick in some places. We first passed through the outermost section, where potatoes, onions, and winter squashes were carefully laid out on either side of a pathway that lead to the interior *cave* where the wine and olives were kept. This much smaller room had no light. The single bulb of the large *cave* altered the darkness just enough to allow us to distinguish the narrow necks of the wine *bonbonnes* from those of the olives. Françoise located the scoop by feel, and because she was the only person to get olives from the *cave,* it was always right where she had left it on her previous trip. She took the cork from one of several *bonbonnes,* and scooped her bowl full of olives—sometimes black, sometimes green, sometimes both. Replacing the cork, we retraced our steps, returning to the kitchen with the bowl.

Although fewer people cure their own olives today than in the past, the strength of the tradition can be noted by the fact that hardware stores, big discount stores, and traveling vendors at open markets continue to sell olive scoops and the *bonbonnes* with their big, flat corks as standard household products alongside rakes, hoes, cookware, hammers, and garden hose.

As in so many aspects of life in Haute Provence, the making of olives takes place within the rhythm of the year. Olives for curing are not all picked in one intense rush, but over a period of six months, as they gradually ripen from green to darkest black. The fully green olives, picked just before they start to blush purple, are harvested in late August or September to make the early season olives, *vertes cassée*. When they have turned violet, but not yet black, they are picked again to make a brined olive. When deepest black they are gathered and packed in salt, and finally, when the last of the olives are wrinkled and black in late winter, they are put into jars alone, to age for at least a year, but preferably for three or four years.

This simplest *produit du terroir* mirrors the seasons. When the green olives are picked and cured, the *potager* is still thick with tomatoes and eggplant, the fields full of lush melons, and the grapes still sweetening on the vines. Lunch is eaten outside under mulberry trees. By the time the olives have turned violet, the garden has been cleared of summer's fruit, and stiff soldiers of leeks and onions line the rows with rounds of winter cabbage beside them. Potatoes have been dug and stored, and the grapes are being cut. When the black olives are picked, the cold winds have blown the dried, crinkled leaves from the trees and vines, and the fields are a blanket of brown earth, seeded deep with winter wheat that has yet to emerge. Thin layers of ice coat the shallow rain pools and smoke curls from the chimneys of houses throughout the day.

Olive making, once a few principles are understood, is quite easy. All olives are first green, then purple, and finally black once fully mature. Whether one eats a green olive or a black depends not upon variety, but upon the stage of maturity at harvest. Regardless of harvest time or color, fresh olives are unfit to eat because they contain a glucoside that makes them extremely and unpleasantly bitter. Thus, they must undergo a process that leaches the bitterness from them. This is traditionally done in one of several ways: by soaking them in frequent changes of water or in a mixture of water and wood ash, or by packing them in salt. The different processes can take anywhere from several days to a month, but all the olives will retain some degree of bitterness, unlike those known as California ripe olives. The latter are in fact picked green, undergo a lye process, then are turned black during a sterilization procedure. They bear little flavor resemblance to the olives cured in the Mediterranean region.

Some olive varieties grown in Haute Provence are cured when green because they are most flavorful then, others preferably when violet or black, and still others at all three stages. In general, though, a good olive for curing, one that makes a good table olive, has thick meat and a small pit. There are a few exceptions to this rule, as there are to most. The Cailletier variety, more commonly known as *olives de Nice* or *Niçoise,* produces small fruits, rarely larger than the tip of a little finger, and quite good.

Over the years olives have come to be called by the name of the area in which they are cultivated as well as by a proper varietal name, so terminology can be confusing. The same olive might be called by a dozen different names, depending upon where it is grown. Also, different olives are called by the same name if prepared in the same way. For example, *à la picholine* can describe any olive packed in a lightly herbed brine. But Picholine is also the varietal name of a specific olive—almond shaped and with a pointed tip—that is one of the most commonly grown on a commercial scale, as well as in gardens and landscapes.

My neighbor Françoise's husband, Maurice, doesn't really know what variety of olives his trees are, and neither does Françoise. "The trees were here before we were," he says. They simply pick their table olives for curing from the trees that bear fruits with small pits and thick flesh. Françoise cures them the way she learned from her mother, an Italian immigrant. My other neighbor, originally from Marseille, cures her olives slightly differently, and she and her husband planted Picholine olive trees, as well as numerous "race de Montfort" types when they inherited their property. They also have a number of trees they planted specifically for oil.

Maurice, who is a *paysan* (farmer), specializes in growing melons and other fruits and sells them at the weekly open markets. He also has a small vineyard whose grapes go to the local wine cooperative, and several acres that he plants with cereal. His olive trees, about twenty in all, are interspersed among his six acres of grapes. In late December, when the olives mature in the Haute Var, the family and relatives pick the olives and Maurice takes between five and six hundred kilos of them, over a thousand pounds, to the cooperative olive mill in a neighboring village, where the oil is extracted. His harvest generally yields sixty to eighty liters of oil, enough to supply his family for the year.

Some small farmers or householders have more oil from their trees than they can use, and it is this oil that is sometimes advertised for sale in country *épiceries* on a handwritten card taped onto the cash register or a window: *"Huile d'olive de pays sur commande."* I order such an olive oil from a local *épicerie,* and return for it the following week after it has been delivered. It is in recycled bottles—often liter-sized lemonade bottles with a small cork wedged into the neck. The color is a lush golden-green and cloudy. It comes, the woman who runs the little grocery store tells me, from somewhere near Aups, or maybe Salernes or Quinson. Never do I learn exactly from where. I love this olive oil, though, and look forward each year to the new crop and to the ritual of acquisition.

The harvest of olives for oil takes place between December and February, depending upon when the oil content of the fruits is at its peak. In the Haut Var, in Tavernes and Salernes, in Cotignac, the harvest typically commences in December and goes into January. But in Entrevaux, in the Alpes-de-Haute-Provence, the olives are not mature until late January or early February, the same time those of Nyons are picked. Nyons, which at the beginning of the twentieth century counted over one million olive trees on its surrounding slopes and was a major oil production center, today has less than thirty thousand trees, most of them in small holdings. The great freezes of 1929, 1956, and 1985 took their toll, and damaged trees were pulled out, not to be replanted.

The olives are traditionally hand picked, usually by family members and friends. Most large commercial plantings today have converted to mechanized harvesting, but the ancestral way is still practiced throughout the small holdings, even in Nyons. Olives that have fallen to the ground are collected, and then tarps are spread beneath the trees. The olives are picked one by one, or by stripping, which takes leaves as well as olives. The fruits fall to the tarp, and any that scatter beyond it are collected. Finally, they are bagged and taken to the mill.

At modern mills the olives are washed and the stones, leaves, and trash separated out. The whole olives, including their pits, are finely ground and mixed into a paste. A centrifuge separates water and a mixture of oil and water from the paste, and a smaller centrifuge removes more water from the mixture, leaving pure olive oil. Modern centrifuges are much simpler and yield more oil than traditional oil presses, but until the last quarter of the twentieth century most of the mills in Haute Provence were still using traditional equipment and methods to obtain the oil.

A few of the old-style olive mills still function, exuding their ambience during the winter months. Many local people recall their childhoods, when they congregated at the mill after school, or at lunch, their bread in hand, to dip into the newly pressed oil.

The olive mill in Entrevaux is a traditional one, and there my family and I appeared with friends from Annot late on a freezing cold February afternoon with our baguettes and a bottle of red wine. Originally water-driven, the mill is on the canyon flank above the river, built atop an ancient flume fed by a mountain stream from a side canyon. The sound of rushing mountain water is constant. Stepping inside the stone building, we entered into a relatively small room with whitewashed walls and a low ceiling. A quarter of the room was consumed by a waist-high stone vat with a large, circular, slowly revolving millstone that turned and crushed the olives. In one corner was a wood-fired boiler that ran pipes to an ancient radiator by the oil press, an element necessary in mountainous country in the winter to keep the oil flowing. Opposite the turning millstone stood the heavy iron-framed press, stacked with more than a dozen shallow cocoa fiber mats filled with olive paste from the millstone. The mats were under several tons of pressure, so liquid was slowly running down their sides, to be collected in a basin below. Originally the freshly pressed oil was put directly into the ceiling-high vats lining one wall, but now it is first run through a small centrifuge. The vats have spigots at the bottom, and over time as the lighter olive oil rises to the top, the water can be drawn off the bottom by opening a spigot.

After explaining the various workings, the miller cut one of our baguettes into three lengths, then split each piece lengthwise. He unhinged the long-handled grill that had been leaning on the wall next to the fire, placed the pieces of bread on one side, and closed it, securing the bread. The grill was held in the fire by the miller just long enough to warm the bread through and to char it slightly. Opening the hinge once again, he removed the bread to a large wooden table, and rubbed the face of each piece with the cut end of a garlic clove. Then, setting down a large dinner plate of olive oil, he instructed us to dip the bread face down into the oil. The bread emerged dripping with the greenish gold liquid. Ceremoniously, our wine was opened, we were handed glasses, and thus we settled back to enjoy the warmth of the room and to savor the toasts and the conversation with other people who had gathered there, guests of the miller and the village, part of a long tradition of hospitality.

ABOUT OLIVE OIL

There are several grades of olive oil recognized by the International Olive Oil Council, defined by law to meet certain requirements. The highest grade is labeled extra-virgin and/or first cold press, and it is extracted without the use of heat, which can alter the character of oil. Extra-virgin, first cold press is without question the most flavorful of the grades and should always be used whenever olive oil is added directly to food, with little or no further cooking. The actual flavor of extra-virgin olive oils varies depending upon the variety of olives used, where and how they were grown, their condition when pressed, and the circumstances and method of the pressing and extraction process.

The next grade is virgin olive oil, and this varies considerably in quality. Generally extracted with the use of heat, the oil has a lower smoking point than that of extra virgin and is typically used for frying and deep-frying. The third level is industrial grade olive oil.

MAKING FLAVORED OLIVE OILS

Olive oil may easily be infused with the flavor of other ingredients, such as rosemary, thyme, juniper, truffle, black pepper, and lemon. Simply put several twigs of the herbs, a handful of juniper berries or black peppercorns, a few truffle shavings, or the zest of several lemons in a jar and add olive oil to cover generously.

I use rosemary, thyme, and juniper oil for grilling and marinades, so a virgin or an inexpensive extra-virgin olive oil is suitable. The black pepper, lemon, and truffle oils are good on salads, for dressing warm vegetables, and for drizzling over dishes that have already been cooked, so I like medium-priced extra-virgin oil for these flavorings.

Sterilize the jar or bottle and make sure that the flavoring ingredients are completely covered by the olive oil. If they are exposed to the air they will mold. Close the jar with a lid or a tight-fitting cork and keep in a warm place. After several days, the oil will begin to take on the flavor of the infusing ingredient. Pour a bit of oil into a saucer and taste it with a piece of bread. Continue the infusing process until the olive oil is flavored to your taste. At that time, remove the infusing ingredient and, if desired, remove the olive oil from the jar and bottle it, storing it in a cupboard or another location away from direct light. Small bottles with corks can be purchased in import stores, at wine-making supply stores, and in the housewares sections of department or specialty stores.

Leaching, Salting, and Brining Olives
Leaching with Water Only
This method is frequently used for the green olives of August and the black-purple ones that follow.

Cracked Green Olives
Choose olives that are green without the slightest hint of purple, and that are meaty with small pits. Crack the skin with a mallet or the back of a wooden spoon, but don't break the pit. Put the olives in a nonreactive vat or crock and cover them with cold water. Change the water every day for at least 10 days or up to 25 days, according to taste. The longer they are in the water, the more bitterness they will lose, but they will always retain some, which is their attraction. When you deem them to your taste, drain the water and put them in a clean, dry jar with a lid. Cover them with cooled brine (page 68) and tighten the lid. Store them in the refrigerator, where they will keep for up to 3 months. They are ready to eat after 1 week.

Black-Purple Olives

Choose plump olives that are purple on their way to black. Prick them all over with pins that have been pushed through a slice of cork to speed the leaching process. Place in water and continue as in Cracked Green Olives. They will be ready to eat in 1 month after having been put into the brine, and will keep for several months in the refrigerator.

Leaching with Lye

I was apprehensive the first time I used this method, though I know many people who always leach their olives with lye. All those warnings on the lye can seemed so intimidating, and I couldn't believe that something so dangerous could be used for something to eat. I was wrong. This is a quick and effective way to leach the olives, taking only 5 or 6 days, and virtually all of the bitterness will be gone. Lye should be used with caution, however, and far, far from the reach of small children. Unlike the plain-water method, the olives must be weighted down so that they are thoroughly submerged in the lye mixture. If they are exposed to the air, they will be discolored and mushy. Green to purple olives should be used.

Place the olives in a nonreactive pot or crock. I use plastic buckets. In another container, also nonreactive, make a mixture of 4 ounces pure lye per 1 gallon of water. Make enough to cover the olives completely. Place a clean towel on top of the olives, and weight them down with a plate topped with a brick. (As primitive as the method sounds, it is effective in keeping the olives submerged.) Every 12 hours, remove the weights and towel and, with a long-handled wooden or plastic spoon, reach down to the bottom and turn the olives, stirring from top to bottom. Green olives will begin to show a color change from bright to darker green almost immediately. Repeat for 4 or 5 days, until it is evident that the lye solution has penetrated to the pit. Check the penetration by slicing an olive at least every day and observing the color change as the lye solution moves through the flesh. Once the olives are done, drain and rinse them, then put them in fresh, cold water for 6 to 12 hours. Repeat for 5 changes of water.

Drain the olives a final time and place them in clean, dry jars. Cover them with cooled brine (page 68) and tighten the lids. These olives have virtually no bitterness. Store them in the refrigerator, where they will keep up to 1 year.

Leaching with Wood Ash

Wood ash, because it contains lye, is a form of leaching with lye. This method is best used for green olives. For 2 pounds of olives, sift enough hardwood ashes to make 5 cups; the finer the ash the better. Combine the ashes with enough water to make a thin paste. Put the olives in a nonreactive vat, crock, or jar and cover with the paste. Stir these daily for 5 or 6 days. As with commercial lye, examine the olives to see penetration toward the pit. When the lye has reached the pit, drain off the wood ash paste, wash the olives, and put them back in the vat, crock, or jar. Rinse them daily in a change of fresh water for from 10 days up to 25 days, or until the bitterness is attenuated. There will be residual bitterness, but less so than when using only the water to leach.

Leaching with Salt

Choose very black olives; even slightly wrinkled ones are acceptable. Pierce them all over with pins that have been pushed through a slice of cork, as this aids in the penetration of the salt and the drawing off of the liquid. Place the olives in a burlap bag and cover thoroughly with salt. Or line a wooden box with burlap and cover the burlap with a 2-inch layer of rock salt. Add the olives and cover with more salt. Place the box or bag above a bucket or sink to dispose easily of the liquid that will drain. Add more salt as needed. The olives will be leached of their bitterness in approximately 20 days, and will not taste of salt because the salt will have dissolved and drained off. Once the olives are leached to your satisfaction, wash and dry them. Place them in a jar with olive oil, salt, dried thyme, and perhaps black peppercorns, dried red chilies, and bay leaves. Take care to cover well with the oil, because thyme, if exposed, will mold. Store the olives in the refrigerator, where they will keep for up to 1 year.

OLIVES & OLIVE OIL

No Leaching

Place very black, shriveled olives in a jar with a tight-fitting lid. Add nothing else. Leave the olives in a cool, dark place for a year before sampling. They will still be quite bitter, but their bitterness is thought desirable by many people. These olives are frequently kept 3 years before eating, and will keep, I have been told, for 10 years, when stored in a cool, dark place.

Brining

A brine of water and salt, with or without additional flavorings, is used to store the olives once their bitterness has been leached. But, unless you have a very cold cellar or similar location, the brined olives should be stored in the refrigerator, where they will keep for several months.

This is a common brine used in Haute Provence, and it serves for green, purple-black, or black olives. Although specific proportions are given here, the rule of thumb is ½ cup salt for 4 cups water. If, on eating, the olives seem too salty, they may be soaked in clean, fresh water for several hours or overnight.

    2 quarts water
    1 cup course sea salt
    3 fresh bay leaves, or 2 dried
    2 flowering fennel heads
    3 or 4 fresh winter savory branches
    3 or 4 fresh thyme branches
    1 piece dried orange peel
    1 tablespoon coriander seed
    1 tablespoon black peppercorns

Combine all the ingredients in a saucepan and bring to a boil over medium-high heat. Reduce the heat to medium and cook, uncovered, for 15 minutes. Remove from the heat and let cool completely before using.

Makes 2 quarts

Peppered Citrus Olives

MAKES 2 CUPS

This is my version of the green olives flavored with pieces of lemon and bay that I see in the markets of Haute Provence.

2 cups brine-cured green olives, mixed sizes if desired
30 black peppercorns
1 lemon, preferably Meyer
6 fresh thyme sprigs
2 tablespoons extra-virgin olive oil

◆ Drain the olives and place them in a glass or other nonreactive container. With a wooden mallet or the back of a wooden spoon, hit the peppercorns just enough to bruise or barely crack them. Add to the olives. Cut the lemon into about 12 or 15 pieces and remove the seeds. Add the lemon to the olives. Rub the thyme sprigs between your hands over the olives, dropping some of the leaves, then add the sprigs and the olive oil. Turn to coat the olives. Cover with plastic wrap and refrigerate for 1 to 3 days before serving. The olives will keep, refrigerated, for up to 6 weeks.

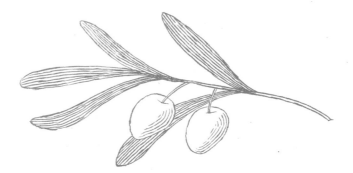

Spicy Black Olives

MAKES 2 CUPS

Set out these olives when serving aperitifs, or add them to spicy sauces. For an even more sizzling version, use fiery bird's-eye chilies. The longer you let the olives stand in this mixture, the hotter they will become.

    2 cups brine-cured or salt-cured black olives
    2 tablespoons crumbled, somewhat mild, dried red chili peppers,
        such as Anaheim, Colorado, or California
    2 tablespoons coriander seeds
    2 tablespoons black peppercorns
    6 fresh thyme sprigs
    3 fresh bay leaves or 2 dried
    ¼ cup extra-virgin olive oil

◆ Drain the olives and place them in a glass or other nonreactive container. Add the crumbled chili. With a wooden mallet or the back of a wooden spoon, hit the coriander seeds and peppercorns just enough to bruise or barely crack them. Add to the olives. Rub the thyme sprigs between your hands over the olives, dropping some of the leaves, then add the sprigs, the bay leaves, and the olive oil. Turn to coat the olives. Cover with plastic wrap and refrigerate for up to 3 days. The olives will keep, refrigerated, for up to 6 weeks.

Black Olive *Tapenade*

MAKES ABOUT 1 CUP

Tapenade can be made in many different ways with virtually any olive, but since the olives must first be pitted, it is more sensible to use those with small pits and thick meat. The heart of the mixture is the olive crushed to a paste. The capers add a tang, the anchovies a salty fish flavor, and the garlic a piquancy. Bread crumbs, ground almonds, mustard, and herbs are occasional ingredients as well and are often used to adjust texture as well as taste. Generally, the saltier the olives, the fewer the anchovies. Different cooks adjust the ingredients to their personal taste, to the occasion, or to what is on hand. This version is a relatively powerful one.

> ½ pound oil-packed black olives, drained
> 6 well-rinsed anchovy fillets, preferably salt-packed
> 3 tablespoons drained capers
> ½ teaspoon minced fresh thyme
> 1 teaspoon fresh lemon juice
> 1 or 2 tablespoons extra-virgin olive oil

◆ Break open the olives by pressing on them with the back of a wooden spoon, then remove the pits. Put the olives, anchovies, capers, thyme, and lemon juice in a blender and process until a paste has formed. With the motor running, add the olive oil a little at a time until the paste is smooth but not oily. (If you prefer, make the *tapenade* in the traditional way using a mortar and pestle.) Use the *tapenade* immediately, or put it into a covered jar and store it in the refrigerator, where it will keep for up to 3 months.

Green Olive and Almond *Tapenade*

MAKES ABOUT 2 CUPS

The first green olives of the year are prepared in August to eat in September, the same time as the almond harvest, making these a seasonal spread that can nonetheless be made throughout the rest of the year as well. The nuts can turn rancid, so this tapenade doesn't store as well. The flavor is of olives and nuts, but if you desire, 5 or 6 anchovy fillets may be added as well. It makes a fine spread on its own, or may be used as a sauce for fish or meat.

½ pound not-too-salty, brine-cured green olives, drained
1 cup blanched whole almonds
1 teaspoon minced fresh thyme
2 teaspoons fresh lemon juice
1 to 2 tablespoons olive oil
2 teaspoons capers

◆ Break open the olives by pressing on them with the back of a wooden spoon, then remove the pits. Put the olives, almonds, thyme, lemon juice, olive oil, and capers in a blender and process until a paste has formed. (If you prefer, make the *tapenade* in the traditional way using a mortar and pestle.) Use the *tapenade* immediately, or put it in a covered jar and store it in the refrigerator, where it will keep for up to 2 weeks.

Poor Man's Foie Gras

MAKES 18 TOASTS; SERVES 4 TO 6 AS AN HORS D'OEUVRE

Mme. Corbet, who lives across the road from me, serves these slightly gamy toasts, full of local flavors, at aperitif time, where they go well with a variety of drinks from pastis to vin de noix.

 2 well-seasoned sausages such as Toulouse or spicy Italian, almost ¼ pound total
 2 chicken livers
 20 salt-cured black olives, pitted
 15 fresh juniper berries, or 10 dried
 18 baguette slices, cut on the diagonal

◆ Preheat an oven to 400 degrees F.

◆ Cut the sausages into chunks, and peel away the skin and discard. Cut the chicken livers into small pieces, discarding any veins. Put the sausages, chicken livers, olives, and juniper berries in a blender or food processor and process to a fairly smooth paste. Spread the paste thinly on the bread and place on a baking sheet. Bake until the edges of the bread are browned and the paste is cooked, 8 to 10 minutes. Serve hot.

Classic Vinaigrette

MAKES 6 TO 7 TABLESPOONS, ENOUGH FOR A SALAD FOR 4 OR 5

Vinaigrette dresses the salads and vegetables of Haute Provence. It might be made directly in the bottom of the salad bowl, as my friend Françoise taught me to do, or made separately and poured over the salad or the vegetables. Minced garlic, onion, or shallot may be added to the vinaigrette with the salt and pepper, as can peeled, seeded, and minced tomatoes or various herbs. Vinaigrette is also made individually, at the table, with each person adding olive oil, vinegar, salt, and pepper to individual taste, although this practice was more common in households of past generations than it is today.

Extra-virgin olive oil should always be used. Vinegars vary in flavor and strength with the latter commonly falling between 4 and 7 degrees in strength; if using a higher strength vinegar, use less in this recipe. Red wine vinegar is typical in most of Haute Provence.

¼ cup extra-virgin olive oil
2 to 3 tablespoons red wine vinegar
½ teaspoon salt
½ teaspoon freshly ground black pepper

◆ Place the olive oil in the bottom of a salad bowl or in a small mixing bowl. With a fork or a spoon, blend in the vinegar, salt, and pepper.

OLIVES & OLIVE OIL [74]

Rice, Tomato, and Olive Salad

SERVES 4

In Haute Provence, this salad, made from the previous night's rice, is served at midday. The olives give their deep flavor to the otherwise bland rice, and the tomatoes—even wintertime ones—add texture and acidity. Other ingredients can be added, too, such as chopped sweet peppers, and basil can be used instead of parsley.

1 ½ to 2 cups cooked long-grain white rice, at room temperature
1 tomato, chopped
1 tablespoon balsamic vinegar
1 tablespoon extra-virgin olive oil
½ teaspoon freshly ground black pepper
½ teaspoon salt
¼ cup minced red or green onion
20 tart green or oil-cured black olives, pitted and chopped
¼ cup minced fresh parsley

◆ Combine all the ingredients in a bowl. Turn gently with a wooden spoon until well mixed.

Olive and Lentil Salad

MAKES ABOUT 6 CUPS; SERVES 5 OR 6

Simple and spare, this salad is a celebration of the taste sensations that can be achieved with a few ingredients of good quality. Use only an extra-virgin olive oil and green lentils. An olive oil that has been subjected to processing will taste so. The small French green or Le Puy lentils are best to use as they retain their shape after cooking, while the more common brown lentils quickly become soft and mushy if even slightly overcooked.

    1½ cups French green lentils
    5 cups water
    2 fresh bay leaves, or 1 dried
    1 teaspoon salt
    12 tart green olives, pitted and chopped
    3 tablespoons extra-virgin, first cold press olive oil
    1 tablespoon red wine vinegar

◆ Place the lentils in a saucepan with the water, bay leaves, and 1 teaspoon salt. Bring to a boil over medium-high heat. Reduce the heat to low and simmer, uncovered, until the lentils are tender, 20 to 30 minutes. Remove from the heat and let cool.

◆ Drain the lentils thoroughly and combine in a bowl with the olives, olive oil, and vinegar. Adjust for salt. Serve chilled or at room temperature.

Olives, Roasted Red Peppers, and Eggplant Salad

SERVES 4 TO 6

This is inspired by Italian caponata, *but is milder, as olives replace the capers and the seasonings are not as astringent. It makes a wonderful summertime accompaniment to grilled meats or chops, and to polenta or rice dishes. The vegetables are chopped, not pureed, and the eggplant retains its firm texture after baking to better absorb the seasonings.*

    1 medium-large eggplant
    3 roasted red sweet peppers (page 150), coarsely chopped
    1 cup pitted, coarsely chopped oil- or brine-cured green or black olives
    1 teaspoon salt
    1½ teaspoons coarsely ground black pepper
    ¼ cup chopped fresh parsley
    2 to 3 tablespoons extra-virgin, first cold press olive oil
    2 cloves garlic, minced
    ½ yellow onion, minced
    Juice of 1 lemon (about 2 tablespoons)

◆ Preheat an oven to 300 degrees F.

◆ Place the eggplant on a baking sheet and bake until tender, about 1¼ hours. Remove from the oven and let cool. Peel the eggplant and chop it coarsely. Place in a bowl.

◆ Add all the remaining ingredients to the eggplant and mix well. Serve warm or at room temperature.

Tapenade, Roasted Red Pepper, and Goat Cheese Sandwiches

MAKES 4 SANDWICHES

Unlike many French sandwiches, these are made not on baguettes or thick slices of country bread, but with pain de mie, *a dense loaf cut into thin slices. Here, a firm-textured sandwich bread from a bakery might be used, or thin slices of country bread. The sandwich, once composed, is grilled until the bread is toasty gold and the cheese melted.*

> 8 slices white bread (see recipe introduction)
> ½ cup Black Olive *Tapenade* (see page 71)
> 4 roasted red sweet pepper halves (see page 150)
> ¼ pound soft fresh goat cheese
> 2 to 3 tablespoons unsalted butter

◆ Spread 4 of the bread slices with the *tapenade* on one side only and lay a roasted red pepper half on top of each slice. Spread the other 4 bread slices with the goat cheese and place the slices, goat cheese side down, on top of the red peppers to form sandwiches.

◆ Melt half the butter in a large skillet over medium-high heat. When it foams, add the sandwiches and cook, pressing lightly with the back of a spatula to flatten. When the first side is golden, in 3 to 4 minutes, add the remaining butter, turn and brown the other side, 2 to 3 minutes longer.

◆ Remove to individual plates and cut in half. Serve hot.

Braised Greens and Black Olives

SERVES 3 OR 4 AS A SIDE DISH

A mixture of spinach, escarole, and chard is simmered to tenderness in a little olive oil and the water that clings to the leaves of the greens as they go into the pan. The olives fill and plump during the cooking and season the greens, which melt into a tender heap.

> 6 cups mixed young spinach, escarole, and chard leaves
> 2 tablespoons extra-virgin olive oil
> 1 clove garlic, minced
> 8 to 10 oil-cured black olives

◆ Rinse all the greens well and remove any coarse stems. Place the leaves in a bowl of cold water.

◆ In a large, deep skillet, warm the olive oil over medium heat. Add the garlic and sauté for a minute or two. Remove the dripping greens from the water—do not dry—and pack them into the skillet. They will seem almost not to fit. Place a cover on the skillet and cook, sliding the pan back and forth over the heat. After a minute or two, remove the cover and toss the greens. Add the olives. Return the cover and continue to cook, stirring the greens and olives, until the greens are thoroughly limp and tender, another 3 or 4 minutes. Serve hot.

Rosemary Pasta with Black Olives and Carrots

SERVES 4

Oil-cured black olives bring their unctuous flavor to this simple wintertime dish, while the rosemary enlivens the sweet taste of the sautéed carrots.

3 tablespoons extra-virgin olive oil
1 tablespoon butter
3 cloves garlic, minced
½ yellow onion, chopped
1 to 2 carrots, peeled and cut into very thin slices
1 teaspoon salt
1 tablespoon freshly ground black pepper
1 teaspoon minced fresh rosemary
½ cup oil-cured black olives
10 ounces dried pasta, such as penne or mostaccioti
¼ cup grated Parmesan cheese (optional)

◆ Bring a large pot of salted water to a boil. Meanwhile, in a skillet warm 2 tablespoons of the olive oil and the butter over medium heat. Add half the garlic, all the onion, and carrots, and sauté until the carrots are easily pierced with the tines of a fork, 7 to 10 minutes. Add the remaining garlic, salt, half of the pepper, half of the rosemary, and the olives. Continue to sauté until the olives are plumped and the edges of the carrots are slightly golden, about 3 or 4 minutes.

◆ While the vegetables are cooking, add the pasta to the boiling water, stir well, and cook until just tender. Drain.

◆ Place the pasta in a warmed serving bowl, and turn it with the remaining 1 tablespoon olive oil and the remaining pepper. Add the contents of the skillet, including the pan juices. Add the remaining rosemary and turn to mix all the ingredients. Adjust the salt. Top with the optional Parmesan cheese if desired. Serve hot.

Chicken Breasts Stuffed with *Tapenade*

Serves 4

Here is a simpler echo of the richer, more elegant chicken dish in which a layer of sliced black truffles is spread between the meat and the skin.

> 4 chicken breast halves
> 2 tablespoons fresh thyme leaves
> 1 teaspoon dried winter savory
> ½ teaspoon salt
> 6 black peppercorns
> 6 to 8 tablespoons Black Olive *Tapenade* (page 71)

◆ Preheat an oven to 375 degrees F.

◆ Loosen the skin on each chicken breast to make a pocket for the stuffing by carefully slipping your fingers between the skin and the meat. Do not detach entirely or tear any holes in the skin.

◆ In a small spice grinder or mortar, combine the thyme, winter savory, salt, and peppercorns and grind to pulverize. Rub the chicken breasts all over with the herb mixture. Using a small knife, spread some of the *tapenade* between the skin and the flesh of each chicken breast.

◆ Place the chicken breasts on a baking sheet, skin side up. Bake until the juices run clear when a breast is pierced with a knife, and the skin is golden brown, 35 to 45 minutes, basting with the pan juices once or twice during cooking. Serve hot or at room temperature.

Chicken Ragout with Black Olives

SERVES 6

This is comfort food in Haute Provence. I have been served it many times over the years and often make it myself, and it is always satisfying. The chicken parts are first browned in a little olive oil in a heavy pan or skillet, then topped with herbed tomatoes and a handful of oil-cured black olives to finish cooking. The olives bring the salt and a mellowness to the dish and add texture and spots of intensity. Brined black or green olives can be used in place of oil-cured olives, and will impart a sharper flavor to the dish. Rabbit, pork, or beef can be prepared this way as well. In Haute Provence, any leftovers appear the following day as a sauce for pasta, polenta, or rice, with perhaps a few mushrooms and some fresh herbs added.

1 fryer chicken, about 3 pounds, cut into serving pieces,
    or a selection of breasts and thighs
1 teaspoon freshly ground black pepper
3 tablespoons fresh thyme leaves
1 teaspoon chopped fresh rosemary
1 tablespoon extra-virgin olive oil
1½ teaspoons unsalted butter
½ cup minced yellow onion
2 cloves garlic, minced
4 to 6 large, very ripe fresh tomatoes, chopped, or 3 cups chopped
    canned Roma tomatoes and their juice
2 fresh bay leaves, or 1 dried
16 oil-cured black olives

◆ Rub the chicken pieces all over with the pepper, half of the thyme, and half of the rosemary. In a skillet large enough to hold all the chicken pieces in a single layer, heat the olive oil and butter over medium-high heat. When it is nearly smoking, add the chicken pieces. Reduce the heat to medium, and sauté for 2 or 3 minutes until lightly browned. Turn the pieces over and cook for another minute or two to brown on the other side. Add the onion and garlic and continue to cook for another minute or two. Pour the tomatoes over the chicken. Add the bay leaves, and stir in the olives. Cover tightly. Reduce the heat to medium-low and cook until the juices run clear when the thickest part of a thigh is pierced with a knife, about 15 minutes.

◆ Remove the cover, increase the heat to medium, and cook for another 5 minutes to reduce and thicken the sauce. Stir in the remaining thyme and rosemary and serve hot.

NOTE: *If skinned chicken pieces are used, add 1 to 2 additional tablespoons olive oil to the pan.*

Rabbit Sauté and Green Olives

SERVES 4 TO 6

Rabbits are an important part of life in Haute Provence. In the countryside many people have a hutch or two to keep a steady supply on hand, and fresh rabbit is standard fare in butcher shops and at the local markets. There the rabbits are sold whole, including the head, which is considered a delicacy. Prepared in a sauce, and served with pasta or polenta, a single rabbit can feed up to six people. Olives added to the sauce enrich the dish with their complexities, contributing a sense of substantialness.

This is an ideal preparation for young rabbit, as the cooking time is short and renders the tender meat succulent. The lemon juice that is used to deglaze the pan combines with the olives to enhance but not overwhelm the meat. A little sauce is made from the pan drippings and chopped tomatoes, and it, too, is aromatic with lemon and olives.

continued

1 young tender rabbit, 2½ pounds
2 tablespoons unsalted butter
1 teaspoon freshly ground black pepper
¼ cup minced yellow onion
16 tart green olives, preferably seasoned with lemon and fennel
Juice of 1 lemon (about 2 tablespoons juice)
¼ cup chicken broth
1 cup chopped very ripe tomatoes, or 1 cup chopped canned
    Roma tomatoes and their juice

◆ Cut the rabbit into serving pieces as described in Sage-Roasted Rabbit and Potatoes (page 48).

◆ In a Dutch oven or deep, heavy-bottomed skillet, melt the butter over medium heat. When it foams, add the rabbit pieces and sauté over medium to medium-low heat for about 15 minutes, turning often. The rabbit will become golden as it cooks. At the end of 15 minutes, sprinkle with the pepper and add the onion and the olives. Cook for another minute or two, then squeeze the lemon juice over the contents of the pan and follow it with the broth. Scrape the pan bottom to dislodge any bits clinging to it, then add the tomatoes. Cover the pan tightly and reduce the heat to low. Cook until the rabbit is tender, about 10 to 15 minutes.

◆ Uncover, increase the heat to medium and continue to cook, stirring occasionally, until the sauce has thickened and reduced, about 5 to 7 minutes. Serve hot.

NOTE: *If only a large, mature rabbit is available, double the amount of the other ingredients and increase the covered cooking time to at least 1 hour, or until the meat is tender.*

Black Olive Bread

MAKES 2 LOAVES

This rustic bread is found at boulangeries *throughout the region. It is a lovely brown color, somewhat soft, dotted with chunks of black olives. This version is from a California friend, a creative home baker who knows and loves the black olive bread of Haute Provence.*

The amount of salt should be adjusted according to the saltiness of the olives.

3 cups skim milk
1½ tablespoons honey
1 envelope active dry yeast (2½ teaspoons)
1 cup rye flour
4 cups whole-wheat flour
2 cups white bread flour, plus 1½ to 2 tablespoons for bowl
    and baking sheet
Extra-virgin olive oil for bowls, plus ¼ cup
½ to 1 teaspoon salt
3 cups pitted oil-packed black olives

◆ In a saucepan combine the milk and honey and heat to lukewarm (105 degrees F). Pour the mixture into a large bowl and sprinkle the yeast over the surface. Let stand for 10 minutes until foamy.

◆ Add the rye flour, 1 cup of the whole-wheat flour, and the 2 cups bread flour and stir with a wooden spoon until a sticky sponge forms. Remove from the bowl to a floured work surface and knead until the dough is supple, 5 to 10 minutes. Oil a large bowl with a little olive oil, place the dough in it, and turn the dough to coat the surface. Cover the bowl with a clean cloth and place in a warm place until the dough has doubled in size, about 2 hours. Remove the dough from the bowl to a floured work surface and work in the remaining 3 cups whole-wheat flour, the salt, and the ¼ cup olive oil. Return to the oiled bowl, cover, and let rise until doubled again, about 30 minutes.

continued

OLIVES & OLIVE OIL

♦ Remove the dough to a floured work surface again and knead in the olives. Return the dough to the bowl, cover, and let rise once again until doubled, about 20 minutes.

♦ Preheat an oven to 375 degrees F. Sprinkle a baking sheet with the 1½ to 2 tablespoons bread flour.

♦ Remove the dough to a floured work surface, divide in half, and shape into 2 oblong loaves, each about 12 inches long, 3 inches wide, and 3 inches high. Place on the prepared baking sheet.

♦ Bake until the loaves form a dark crust and a knife inserted into the center comes out clean, 50 to 60 minutes. Transfer to a rack to cool.

Wild
Mushrooms
&
Truffles

RECIPES

Warm Potato and Truffle Salad

Brouillade of Truffles

Green Salad with Truffled Oil Dressing

Sanguins Grilled with Garlic and Parsley

Creamy Mushroom Soup

Gratin of Forest Mushrooms

Baked Pasta with Chanterelles

Tart of Leeks and Dried Morels

Beef Daube with Dried Cèpes

Cannelloni Filled with Next-Day Daube

WILD MUSHROOMS AND TRUFFLES ARE significant ingredients in the kitchens of Haute Provence, where they are used fresh, dried, and pickled. Dozens of edible fungi species, including the legendary *rabasse,* the black Périgord truffle, can be found in the scrubby underbrush of the hillsides, in the forests of oak and pine, in abandoned chestnut orchards, and along the edges of valley and mountain streams. Wild mushrooms and black truffles are more than seasonal delicacies—they are objects of desire. Once the mushrooms start to appear in the fall, people are seized with excitement and enthusiasm, by a passion for the chase. Every weekend from late September through early November, the cars of mushroom hunters are parked, helter-skelter, along the shoulders of rural roads, while their inhabitants, armed with baskets, roam the countryside, seeking the wild quarry.

I share the French passion for mushroom hunting. Ducking beneath the outermost oak and pine trees that border the road's edge to enter into the shelter of the forest, to be nearly overcome by the compelling, primeval scent of damp earth, rotting leaves, and fungi, and then to spot the clumps and rings of mushrooms, is an exhilarating experience. Moss and earth bulge, layers of leaves lift to reveal caches of creamy white *pieds de mouton,* nodding heads of *petits gris,* and firm, round caps of cèpes, all deliciously edible. I quickly cut them free, drop them into my basket, and plunge on, looking for more. There is also the lure of the unknown mushrooms, those of striking colors, small or large, sturdy or fragile, whose odors tantalize. Perhaps they are rare and wonderful edibles. These I put into a separate bag in the basket to be taken later to the village pharmacy for identification. By an endearing custom—and by law—French pharmacists are trained in mycology and enthusiastically identify mushrooms brought to them. More often than not the pharmacists, at least in Haute Provence, are avid mushroom hunters themselves, and as baskets are perused and the fine edible specimens exclaimed over, they will try to discover where they were found or suggest a favorite recipe.

When mushroom hunting in a group, everyone tends to scatter, bent on the hunt, rather than on sociability. Triumphant finds are shouted out through the forest and underbrush. Conversation does not resume until the agreed upon meeting time, and even then the topic is the bounty in the basket. It is not uncommon to see local people, those who know exactly where to go, returning home from a day in the forest with ten to fifteen pounds of mushrooms of several different kinds.

During the season, supermarkets in Haute Provence dazzlingly display huge piles of a dozen different wild mushrooms, while in the open markets, local people sell their own gatherings, albeit displayed in a less flamboyant fashion. Then, suddenly, the weather turns, the first freeze comes and the season is over, to be remembered though, when a handful of dried cèpes or *girolles* release their aroma to a winter stew.

Although mushrooms are found in spring, fall has the greater abundance and greater variety. Cèpe, *pied de mouton, petit gris, sanguin, girolle,* and *pied bleu* are among the most delectable finds in Haute Provence. Where and when they are found, though, varies from place to place, depending upon altitude and the vegetation. As an example, in the mountainous region of Annot and Entrevaux, the abandoned chestnut orchards and oak and pine forests can become a veritable carpet of cèpes during August and September. In the Haut Var and in the vicinity of Moustiers-Ste.-Marie and the slopes of the Plateau de Valensole, however, the mushroom season is generally considered to be October, and although cèpes and their relatives are found there, they are less abundant than at the higher altitudes.

The *sanguin (Lactarius deliciosus,* the Delicious Milk Cap) is pursued in the lower altitudes, where it populates the forest floors. Its concave cap, ringed in orange and cream and tinged with iridescent green, oozes a bloodlike red when broken. Well seasoned with minced garlic, olive oil, and salt and pepper, and cooked on a grill over hot coals flavored with grapevine cuttings, *sanguins* are a seasonal marker. In a good year, though, when they are plentiful, they are pickled by the jarful and then served throughout the year, as part of the hors d'oeuvre selection.

The thick, meaty cèpe *(Boletus edulis)* belongs to the extensive *Boletus* genus, whose members are easily distinguishable by the spongelike undersurface of the cap. King boletus, as it is sometimes called, has a firm, rounded brown cap, rather dry to the touch, and an underside of pale cream. Considered to be one of the finest of wild mushrooms, it is consumed fresh in sautés, soups, stews, and omelets. Once dried, it is extraordinarily aromatic, and a scant seven or eight dried slices are enough to dominate and to enrich a sauce or flavor a stew. The cèpes relatives include the poisonous *diable* or *Boletus satanas,* whose grayish-white cap and spongy yellow-red underside bruise an ugly dark blue when touched, and the lowly, watery *pisacan,* always prolific, but with only a passable flavor.

Throughout springtime in Haute Provence, mushroom hunters seek the morel. Dark brown, craterous, hard, and chewy, it is held in high esteem along with the cèpe and the *sanguin* of fall. Although I have been taken to secret truffle grounds, not one of my acquaintances has ever invited me along when hunting for morels. These highly perfumed mushrooms are cooked in stews and sautéed to surround chops and roasts, to which they impart their nutty, earthy flavor. Like cèpes, they are easily dried and are pungent and powerful.

The noble black truffle of Périgord *(Tuber melananasporum)* is found throughout Haute Provence, and today truffles from Provence, not from the Périgord, account for approximately 80 percent of truffle sales in France. They have the appearance and texture of the roughly patterned surface of a dog's nose, an expandingly pungent perfume that is at once musky and earthy, and a weight ranging from half an ounce to two pounds. A common local name is black diamonds, a reference to the high esteem in which they are held by gastronomes, and perhaps to the high prices they bring as well. Unfortunately for the amateur, truffles are far more difficult to find than wild mushrooms. Unlike mushrooms, which rise out of the ground, truffles grow to maturity obscured by the earth, primarily in association with the roots of oak trees. Filaments emerge from the spores of the truffle that elongate and attach to the roots of the host trees—oaks, hazelnuts, pines, and lindens. From this union mycorrhiza are formed, and eventually the tree's root system is invaded. In approximately ten years, the first truffles will form and can be dug. *Truffière,* or truffle-producing grounds, may be found extensively in the wilds of Haute Provence, but the *truffière* may also be cultivated grounds grown from hand-planted acorns, or more recently from commercially inoculated seedlings.

Three means are used to locate truffles: flies, a pig, or a dog. One must first know where to look, and it is not obvious to the untrained eye. Truffle-bearing trees are marked by a circle around their base where no grass grows. This is called a *brûle* or "burn," and is thought to be caused by the truffle's secretion of herbicidal substances. To hunt using the fly method, a branch of Aleppo pine is stripped of all but the needles at its tip. The needles are brushed over the *brûle,* and if there are truffles hidden there, little flies will jump up because they are in the process of laying their eggs. If flies jump up, then the hunter's next job is to sniff the ground, and to dig deeply, up to one and a half feet, where the truffle aroma is strongest. I have heard much about this method, but have never practiced it with any success, although I vainly keep trying.

Trained pigs and dogs can scent the truffles' powerful aroma beneath the earth, thus locating the truffles for their masters. I once saw a dog pause at a crumbled rock wall near an oak tree. He sniffed a stone, scratched the earth next to it, and then stood aside. The dog's owner moved the stone, which weighed at least twenty pounds, then dug down a good eighteen inches to pull out a black truffle the size of a lemon.

Although there is much historical association of truffle hunting with pigs, dogs are more commonly used today. Room, board, and transportation for a three-hundred-pound pig may be a factor, yet some *rabassiers* still use pigs. One such hunter, M. Capretti, took me with him. He was eighty-three years old at the time and, after sharing coffee with him and his wife in their well-appointed dining room, we walked several doors down to the urban, but still medieval, stone garage, which turned out to be the building, with accompanying yard, where his recently acquired *truie*—a four-foot-long, pale-rose pig—was installed. He backed his shiny new Renault van close and opened the rear door, revealing an interior bedded with fresh straw. A ramp was slid out and the sow lured onto it with a handful of dog biscuits. As she gulped the biscuits, her leash was quickly attached, then she clambered up the ramp and into the straw at the rear, where she was rewarded with more biscuits. For fifteen minutes I followed the van to the outskirts of town, where we climbed a winding road to M. Capretti's *cabanon,* a summer house on a hillside, with a modern glassed-in porch, surrounded by mounds of lavender and rosemary. Down and across the gravelly slope was half an acre or so of pubescent oak trees in neat rows. He had planted them himself, M. Capretti told me, from acorns gathered in the forest from known truffle trees. He had been truffle hunting since he was fifteen, starting in the forests; then when he realized their relative values, he tore out his inherited grapevines and replaced them with truffle oaks. He had no other profession.

Off we went to the field below, the pig pulling on her leash, rushing headlong from tree to tree, while I scrambled behind. All the time, he was talking softly, encouraging his pig, *"Ma petite cherie, cherches, cherches."* Suddenly the pig stopped and nuzzled the ground. Then she began to dig furiously with her powerful snout, throwing dirt in every direction with her master crouched next to her, his eyes focused on the hole. At a finely timed moment, when the truffle was evident, but before the pig could seize it, in one fluid movement, M. Capretti jerked back on the leash, distracted the pig by tossing a few biscuits to one side, then loosened the truffle with his stick and slipped it into his bag so quickly I never saw it. After forty minutes of such hunting, the pig had located several dozen truffles, mostly small, but by then the aroma from the bag was nearly overwhelming.

After a stroll around the property, with a peek at the inside of the *cabanon,* we returned to the village to put the pig away. We went back to the house, through the ground floor cellar to select a bottle, then upstairs for tea, Bordeaux, hard almond cookies, and conversation to cap a memorable afternoon. I was sent off with a bag of truffles, "enough to make a good *brouillade"*— which I did.

Truffles can be eaten either raw or cooked, but there seems to be consensus that a little warmth or heat brings out the full and powerful perfume that is their hallmark. A few thin slices heated only for a moment or two in a skillet, sprinkled with salt and pepper, and then placed atop a well-seasoned sauté of potatoes, or as I once had them at the Grand Hôtel in Valensole, over a sauté of Jerusalem artichokes, are sufficient to demonstrate the truffle's intoxicating reputation. Adventuresome and skilled cooks, such as the chef of the Grand Hôtel, can create adventuresome truffle pairings with a deft hand. I tried to re-create, for example, a *pain grillé* that I had sampled there. It had been spread with black olive *tapenade,* topped with two generous slices of truffles, and then broiled briefly to warm the truffles and crisp the edges of the toasts. My *tapenade* had too strong a character, and it overwhelmed the truffle, whereas the one I sampled in the restaurant was more delicate, allowing the flavor of both the olives and the truffle to be equally present.

If you ask ahead, you can bring your own truffles to many restaurants in Haute Provence and the chefs will prepare them for you. On a late-January visit to the uppermost regions of the area, at the height of truffle season, my friends called ahead to ask a *charcutier* of their acquaintance who specialized in truffled pâtés to suggest a good local restaurant where we might have a simple lunch that would include a *brouillade* of truffles. Hôtel-Restaurant de la Poste was the answer. Shortly after one o'clock we arrived at our destination, which, like so many similar hotel restaurants dating from the nineteenth century, was built directly on what are now country roads but were once stage stops for the *diligences,* the horse-drawn travelers' coaches. We were greeted, then ushered through the bar past tables set for lunch, where a number of people were eating, to the dining room, which was completely empty. The busy season, we were told, is summer.

The proprietors, representing three generations, told us that the truffles and freshly laid eggs had been brought down to them that morning by the *charcutier* himself. Then they asked if we would like to visit the kitchen and watch our *brouillade* being made. Of course we said yes, but first we were brought an aperitif. When it was finished, we were escorted into a huge kitchen where a white-clad young man, the son, was standing over a massive wood-burning stove upon which was set a pan of mythic proportions to serve as a *bain-marie*. Nearby were the eggs, their deep gold yolks pooled in a glass bowl, heavily flecked with black bits of truffle. A tablespoon of butter was dropped into a long-handled black skillet, which the cook held in place on the surface of the gently simmering water. Once the butter melted, he poured the egg-and-truffle mixture in and then whisked it continuously until the eggs set into a small, creamy curd. At the last minute, a tablespoon of crème fraîche was swirled in along with a little salt and a grind or two of white pepper (to not confuse the black pepper with the truffle bits!). We scurried to our table, and were told we must eat it hot, now. The table had been set with heavy linens, the breadbasket was brim full of baguette slices, and a trivet was posed in the center. The hot skillet was set down upon the trivet and we commenced to serve ourselves. M. Rodier, the father of the cook, suggested we might like to try a rosé wine from one of the few remaining *domaines* of the region. We did indeed. The wine was served chilled but not icy, a full rose color, dry and light yet fruity, and it went very well with the truffled *brouillade*. More courses followed, and each generation came from the kitchen with his or her *specialité,* concluding with *la grandmère* offering us spoonfuls of her homemade *confiture de pastèque* (watermelon jam). Late in the afternoon, after being immersed in simple flavors, we had a final *café express,* then fondly said good-bye.

It is not easy to buy truffles in small quantities. They are not sold in the supermarkets, like wild mushrooms, and almost never in the open markets. Although formal truffle markets exist, they bear no resemblance to weekly open markets, where lively discourse, cries, and shouts are part of the panoply. In one of the important truffle market towns of Haute Provence, the only clue to a market in progress may be as subtle as a larger-than-usual gathering of people standing around the town square, at a café, or perhaps, as in Aups, near a specified building.

In Aups, the truffle market occurs on Thursday mornings from late November through late February at the Salle des Jeunes. Silently, some of the truffle sellers position themselves behind folding tables with a canvas bag or a wicker basket open on the table to reveal their wares. Others stand or circulate, holding opaque plastic bags with the telltale bulges of truffles. Those who have come to buy at this wholesale market, the *courtiers* (brokers), *charcutiers,* restaurant chefs, and others who are prepared to buy truffles in large quantities, stand singly or in small groups, chatting softly, sometimes going into a café or just walking about. Careful scrutiny of the scene reveals little or no overt activity until nearly eleven o'clock. Then a mute flurry of activity occurs. As if from nowhere, scales suddenly emerge to weigh the truffles, and quickly money and truffles change hands. Some sellers even prevail upon nearby *épiceries* for their produce scales, so that the truffles might be accurately weighed. Before noon and aperitif time, all evidence is gone of the tens of thousands of francs that have been passed. The expensive cars with license plates indicating they are from the rich enclaves of the Cote d'Azur, the Bouches-du-Rhône, from Paris and Monaco have gone, taking with them the fur-wrapped women and well-dressed men who only a short while before were milling about with the country folk.

A great part of the mysterious air that surrounds the buying and selling of truffles is that often the money is not declared legally as income, and it can be substantial. I wish I could have seen the markets in days past, into the 1970s and early '80s, when buyers flipped up the trunks of their cars, so I have been told, to reveal open cartons and suitcases containing thick packets of banded banknotes ready to be handed over in exchange for truffles.

In the culture of Haute Provence, truffles are more than just a business enterprise affecting a few; they are part of wintertime life. From November through February, walks in the forest will reveal holes dug by wild boars rooting for truffles. An unusual number of people, mostly men, will be seen driving over the back roads with a dog, but without hunting garb. Signs are posted against poachers, and yet for some, part of the game is to see who can poach from whom. During this season virtually every restaurant offers at least a *brouillade* of truffles, while other restaurants are well known for their chefs' way with these prized black knobs. In those restaurants, multicourse meals, each course featuring the truffle in a different presentation, are on the winter menu. With a knock on the back door, restaurateurs are offered bags of truffles for sale, usually from someone in their village, and near Christmastime, nearly everyone manages to buy a few truffles from a friend who knows where and how to find them. Truffle hunting and selling, although more open than it was in the 1980s and earlier, remains arcane.

CLEANING TRUFFLES

The freshly unearthed truffle is covered with dirt or, if the ground is still wet from recent rain or snowmelt, mud. To remove, gently wash the truffle under running water, scrubbing lightly with a small brush, such as a toothbrush, to remove any traces caught in the miniscule craters of the truffles' exterior. Dry the truffle gently with a clean cloth. It is now ready to use. For a refined presentation, some people scrape off the bumpy exterior, reserving the scrapings for another use, such as a *brouillade*. Truffles may also be purchased preserved, in which case no cleaning is necessary, but these lack the intense fragrance and flavor of fresh truffles. Fresh truffles are also occasionally sold cleaned, packed with rice, in a jar or plastic container.

GRATING TRUFFLES

Once a truffle has been cleaned, it can be grated in the large holes of a hand-held grater.

CLEANING MUSHROOMS

Avoid washing mushrooms whenever possible, as they absorb the water, which dilutes their flavor. Instead, use a brush to remove clinging bits of dirt or leaves. Any damaged spots should be cut away and discarded.

Hunting Wild Mushrooms

Under no circumstances should anyone gather wild mushrooms for eating unless accompanied by an expert. Many wild mushrooms are deadly, while others can cause severe illness. Some edible mushrooms so closely resemble poisonous ones that even experts shy away from collecting these.

Wild mushrooms, such as morels, cèpes, and chanterelles, that have been foraged by experts are available in many markets. Additionally, cultivated mushrooms such as shiitakes and portobellos may be substituted for wild mushrooms in many dishes. The flavors, of course, will be different, but will nevertheless have the richness associated with wild mushrooms.

Drying Mushrooms

Cépes, *sanguins,* and other large, meaty mushrooms are particularly suitable for drying. Of the cultivated varieties, the portobello, white button, and shiitake are good choices. Slice the mushrooms lengthwise from top to bottom, including the stem. The slices should be about ¼ inch thick. Spread on racks in the sun, bringing the racks to a sheltered spot in the nighttime to avoid evening and morning moisture. Mushrooms may also be strung on strings, using a needle and button thread. In the homes of Haute Provence, the strings are hung near the fireplace or an oil-burning stove to dry. If the mushrooms no longer exude any juice when squeezed between your fingers and are nearly brittle, they are sufficiently dried. Place them in a paper or plastic bag or a closed tin and store them in a dry place, where they will keep for a year.

PICKLING MUSHROOMS

Meaty mushrooms such as sanguins *and cèpes are the ones typically used for pickling. Portobello, white button, and shiitake are good choices among the cultivated varieties.*

> ½ cup extra-virgin olive oil
> ½ cup red wine vinegar
> ¾ teaspoon salt
> ½ teaspoon black peppercorns
> 4 fresh thyme sprigs
> ½ pound firm fresh mushrooms (see recipe introduction),
>   sliced ¼ inch thick

Combine ¼ cup each of the olive oil and vinegar in a stainless steel, nonreactive saucepan. Add the salt, peppercorns, and thyme and bring to a boil over medium high heat. Boil for 2 minutes, then add the sliced mushrooms and reduce the heat to very low. Cook for 2 minutes only, turning the mushrooms constantly.

Ladle the hot mushroom mixture into a dry, sterilized jar. Add the remaining olive oil and vinegar and cover the jar loosely with aluminum foil or waxed paper. Let cool to room temperature. Discard the foil or waxed paper and cover the jar with a tight-fitting lid or cork. Refrigerate for at least 24 hours before using to allow the flavors to develop. The oil will solidify somewhat, but will liquefy again at room temperature. The mushrooms may be stored in the refrigerator for up to 3 months.

Makes 2 cups

Mushroom Broth

Mushroom broth is a good, all-purpose vegetable broth to have on hand. If one wishes, it can be substituted for beef or chicken broth in many instances.

½ pound cultivated fresh white or brown mushrooms
8 dried cèpe slices
4 carrots, carefully rinsed and cut into 2-inch lengths
2 large leeks, carefully rinsed and cut into 2-inch lengths
1 large celery stalk, cut into 2-inch lengths
5 whole cloves
2 quarts water
1 teaspoon salt

◆ Coarsely chop the fresh mushrooms. Combine all the ingredients in a medium-sized soup pot or stockpot. Bring to a boil over medium-high heat. Cover, reduce the heat to low, and simmer until the vegetables have imparted their flavor to the broth, 45 minutes to 1 hour.

◆ Remove from the heat and strain the broth through a fine-mesh sieve into a clean container. Discard the contents of the sieve. Cover the broth and refrigerate or freeze if not using immediately.

Makes about 6 cups

Warm Potato and Truffle Salad

Warmth releases and intensifies the perfume and taste of the truffle, and potatoes, like eggs, are a good background against which it can star. The potatoes, once boiled and peeled, are gently dressed with only a fine-quality olive oil, salt, and freshly ground pepper, and then the grated truffles are folded in. Serve this on its own as a first course.

6 waxy boiling potatoes, such as Bintje, Yellow Finn, or Yukon Gold,
  or new potatoes, about 1½ pounds total
¼ to ⅓ cup extra-virgin olive oil
1 teaspoon salt
1 teaspoon freshly ground black pepper
2 or 3 walnut-sized truffles, cleaned and grated (page 97)

◆ Boil the unpeeled potatoes in salted water to cover until just tender when pierced with the tines of a fork, about 20 minutes. Do not overcook them. Drain well and, as soon as they are cool enough to handle, peel them. Cut into ¼-inch-thick slices or ½-inch cubes. Place in a bowl; they should still be hot. Pour the olive oil over the potatoes and turn gently with a wooden spoon to coat them. Add the salt, pepper, and grated truffles. Turn gently to distribute the ingredients.

◆ Serve immediately, while nice and warm, spooned onto warmed plates.

Brouillade of Truffles

Calling this scrambled eggs, a familiar breakfast dish for Americans, doesn't describe the French version, which is not a breakfast dish but a first course or main course for lunch or dinner. In the French manner, the eggs are cooked very slowly over low heat or over simmering water in a double boiler, with butter or crème fraîche. They are stirred constantly during cooking until they separate into tiny pieces, like creamy cottage cheese curds. In Haute Provence, brouillades *are the preferred home-style way to cook winter's truffles and early spring's wild asparagus. The eggs essentially act as carriers for the powerful flavor of the truffle, which, even though used in small amounts, makes an impact.*

Classically, a bocal, *or glass canning jar with a hinged lid and a rubber sealing ring, is filled with unbroken raw eggs (a 1-quart jar holds six to eight eggs) and several truffles. The jar is closed and left in a cool, dark place or in the refrigerator for five days to a week. Four or five walnut-sized truffles are enough to perfume and flavor the* brouillade. *If you do this, open the lid of the jar every day once or twice and take a deep breath of the aroma, just to prepare yourself for what is to come when at last you sit down to eat your* brouillade aux truffles.

In the various villages and districts of Haute Provence, brouillades *are prepared with butter, absolutely with olive oil or absolutely not, with milk or crème fraîche or never, or with only butter, depending upon local and family traditions. I prefer the lighter flavor of the butter to the more powerful character of the olive oil in this dish. Serve with plain or toasted slices cut from a baguette or a country-style loaf, and pour a chilled French-style rosé or a light dry wine.*

8 eggs

4 or 5 walnut-sized truffles, about 40 grams (about 1⅓ ounces),
   cleaned (page 97)

½ cup unsalted butter, cut into 1-inch pieces, or 2 tablespoons crème
   fraîche and 2 tablespoons unsalted butter

1 teaspoon salt

2 teaspoons white pepper

◆ Combine the eggs and truffles in a glass jar as described in the recipe
introduction and keep for 5 days.

◆ Crack the eggs into a bowl. Finely chop the truffles and add them to the
eggs. Let stand together for 1 hour to perfume the eggs further. Place the
lower pan of a double boiler over medium high heat and bring to just below
a boil. Reduce the heat to low and place the upper pan of the double boiler
atop the lower. Add the eggs, truffles, and the ½ cup butter, if using. Whisk
the eggs continuously until they have thickened into a creamy mass of tiny
curds. This will take about 15 minutes. If using the crème fraîche and butter
variation, whisk them in a few minutes before the tiny curds have formed.

◆ Whisk in the salt and white pepper and serve immediately, piping hot,
onto warmed plates.

Green Salad with Truffled Oil Dressing

SERVES 4

Truffles are such a strong flavoring element that any trimmings, once free of dirt, are saved. Even a scant teaspoon of minced truffle will imbue a half cup of olive oil with its flavor. The flavored oil, which must sit for a month to develop its full bouquet, may then be used to season vegetables or salads, for example. If available, minced truffles are added to the salad as well, after first being warmed just a minute or two in a skillet or on a griddle. Truffled oil is available for purchase, too, in fancy food stores.

FOR THE TRUFFLE OIL:
½ cup extra-virgin olive oil
1 or 2 teaspoons minced truffle

3 tablespoons Champagne vinegar
1 tablespoon minced shallot
½ teaspoon salt
¾ teaspoon freshly ground black pepper
4 cups mixed escarole, frisée, and young spinach leaves,
    torn into bite-sized pieces
1 walnut-sized truffle, minced (optional)

◆ To make the oil, place the olive oil and the minced truffles in a dry, sterilized jar with a lid. Cover the jar and put it in a cool, dark place or in the refrigerator for 1 month. At the end of that time, the oil is ready to use. It will keep for up to 3 months.

◆ To make the salad, pour ¼ cup of the truffled oil into the bottom of a bowl. (Reserve the remaining oil for another salad.) Using a fork or spoon, stir in the vinegar, shallot, salt, and pepper. Add the torn salad greens and let stand 30 minutes before serving.

◆ Just before serving, using two large spoons, turn the leaves over and over in the bowl, adding the minced truffle, if using, and coating the leaves thoroughly with the dressing. To serve, spoon onto salad plates.

Sanguins Grilled with Garlic and Parsley

SERVES 4 OR 5

Tossed with a handful of freshly gathered thyme and then doused with olive oil before grilling, these meaty, full-flavored mushrooms are cooked over grapevine-fired grills in fireplaces, indoors or out, every fall in Haute Provence. The usual presentation is to serve them directly off the grill, either to accompany an aperitif or as the first course of a meal, but they might also be served atop a salad of mixed greens or piled high on a grilled steak or chop.

16 medium to large fresh *sanguin* mushrooms (see note)
5 or 6 large fresh thyme sprigs, or ¼ cup fresh thyme leaves
1 teaspoon salt
2 teaspoons freshly ground black pepper
¼ cup extra-virgin olive oil
3 or 4 cloves garlic, finely minced
¼ cup minced fresh flat-leaf parsley

◆ Place the whole mushrooms in a bowl. Add the thyme sprigs or leaves, the salt, pepper, and olive oil and turn the mushrooms to coat. Let stand for 1 hour before grilling. Combine the garlic and the parsley in a small bowl and stir together. Prepare a fire in a charcoal grill, or in a fireplace or a firepit fitted with a grill. Let the charcoal or wood cook down until medium-hot. If available, add a handful of dried grapevine prunings. Let these burn down to coals, which they will do quickly.

◆ Place each mushroom cap side down on the grill rack. Sprinkle the interior of the cap with a little of the garlic parsley mixture. Cook for 2 to 3 minutes, then, using tongs, turn over and cook until tender, another minute or two. Remove with tongs to a platter or to individual plates and serve immediately.

NOTE: *If sanguins are unavailable, 16 fresh shiitake mushrooms or 4 fresh portobello mushrooms, quartered, can be substituted.*

Creamy Mushroom Soup

Serves 4 to 6

Made from a mixture of mushrooms, seasoned with juniper, and thickened with cream, this rich soup tastes of the forest. It can be spooned over garlic-rubbed toasts to make a heartier dish, if desired.

2 tablespoons unsalted butter
1 shallot, minced
2¼ cups minced mixed meaty fresh mushrooms such as
    cèpe, chanterelle, and button
1 dried juniper berry, ground
1 teaspoon minced fresh thyme
½ teaspoon salt
1 teaspoon freshly ground black pepper
½ cup dry white wine
3 cups Mushroom Broth (page 100)
1 cup water
¼ cup heavy cream, whipped

◆ In a heavy-bottomed saucepan melt the butter over medium heat. When it foams, add the shallot and sauté until translucent, 4 or 5 minutes. Add all but ¼ cup of the mushrooms, the juniper, thyme, salt, and pepper, and sauté until the mushrooms change color slightly, 3 or 4 minutes. Remove to a dish.

◆ Raise the heat to medium-high, add the wine, and deglaze the pan by scraping up any bits that cling to the bottom. Boil for 2 minutes. Add the broth and water and return the mushrooms and their collected juices to the saucepan. Reduce the heat to medium-low and cook, uncovered, for 15 minutes.

◆ Stir in the cream and ladle immediately into warm bowls. Garnish with the reserved raw mushrooms, placing a tablespoon in the center of each bowl of soup.

Gratin of Forest Mushrooms

SERVES 6 AS AN ACCOMPANIMENT, 3 OR 4 AS A MAIN DISH

*This gratin can combine a number of different mushrooms collected during
a day's foray, or consist of just a single variety that was particularly abundant.
It can either be prepared with a creamy béchamel to bind the mushrooms together
as they bake between thin layers of garlic-rubbed toasts, as here, or be made with
an egg, milk, and stale bread combination that results in a
fluffy, soufflélike dish. In either preparation, the gratin
might be served as an accompaniment to grilled
or roasted meat, where the juices from the meat blend
and mingle on the plate with the gratin, or it may be
served as a main dish.*

6 to 8 thin slices country-style bread, or as needed

2 cloves garlic

2 tablespoons extra-virgin olive oil

7 tablespoons unsalted butter

1 pound fresh mushrooms, either a mixture of chanterelle, cèpe,
    pied de mouton, oyster, and *petit gris* or a single variety (see note)

2 tablespoons minced shallot

1½ teaspoons salt

½ teaspoon freshly ground black pepper

2 tablespoons dry white wine

2 tablespoons all-purpose flour

¼ teaspoon cayenne pepper

2 cups milk

¼ cup minced fresh flat-leaf parsley

continued

◆ Preheat an oven to 350 degrees.

◆ Place the bread slices on a baking sheet and bake until their surface is dried, about 15 minutes. (If you have day-old bread on hand that is already dried out, this step can be skipped.) Remove from the oven, and when cool enough to handle, rub both sides of the dried bread slices with the garlic cloves. Drizzle with the olive oil on the top side, and return to the oven to toast until lightly browned, about 10 minutes. If necessary, place under the broiler to complete the toasting. Remove and set aside.

◆ Raise the oven temperature to 400 degrees F. Using 1 tablespoon of the butter, grease an oven-to-table, 8-by-9-inch baking dish. Slice or chop the mushrooms into 1-inch pieces. In a skillet, melt 2 tablespoons of the butter over medium heat. When it foams, add the shallot and sauté until just translucent, 1 to 2 minutes. Add the mushrooms and continue to cook, stirring, until the mushrooms have rendered their juices, their color is slightly changed, and they have become shiny, 4 to 5 minutes. The amount of juice will depend upon the variety of mushrooms, with oyster, *pied de mouton,* and *petit grise* varieties releasing more, and the meatier cèpe and chanterelle releasing less. Sprinkle with ½ teaspoon of the salt and ¼ teaspoon of the black pepper, and stir the mushrooms to blend. Remove the mushrooms with a slotted spoon to a bowl.

◆ Raise the heat to high. Add the white wine, and boil to reduce the juices to about 2 tablespoons, about 5 minutes. Pour the juices into the bowl with the mushrooms and set aside.

◆ To make a béchamel sauce, melt 3 tablespoons of the butter in a heavy-bottomed saucepan over medium heat. When it begins to foam, remove the pan from the heat and whisk in the flour, the remaining 1 teaspoon salt and ¼ teaspoon black pepper, and the cayenne pepper until a paste forms. Return the pan to medium heat and gradually whisk in the milk, adding it in a steady stream. Reduce the heat to low and stir until there are no lumps. Then simmer, stirring occasionally, until the sauce becomes thick enough to coat the back of a spoon, about 10 minutes. Remove from the heat.

◆ Add half of the béchamel sauce to the mushrooms and their juices along with half of the parsley. Stir to mix together. Place all but two of the toasts in a single layer on the bottom of the gratin dish, and top with the mushroom mixture. Sprinkle with the remaining parsley. Break the reserved toasts into pieces about 1 inch square and place them atop the mushroom mixture. There will not be enough to cover completely. Pour the remaining béchamel sauce over the top, blanketing the dish from edge to edge. Dot with the remaining 1 tablespoon butter and bake until the surface has formed a golden crust and is bubbling, 10 to 15 minutes. If necessary, slip the dish (make sure it is flameproof) under the broiler for 2 or 3 minutes to achieve the desired result.

◆ Remove from the oven and serve hot from the baking dish, spooning up portions that include some of the toasty bottom and top.

NOTE: *If wild mushrooms are unavailable, a mixture of cultivated fresh button, shiitake, and portobello mushrooms can be used.*

Baked Pasta with Chanterelles

SERVES 4

A thick, rather chewy pasta such as orecchiette or some type of wide noodles is combined with sautéed chanterelles and their sauce, placed in a gratin dish, topped with a little Gruyère cheese and parsley, and baked just until a light crust forms.

2 tablespoons unsalted butter

1 pound fresh chanterelle mushrooms (see note)

1 tablespoon olive oil

¼ cup minced shallot

2 cloves garlic, minced

¼ cup dry white wine

¼ cup chicken broth

2½ teaspoons minced fresh thyme

1½ teaspoons salt

1 teaspoon freshly ground black pepper

8 to 10 ounces pasta (see recipe introduction)

2 ounces fresh goat cheese

½ cup shredded Gruyère or Swiss cheese

¼ cup chopped fresh flat-leaf parsley

◆ Preheat an oven to 375 degrees F.

◆ Butter a 12-inch-long gratin dish with ½ tablespoon of the butter. Bring a large pot of salted water to a boil. Meanwhile, cut the large mushrooms into halves or quarters, and leave the small ones whole. In a skillet, melt 1 tablespoon of the butter with the olive oil over medium heat. When it foams, add the shallot and garlic, and sauté just until translucent, about 3 minutes. Add the mushrooms and sauté until they have released their juices, 4 to 5 minutes. Raise the heat to high, add the white wine, and deglaze the pan by scraping any bits that cling to the bottom. Add the chicken broth and cook until the juices are reduced by one-third, 2 to 3 minutes. Stir in the thyme, salt, and pepper and remove from the heat.

◆ Add the pasta to the boiling water, stir well, and cook until barely tender. Drain well and place in a large bowl. Reheat the mushrooms and their juices and stir in the goat cheese. Continue to stir until the cheese has melted and a sauce forms, 2 or 3 minutes. Add the mushrooms and their sauce to the pasta and toss to coat.

◆ Transfer the pasta to the prepared gratin dish. Scatter the Gruyère or Swiss cheese evenly over the top and dot with the remaining ½ tablespoon butter. Sprinkle with the parsley. Bake until the cheese melts and a crust is formed, 10 to 15 minutes. Serve hot, scooped directly from the baking dish.

NOTE: *If chanterelles are unavailable, substitute portobello mushrooms.*

Tart of Leeks and Dried Morels

SERVES 4 OR 5

Although puff pastry, leeks, and dried morels are the components of the tart, this is a versatile dish in which many substitutes are possible. In France, supermarkets, even the small ones in the rural areas, have fresh or frozen puff pastry, which is also available in the United States, but not as readily. Pizza dough (page 137) is an alternative to the puff pastry. Unlike puff pastry, it is easily made even by the most unskilled hands.

The delectable topping, with its undertone of sweetness from the leeks' natural sugar, is made of thin slices of leeks that have been simmered in a little butter, then combined with fresh goat cheese and rehydrated morels and seasoned with thyme. One can substitute onions, which also have natural sugar, for the leeks, and dried cèpes or shiitakes might be used in place of the morels, as might fresh mushrooms.

Although the tart makes a fine first course, I find that accompanied with a green salad and red wine it makes an excellent meal in itself.

25 dried morels, about ½ ounce

3 cups warm water

6 large leeks, carefully rinsed

2 tablespoons plus 1 teaspoon unsalted butter

1 tablespoon fresh thyme leaves

2 fresh bay leaves, or 1 dried

¼ cup sour cream

¼ cup crumbled fresh goat cheese

¾ teaspoon salt

1½ teaspoons freshly ground black pepper

2 tablespoons white wine

¼ cup chicken broth

1 sheet prepared puff pastry, 10 x 12 inches and ¼ inch thick, thawed if frozen

◆ Put the dried mushrooms in 2 cups of the warm water to rehydrate them. This will take about 15 minutes. Finely slice the white parts of the leeks plus 1 inch of the pale green.

◆ Meanwhile, melt 2 tablespoons of the butter in a skillet or saucepan over medium heat. When it is foamy, add the leeks and sauté until translucent, about five minutes. Add the thyme, bay leaves, and the remaining 1 cup warm water. Cover and simmer until the leeks are nearly tender, about 15 minutes. Remove the cover and continue to cook until virtually all of the liquid has evaporated, about 15 minutes longer. Remove and discard the bay leaves. Stir in the sour cream and goat cheese, and add the salt and pepper. The sauce should be creamy and thick. Preheat an oven to 400 degrees F.

◆ Drain the morels and cut them in half lengthwise. Melt the remaining teaspoon of butter in a small skillet over medium heat. When it is foamy, add the morels and sauté for 5 or 6 minutes. Add the white wine and chicken broth and continue to cook until all but approximately 1 tablespoon of the juices has evaporated. Remove from the heat and set aside.

◆ On a lightly floured work surface, roll the puff pastry into a rectangle ¼ inch thick and approximately 12 by 18 inches. Place it on a floured baking sheet. Spread the leek mixture evenly over the surface to within 1 inch of the edges. The paste will be almost ½ inch thick. Fold the edges over the leek mixture, crimping them to make a free-form tart. Place in the oven and bake until the crust has puffed and the leeks are golden, 12 to 15 minutes. Add the morels and bake another 5 minutes. Serve hot, cut into rectangles or wedges.

Beef Daube with Dried Cèpes

SERVES 6 TO 8

Slow-simmering and full of rich flavor, the daube—a wine-based stew—is a classic dish that has many variations. Daubes were once prepared in terra-cotta daubières, then set to braise in a bed of coals in the rear or to the side of the chimney heart where they would cook slowly over eight or ten hours. Today's daubes are prepared on the stove top. The beef is marinated, preferably overnight, in local red wine and herbs, simmered the next day, and can easily wait, its flavors ever deepening, for the day after to be served.

Traditionally a piece of roulade is used to start off the sauté, although salt pork is also suggested. The roulade, which is much like Italian pancetta, starts out flat, like bacon, but then is heavily peppered, salted, and packed with wild herbs, rolled up, and tied with string before curing. This brings a fine peppery flavor to the finished dish, which here is accomplished by the use of freshly ground black pepper and abundant herbs. Dried cèpes bring a fulsome taste and further meatiness.

Daubes require the less tender cuts of beef that have gelatinous sinews and tendons that thicken and flavor the sauce. A fine, tender cut such as top sirloin will be wasted here, and its daube will be thin and pallid. Instead, choose boneless chuck or a combination of boneless chuck and beef shank, which become meltingly tender and flavorful with slow cooking and contribute fully to the sauce's construction.

The daube can be served directly from its pot, and its juices ladled over pasta. A wedge of Parmesan or of Gruyère and a hand grater passed from person to person at the table adds to the simplicity and casual sharing of the dish.

4 pounds boneless beef chuck roast or a combination of
   boneless chuck and beef shank
2 yellow onions
3 carrots
8 fresh thyme branches, each about six inches long
2 dried bay leaves
1 fresh rosemary branch, about 6 inches long
2 teaspoons salt
2 tablespoons freshly ground black pepper
   (reduce to 1½ if using *roulade)*
4 cloves garlic
1 orange zest strip, 4 inches long by ½ inch wide
1 bottle (750 ml) dry red wine such as a Côte du Rhône, Zinfandel,
   or Burgundy
⅓ cup minced *roulade* (pancetta) or salt pork
2 tablespoons all-purpose flour
1 cup water
2 ounces dried cèpes, some broken into 2 or 3 pieces, others left whole
1 pound wide, flat, dried pasta noodles
½ to ¾ cup grated Parmesan cheese
½ cup chopped fresh flat-leaf parsley

◆ Cut the beef chuck into 2- to 2½-inch squares. Trim off and discard any large pieces of fat. If using beef shank, cut the meat from the bone in pieces as large as possible. Place the meat in a large enamel, glass, earthenware, or other nonreactive bowl. Quarter 1 of the onions and add the pieces to the meat along with the carrots, thyme, bay leaves, rosemary, 1 teaspoon of the salt, 1 tablespoon of the pepper, 2 cloves of the garlic, and the orange zest. Pour the wine over all and turn to mix and immerse the ingredients. Cover and marinate in the refrigerator for at least 4 hours, but preferably overnight.

◆ To cook the daube put the *roulade* or salt pork in a heavy-bottomed casserole or Dutch oven large enough to hold the marinating mixture. Place over medium-low heat and cook, stirring occasionally, until the fat is released, about 5 minutes. Discard the crisped bits of *roulade* or salt pork.

continued

◆ Dice the remaining onion and mince the remaining 2 garlic cloves, and add to the fat. Sauté over medium heat until translucent, 3 to 5 minutes. Remove with a slotted spoon and set aside.

◆ Now, drain the meat and reserve the marinade. Pat the meat as dry as possible. Do not be alarmed by its purplish color, as the wine is responsible. Add the meat to the pot a few pieces at a time and sauté for about 5 minutes, turning them once or twice. The meat will darken in color, but will not truly "brown." Remove the pieces with a slotted spoon and continue until all the meat has been sautéed. When the last of the meat pieces have been removed, add the flour and cook it until it browns, stirring often. Raise the heat to high and slowly pour in the reserved marinade and all its ingredients. Deglaze the pan by scraping up any bits clinging to the bottom. Return the sautéed onion, garlic, meat, and any collected juices to the pan. Add the remaining 1 teaspoon salt and the remaining pepper, the water, and the mushrooms and bring almost to a boil. Reduce the heat to very low, cover with a tight-fitting lid, and simmer until the meat can be cut through with the edge of a spoon and the liquid has thickened, 2½ to 3 hours.

◆ Remove from the heat. Discard the carrots, herb branches, and onion quarters. Skim off some, but not all, of the fat, as some is necessary to coat the pasta.

◆ Meanwhile, bring a large pot of salted water to a boil. Add the pasta, stir well, and cook until just tender. Drain.

◆ Put the pasta in a warmed serving bowl and ladle some of the sauce from the daube over it, adding more salt and pepper if desired, and topping with ¼ cup of the Parmesan cheese and the parsley. Serve the daube directly from its cooking vessel, or from a serving bowl. Pass the remaining cheese at the table.

Cannelloni Filled with Next-Day Daube

SERVES 6 TO 8

At charcuteries and traiteurs *in the area of Digne and Puget-Théniers, ready-to-cook ravioli are sold stuffed with minced bits of the meat from a daube, mixed with a little spinach and some of the sauce from the daube to bind the ingredients. Restaurants list* ravioli au daube *on their menus, and at Saturday markets, sheets of twenty-four ravioli, dusted with flour, can be bought from the traveling* traiteur. *Farther south and west, the home-style preparation is cannelloni filled with the leftovers from the daube of the day before. Manicotti shells can be substituted for the cannelloni shells, but remember that the former are thicker than the latter and thus belie the lightness of this simple preparation.*

1 pound spinach

2 tablespoons unsalted butter

½ yellow onion, finely minced

2½ cups finely minced meat and some of the mushrooms,
   if possible, from leftover Beef Daube with Dried Cèpes (page 114)

2 cups leftover daube sauce

24 cannelloni shells, each 4 inches long, or 12 manicotti shells,
   precooked according to package instructions and cooled

½ cup grated Parmesan cheese

◆ Thoroughly rinse the spinach and trim and discard the root ends. Plunge the spinach into boiling water for 1 minute, just until it turns limp but is still bright green. Remove and drain it, then rinse under cold water. With your hands, squeeze all the water from the spinach, then finely chop it by hand or in a food processor. Squeeze again after chopping.

◆ Preheat an oven to 350 degrees F. Using 1½ tablespoons of the butter, grease an oven-to-table baking dish large enough to hold all the cannelloni or manicotti in a single layer.

continued

◆ To prepare the filling, combine the spinach, onion, and minced daube in a bowl. Add ⅔ cup of the daube sauce, and mix together until well integrated and a soft paste is formed.

◆ Using a knife, spoon, or your fingers, fill each cannelloni or manicotti shell with an equal amount of the beef mixture. Arrange the filled shells in the prepared dish. Pour the remaining 1 ⅓ cups daube sauce over the shells. Sprinkle evenly with the cheese. Cut the remaining ½ tablespoon butter into small pieces and use to dot the surface.

◆ Bake until the shells are tender when pierced with the tines of a fork, the sauce is hot and bubbling, and the cheese is melted and slightly golden, 25 to 30 minutes. Serve hot directly from the baking dish.

RECIPES

Frisée Salad with Pan-Grilled Goat Cheese

Fennel, Black Pepper, and Dried Goat Cheese Salad with Lemon Vinaigrette

Tomato, Minced Onion, and Sheep Cheese Platter

Pear, Grape, and Dried Goat Cheese Salad

Eggplant Rolls with Goat Cheese and Tomato Concassé

Omelet of Goat Cheese and Sweet Red Peppers

Pizza Provençal

Cherry Tomato Pasta with Fresh Goat Cheese

Warm Polenta Crêpes with Peaches and Fresh Goat Cheese

Warm Fig and Goat Cheese Dessert

WHEN ANYONE LEAVES FRANCE, ONE of the most powerful images they take away with them is of the passion with which people examine, buy, serve, and eat French cheeses. In Haute Provence, *les petits fromages des collines et des montagnes* are considered especially desirable. These cheeses are made primarily by families and extended families from the milk of goats and sheep they keep themselves. Varying from type to type and from farm to farm, these cheeses, made by artisanal methods, might be small, medium, or large, drippingly fresh, completely dry, or covered with a velvety slipskin of creamy yellow mold. Shapes might be round and thin, round and fat, slender logs, simple or truncated pyramids, or squares. The flavor and consistency of each cheese is affected by where the goats or sheep were grazing, and whether the milk was curdled swiftly in the *caillé doux* method of the Mediterranean, or slowly in the *lactique* method used in the north, where more acidic cheeses are produced. The taste is further determined by the temperature of the cheese in the molds, and by the temperature of the cheese and how long it is left standing once it is removed from the molds. Of course, the taste may be further altered by additions of fresh or dried herbs, a dusting of cinders, or a wrapping of leaves. An individual cheese maker may make only one or as many as ten different types of cheese.

All over Haute Provence are signs reading *Fromage de Chèvre* or *Fromage de Brebis,* often hand lettered and with an arrow pointing down a rough dirt road, almost always indicating an artisanal cheese maker with wares to sell at the farm. It is well worth following the signs, but be prepared for an adventure.

In St.-Julien-le-Montagnier, just before the steep one-way road that leads to the old village at the top of the hill, is a sign reading *Le Pastoral Fromage Fermier de Tradition,* with an arrow pointing down a road heading off into the countryside. One icy morning, while driving with a friend, I followed the arrow. After a mild, flat stretch bordered on one side by an empty field and on the other by scrubby green oak, the road veered off into the woods and began to climb. As we climbed higher, the trees became larger, until we were deep into a thick forest of oaks and pines. The road, now dirt, had become increasingly narrow and deeply rutted. Sometimes there were arrows, apparently indicating turns to take when the road forked, sometimes not. At the end, after four miles of driving, we emerged into a vast clearing that held a huge, several-hundred-year-old farmhouse with a sweeping view down across the forest, plus extensive barns and stables that housed not only goats, but also sheep, cows, geese, ducks, and boars. Invited into the cheese rooms, we discovered impeccably clean stainless steel equipment and temperature-controlled rooms, where the shelves veritably groaned with the weight of huge wheels of cow's milk cheese, some weighing over two hundred pounds. On other shelves were infinitely smaller cheeses made from goat's or sheep's milk. The cheeses, we were told, had been made the previous summer in the alpine regions of Colmars and the Col d'Allos, where the animals spent the season in the high pastures. The larger cheeses bore labels indicating the altitude at which they had been made.

In a tiny hamlet near Baudinard, not far from the Lac de Ste.-Croix, the scene was repeated, but on a much smaller scale, at the farm of Luc and Nelly Chaffard. Posted along the edge of the road running from Aups to Baudinard is a sign with an arrow pointing down the dirt lane that leads into their farm. After traveling about a mile and a half, a collection of stone buildings comes into view, as well as a modern barn. No sheep or cows are found here, though, just one hundred goats. Starting in early spring, when the first kids are dropped, and continuing into late fall, the goats are milked twice a day, first in the morning before they go out to graze in the forest, and again in the evening when they file back into the barn to be fed barley. The milk is directly curdled and made into cheese to be sold to restaurants and at regional open markets, and at the farm, where visitors are encouraged.

In the early 1970s, when I moved to Haute Provence, families still kept pigs, but they had ceased the tradition of keeping a goat or two for milk and cheese. The grandparent generation had kept goats, and although their children, then in their thirties and forties, no longer kept goats, many had fond childhood memories of cheese being made in the kitchen and the glazed terra-cotta molds lined up to drain. They recalled having fresh curds with honey or jam, and drinking glasses of the fresh, warm milk.

Shepherds, of course, still made their own cheese, and there were some large enterprises that used modern milking machines on herds of a hundred or more goats, but in the Haute Var around the villages of Barjols, Pontevès, and Artignosc, where we sold our cheeses, fresh, locally made cheeses were a rarity, a memory from the past. When we began to make our first cheeses, people would buy them a half dozen or more at a time, especially the very fresh ones, only a day or two out of the mold. When I casually inquired what they were going to do with so much cheese—"Oh, you must really like goat cheese," was my clever ploy   my customers told me they took them as a special treat when invited out for lunch or for dinner, or that in fact they ate the cheese twice a day and did indeed like it very much, or that they kept one or two cheeses in a cool, aerated place to age. People who heard about us would come to our house to buy cheese, and also to watch the goats being milked, which, unlike Luc and Nelly Chaffard, I found quite disconcerting. A whole-saler from Toulon found our tiny little *élevage*—we had only forty goats at our largest—and bought our cheeses, too, taking much of what we produced.

We made our cheese the old way, as we had been loosely instructed by the shepherds from whom we bought our goats, and by one or two experienced *mémés* of the countryside who remembered making cheese. After milking, the still-warm milk was immediately filtered into a vat and *présure*—liquid rennet made from the lining of a cow's fourth stomach—was introduced. It was left, covered, in the vat, where it curdled, until the next milking time. Then, after the new milk had been filtered into another vat and the *présure* has been added to it, the curds in the other vat were cut into chunks, ladled into molds with large holes, and set on racks to drain. Approximately twelve hours later they were taken out of their molds, turned, put back in and lightly salted. Twelve hours later they were unmolded and placed on racks to dry, and the next day the fresh cheeses could be sold. We ate vast quantities of fresh cheese for breakfast, spread with a little jam on slices of bread or on pancakes, for lunch with tomatoes and onions, for dessert with sugar or honey, and in cooking wherever the recipe called for cheese. Twice daily, Lucretia, our pig, was fed a mixture of whey and bran, which she gobbled. We did all this in a very tumbled old farmhouse, boiling water from the well to wash our molds and our equipment, and relying on the thickness of the stone walls, and occasionally heavy blankets, for temperature control. Our distant neighbors gave us permission to graze on their forest land, where our goats fed on oak, juniper, grasses, thyme, and other sylvan plants.

By the time we returned to California, more people, especially young ones, were establishing themselves in the regions of the Alpes-de-Haute-Provence and the Haut Var to keep animals and to make artisanal cheese. Some were French, some came from European countries, and some, like us, came from the United States. A goat herd could be established with a relatively small investment, and within a year there would be income from selling cheese and kids. Because sheep give less milk than goats do, making cheeses from sheep's milk requires having a larger herd, although one can also sell the wool and the lambs. Cows are much more expensive to buy than either goats or sheep, and require more maintenance, because grazing on the scrubby brush of the hillsides does not feed them adequately. Nevertheless, some people choose to keep cows, moving them to alpine pastures in summer or feeding them hay. Cows, when properly nourished, give a far larger quantity of milk than do goats.

Rules and regulations have changed dramatically in the last twenty-five years, as France and the European Union (EU) have sought to exert more stringent controls and taxation on cheese making. I have American friends who have kept goats for twenty years on a farm that could initially be reached only by donkey or by foot, and who would bring their cheeses out to market twice a week. They had modernized in 1989 to meet the first round of new EU requirements, but have now, like many small cheese makers in Haute Provence, decided to quit making cheese and have sold all their goats. A substantial investment is needed in order to comply with the new regulations, requiring aggressive marketing and going further afield than the regional open markets, restaurants, and small *épiceries,* which were the traditional outlets for small manufacturers. The time is over, I have been told, when a couple and their children could make a living by buying a small herd of goats and making cheese in their kitchen or *cave* and selling it at a few local markets. A family might instead sell its curdled milk to a cheese maker who has facilities that comply with the regulations, but in that case the cheese could not be labeled *fermier,* the government-regulated designation that the cheese was made on a farm from the milk of the farm's animals. Today, a herd of at least one hundred goats is necessary, plus the capital to bring the dairy, cheese-making room, and the aging rooms in compliance with the EU regulations. Some small farmers are investing the money necessary to meet these new requirements, and will continue to make the beloved cheese of Haute Provence in the old way.

Probably the most well-known cheese of the region takes its name from the village of Banon. It is a style of cheese typically aged in chestnut leaves that have been soaked in eau-de-vie or vinegar. Manufacturers of Banon have been trying for many years to get the French government to award the Banon cheese an *appellation d'origine controllée.* This would mean that only cheese made in a designated area of Haute Provence, from milk collected from goats feeding on the regional plants and using very specific methods of fabrication could be called Banon. *Le vrai Banon de tradition* bears little resemblance to its imitators. It is made only from raw goat's milk that has been curdled using the *caillé doux* method. The cheeses are then drained and, when firm enough to handle, are removed from the molds and placed on racks in a drying room. After twenty-four hours they are moved to the *chambre d'affinage,* which now is a temperature-controlled aging room, though it was once simply a *cave.* The cheeses are kept for two weeks before they are wrapped in brown chestnut leaves, collected the previous autumn, that have been dipped in vinegar diluted with water, or in eau-de vie. Three or four leaves are wrapped around each cheese, and the little packets are tied with raffia or twine. They are then returned to the *chambre d'affinage* for six weeks. By then, the ripe Banon, when unwrapped from its leaves, is crusty on the outside, and so creamy on the inside that it can be eaten *à la cuillière,* "with a spoon." Brown chestnut leaves will infuse the cheese with a mild tannic flavor, but if green leaves are used, the cheese will develop a strong, almost bitter taste due to the much higher amount of tannin in the leaves.

Currently, cheeses labeled Banon may be made from the milk of sheep or cows, curdled either *caillé doux* or *caillé lactique,* wrapped in green or brown chestnut leaves, and made anywhere. Obviously, the resulting tastes are very different.

Probably the least known of the cheeses of Haute Provence are the fermented ones, called *broussin,* or sometimes *fromage couillin,* made from sheep's milk and *la cachaille,* made from either goat's or sheep's milk. Classically, these were made both by shepherds and households. To make *broussin, présure* is added to sheep's milk directly after milking. Once curdled, the curd is placed into molds to drain for twenty-four hours. When removed from the molds, the cheeses are left to dry until they are hard. The cheese is then broken into pieces and put in lidded or corked pots with glazed interiors and kept in a warm place. In the days when the cooking was done in a fireplace, the mantle above held the pot, or it was kept in a nearby cupboard. A few drops of eau-de-vie were added, plus salt and pepper, and often some old *broussin* was stirred in as well. The cheese fermented in the warmth, and after several months, developed a very strong, complex flavor. This cheese was tradionally spread thinly on toasted bread slices, never fresh bread, and preferably those toasted over an open fire.

A similar version, called *la cachaille, la caseille,* or *cachat,* is made from either goat's or sheep's milk. The odds and ends of leftover cheeses, both fresh and dried, are put into the same type of glazed, lidded jar and a little salt, pepper, maybe herbs, and a dash of eau-de-vie or of vinegar are added. As with *broussin,* the fermentation may last up to several months before the cheese is considered ready, and the fermentation may continue for a number of years.

Although there are many different kinds of goat cheeses, it is perhaps most useful to categorize them as fresh, soft, semisoft, or dried. The fresher the cheese, the milder the flavor, and the more versatile it is. As the cheese begins to ripen or age, the flavor becomes stronger and more distinctively peppery, so a dry goat cheese can be quite strong. Very fresh cheese, soft by definition, and only a day or two out of the mold, can be served with honey or sugar, but one that is even three or four days old will have developed enough of the characteristic peppery taste to require the addition of more complex flavors to serve it as a sweet. As a savory, however, goat cheese has many roles, and one of the most pleasing and satisfying ways to enjoy it is to have a slice at the end of a meal, accompanied with bread and red wine. Soft, semisoft, and dried goat cheeses can also be used to flavor and thicken sauces, to add to salads, and in baking tarts.

Sheep cheese also may be categorized into fresh, soft, semisoft, and dried, although it is more often found dried and semisoft than fresh. Its flavor is less sharp and acrid than that of goat cheese, a difference that is especially noticeable when the cheeses are dried. *Brousse,* the fresh curd of sheep's milk cheese, used to be available throughout Provence, but it virtually disappeared in the 1970s. Lately it is making a resurgence, and should you find some, know that it goes well with lavender honey.

The cow's milk cheeses of Haute Provence are generally dense and in the shape of a wheel. They may be fresh, or aged anywhere from a month to two years, and since the flavor changes dramatically, I would urge you to try a sampling, again following the simple guideline that the fresher the cheese, the milder it will be, and the longer it is aged, the drier and more pronounced the flavor will be.

Although a century ago cheeses other than those made locally were rarely used in cooking, today many other cheeses are commonly served or used in the kitchens of Haute Provence. Even the *épiceries* of tiny villages have Gruyère, Camembert, Gorgonzola, Parmesan, and *rouge* for sale, the latter a red-wax-encased cow's milk cheese rather like a Dutch Edam, that is used as a dry grating cheese. Of course, many other cheeses may be purchased, but these, along with local goat and sheep cheeses, and cow's milk cheeses where available, are the most commonly used.

MAKING FLAVORED CHEESE SPREADS
Flavored spreads may be made by mixing finely chopped herbs, nuts, or ground spices into any soft fresh cheese. Once prepared, the cheese should be wrapped and stored in the refrigerator. Herbs and spices may also be pressed into the surface of a fresh cheese to flavor it.

Frisée Salad with Pan-Grilled Goat Cheese

SERVES 4

These days, French supermarkets stock plastic boxes of three or six small goat cheeses, each about one inch in diameter and height, called crottins de chavignol, *with instructions for grilling or broiling them to top salads. They are also sold individually, unwrapped, but with an identifying sticker at the cheese counter, as these are protected by an* appellation d'origine controllée. *In Paris and in the north, one is almost always served this cheese when ordering* frisée avec fromage de chèvre chaud.

But in Haute Provence, markets sell only cheese of the terroir, *two to three inches in diameter, only an inch thick if slightly aged, a little thicker if fresh. Fresh cheeses might be rolled in seasoned bread crumbs before broiling. In California, because it is so widely available, I often buy goat cheese in a four-ounce roll, cut it into four pieces, flatten each piece to make a patty about three inches in diameter and half an inch thick, and then roll the patties in bread crumbs. In France, I buy medium-aged cheese, let the loose skin turn brown under the broiler, then slip it off, revealing the creamy, hot round underneath.*

> 4 ounces fresh goat cheese
> ½ cup dried medium-fine bread crumbs
> ¼ teaspoon salt
> ½ teaspoon freshly ground black pepper
> ½ teaspoon fresh thyme leaves
> 4 cups frisée, pale yellow interior leaves only, torn into bite-sized pieces
> Classic Vinaigrette (page 74)
> 1 tablespoon extra virgin olive oil

◆ Shape the cheese into 4 patties, each about ½ inch thick and 3 inches in diameter. If using a log-shaped cheese, cut it into slices ¾ inch thick. Mix together the bread crumbs, salt, pepper, and thyme and spread the mixture on a piece of waxed paper. Press both sides of each patty into the mixture. Set aside.

continued

◆ In a large salad bowl, toss the frisée with the vinaigrette until well coated. Divide the dressed salad among 4 individual salad plates and set aside.

◆ Put the olive oil in a small skillet just large enough to hold the 4 patties and place over medium heat. When hot, add the patties and cook briefly, just a minute or two, then turn and cook for another minute. The cheese will begin to melt and spread slightly. Quickly slip a spatula under each patty, and place on the dressed salads. Serve immediately.

Fennel, Black Pepper, and Dried Goat Cheese Salad with Lemon Vinaigrette

SERVES 4

Big flavors are the order here, yet the treatment is light. The peppery taste of the dried goat cheese is complemented by the coarsely ground black pepper, and both are held together by the sharp, yet mellow tang of the lemon and olive oil dressing on the crunchy, slightly licorice-like fennel.

    2 fennel bulbs
    1 ounce dried goat cheese
    4 tablespoons fresh lemon juice
    ½ teaspoon salt
    ½ cup extra-virgin olive oil
    ¼ cup minced fresh flat-leaf parsley
    2 teaspoons freshly ground black pepper

◆ Remove any tough or discolored leaves from the fennel bulbs and discard them, as well as the stalks and feathery tops. Remove the tough core portion, slice the fennel bulbs in half lengthwise, and then slice each half crosswise into paper-thin slices. You should have 4 cups of fennel. Set aside. Using a sharp knife, shave the goat cheese paper-thin. You should have about ¼ cup of cheese.

♦ In a small bowl, stir together the lemon juice, salt, and olive oil to form a vinaigrette. Stir in the parsley. Put the fennel in a bowl, add the vinaigrette, and toss to coat. Let stand 45 minutes to an hour so the flavors can develop. Mound the fennel on a serving platter or on individual salad plates. Sprinkle on the pepper and the shaved cheese. Serve at room temperature.

Tomato, Minced Onion, and Sheep Cheese Platter

SERVES 4

An artful arrangement of these simple ingredients becomes an appetizer or first course for any meal.

    2 tomatoes, peeled, seeded, and minced
    1 tablespoon extra-virgin olive oil
    1 tablespoon red wine vinegar
    ½ red or yellow onion, minced
    ¼ cup finely minced fresh basil or tarragon
    4 ounces soft or semisoft sheep cheese
    Salt and freshly ground black pepper
    12 baguette slices, cut on the diagonal and toasted

♦ Put the tomatoes on a small plate and drizzle them with the olive oil and vinegar. Put the onion on a small plate, the basil or tarragon on another small plate, and the cheese on a third. Place the plates on a platter, along with salt and pepper. Arrange the baguette slices.

♦ To serve, each person spreads some cheese on a piece of toast, adds a topping of tomatoes, onions, and herbs, and then sprinkle salt and pepper on the top.

Pear, Grape, and Dried Goat Cheese Salad

SERVES 4

This simple preparation, in which the combination of sweet and salty triumphs, can be served as a first course, as an accompaniment to strong-flavored meats such as duck or venison, or as a light cheese course.

> 1½ cups sweet red, purple, or green grapes
> ¼ cup extra virgin olive oil
> ¼ cup balsamic vinegar
> ½ teaspoon freshly ground black pepper
> 2 cups mixed young salad greens, preferably including frisée and
>   roquette (arugula) or other bitter greens, carefully rinsed
> 3 pears, any kind
> ⅓ cup grated dried goat cheese

◆ Cut the grapes in half, leaving a few whole for garnish. Set aside. In a bowl, stir together the olive oil, vinegar, and pepper to form a vinaigrette. Set aside.

◆ Arrange about ½ cup greens on each of 4 salad plates. Halve the pears, then peel and core them. Cut each half lengthwise into slices about ¼ inch thick. Divide them among the 4 plates and then scatter on the grapes, again dividing equally. Sprinkle each serving with some of the grated cheese, and drizzle with a little dressing. Serve at once.

Eggplant Rolls with Goat Cheese and Tomato *Concassé*

MAKES 8 ROLLS; SERVES 4 AS A FIRST COURSE

For a first course, herbed and grilled eggplant slices are spread with goat cheese and basil, then rolled and fastened with a toothpick and served with a dollop of tomato concassé alongside. Zucchini rolls may be made the same way. For a hot dish, cover the rolls with a tomato sauce and a sprinkling of Gruyère cheese and bake until hot and bubbly.

> 1 large eggplant, cut lengthwise into ¼-inch-thick slices (8 slices)
> 2 teaspoons *herbes de Provence* (page 35)
> ½ teaspoon salt
> 1 teaspoon freshly ground black pepper
> ¼ cup plus 1 teaspoon extra-virgin olive oil
> 2 ounces fresh goat cheese
> ¼ cup minced fresh basil
> 6 small tomatoes, peeled, seeded, coarsely chopped, and drained

◆ Place the eggplant in a baking dish or bowl and add the *herbs de Provence*, salt, and pepper. Turn the slices to coat them well. Pour the ¼ cup olive oil over them and turn again. Let marinate for 1 hour.

◆ Prepare a wood or charcoal fire. When the coals are medium-hot, place the eggplant slices on the grill rack and cook until golden, 4 to 5 minutes. Turn and grill on the other side until golden and the centers of the slices are creamy, about 4 minutes longer. Remove to a platter and let cool for 10 minutes.

◆ Spread each eggplant slice with 1 tablespoon of the cheese to within ¼ inch of the edges. Set aside 1 tablespoon of the basil, then sprinkle the remaining basil evenly over the slices. Roll up each slice to make a plump roll. Secure with a toothpick and set aside.

continued

◆ To make the tomato *concassé*, put the tomatoes in a bowl, add the reserved basil and remaining 1 teaspoon olive oil, and stir together.

◆ Place 2 eggplant rolls on each plate and spoon a mound of the tomato mixture alongside as a garnish.

Omelet of Goat Cheese and Red Sweet Peppers

SERVES 2 OR 3

In the United States, omelets are generally thought of as breakfast or Sunday brunch food. In Haute Provence, however, as well as elsewhere in France, an omelet preceded by a charcuterie plate, or a plate of sliced tomatoes with red onions, accompanied by a green salad, pommes frites, and red wine, and followed by a little cheese and fruit, is considered an excellent dinner. The omelet might be quite simple, flavored only with salt, pepper, and herbs, or a bit more elaborate, such as the filling of goat cheese and red peppers included here. If made with a regional delicacy such as truffles, wild asparagus, cèpes, or other mushrooms, the omelet becomes the centerpiece of a celebratory meal.

1 ½ tablespoons butter

1 clove garlic, minced

2 tablespoons minced yellow onion

½ cup minced roasted red sweet pepper (page 150)

6 eggs, lightly beaten

1 teaspoon salt

1 teaspoon freshly ground black pepper

1 teaspoon minced fresh thyme

1 ounce semisoft or soft goat cheese

◆ In a medium-sized skillet, melt half of the butter over medium heat. When it foams, add the garlic and onion and sauté for a minute or two. Remove the onion and garlic with a slotted spoon to a bowl and add the sweet pepper to them. Set aside. Add the remaining butter to the skillet and place over low heat. When it is foamy, add the beaten eggs, salt, pepper, and thyme. Let cook slowly until a firm edge forms. Using a spatula, lift up the edge and allow the egg to run beneath. When the surface of the eggs is still runny, but is beginning to firm, drain the vegetables and scatter them over half the omelet. Dot them with the cheese. Flip the uncooked side atop the garnished side. Cook for just long enough to melt the cheese, another minute or two. Serve hot.

Pizza Provençal

I first saw pizza provençal listed on a menu at a popular pizza restaurant in Aups, where it appeared alongside the more traditional—and more predictable— offerings of Marguerite (cheese and tomato), la reine (capers, anchovies, olives), and quatre fromages (four cheeses). It was described as tomato sauce, goat cheese, capers, and olives, and it was delicious. Now I not only always order it in Aups, but I also make it at home, both in France and in California.

Pizza making is easier in France, because if I ask the boulangerie a day ahead, I can pick up the risen pizza dough ready to roll out. In California, I make my own dough, but it is only slightly more work because I use a food processor. Sometimes I make a more severe goat cheese pizza, omitting the tomato sauce and brushing the rolled dough with olive oil, then adding minced garlic and chopped oregano. It is then dotted with goat cheese and a tablespoon or so of freshly grated dry cheese, such as Parmesan or dry Monterey Jack. When it emerges from the oven it gets another drizzle of olive oil and a fresh sprinkle of the marjoram. For deluxe occasions, I put on fresh scallops with the goat cheese.

For the dough:

2 envelopes active dry yeast (2½ teaspoons)
1 cup lukewarm water (105 degrees F)
1 teaspoon sugar
1 teaspoon salt
2 tablespoons extra-virgin olive oil
About 3½ cups all-purpose flour
Cornmeal for pans

For the topping:

¼ cup olive oil
½ cup Tomato *Coulis* (page 151)
6 ounces soft goat cheese
2 tablespoons minced fresh thyme
¼ cup freshly grated Parmesan or dry Monterey Jack cheese (optional)
¼ cup chopped fresh oregano

♦ To make the dough, in a small bowl, sprinkle the yeast over the warm water. Add the sugar and let stand until foamy, about 5 minutes. In a food processor combine the yeast mixture, salt, 1 tablespoon of the olive oil, and 3 cups of the flour. Process until the ingredients come together into a ball. If the dough is too wet, add flour, a little at a time, until a smooth, firm-textured ball is formed. If the dough is too dry, add dribbles of warm water until the ball forms. Continue to process after the ball has formed until the dough is silky but firm, 3 to 4 minutes. Turn out the dough onto a well-floured work surface and knead until it becomes elastic, 4 or 5 minutes.

♦ Oil a large bowl with the remaining 1 tablespoon olive oil. Place the dough in the bowl and turn the ball to coat the surface with olive oil. Cover the bowl with a clean cloth and let stand in a warm place until the dough has doubled in size, 1 to 1½ hours. Punch down the dough in the bowl, re-cover it with the cloth, and let it rest for another 30 minutes.

♦ Meanwhile, preheat an oven to 500 degrees F.

continued

◆ Divide the dough into 4 equal portions. On a lightly floured work surface, roll out each portion into a round ⅛ inch thick and about 6 inches in diameter. Alternatively, divide the dough into 2 portions and roll out each portion into a round about ⅛ inch thick and 12 inches in diameter. Sprinkle pizza pans or baking sheets with the cornmeal and transfer the dough rounds to the pans.

◆ To top the pizzas, brush or drizzle them with about half of the olive oil, then spread with the *coulis*. Dot with the goat cheese and sprinkle with the thyme and the grated cheese, if using. Bake on the upper rack of the oven until the crusts are crisp on the bottom and the edges are lightly browned, 10 to 12 minutes. Remove the pizzas from the oven. Drizzle with the remaining olive oil, then sprinkle with the oregano. Serve immediately.

Cherry Tomato Pasta with Fresh Goat Cheese

SERVES 3 OR 4

The fresh goat cheese added to the hot pasta and fresh tomatoes will melt and bind with the tomatoes' juice and olive oil to form a creamy yet delicate sauce.

    1½ cups halved, very ripe, sweet cherry tomatoes, preferably a
        mixture of red and yellow
    2 cloves garlic, minced
    1 teaspoon salt
    1 teaspoon freshly ground black pepper
    ¼ cup minced fresh basil
    2 tablespoons extra virgin olive oil
    10 ounces dried fettuccine or other pasta
    2 ounces fresh goat cheese, crumbled

◆ Place the cherry tomatoes in the bottom of a pasta serving bowl and stir in the garlic, salt, pepper, half of the basil, and the olive oil. Set aside.

◆ Bring a large pot of salted water to a boil. Add the pasta and cook until just tender. Drain.

◆ Immediately add the hot pasta to the bowl holding the tomatoes and stir in the goat cheese. Toss until the cheese has melted and a sauce has formed.

◆ Garnish with the remaining basil and serve at once.

Warm Polenta Crêpes with Peaches and Fresh Goat Cheese

MAKES 24 TO 26 ROUNDS; SERVES 7 OR 8

The flavor and texture of the juicy fruit, the fluffy cheese, and the soft polenta combine to make the simplest of farmhouse desserts. The goat cheese melts into the warm polenta, giving it a light, slightly tart flavor, and a dab of cheese is added to the finished crêpes as well, all helping to balance the sweet fruit. Other fruits, such as pears, apricots, plums, apples, or homemade jam can be used in place of the peaches.

4 cups water
1 teaspoon salt
1 tablespoon unsalted butter
¾ cup polenta
¾ cup fresh goat cheese
3 or 4 peaches, peeled, pitted, and thinly sliced
Sugar for sprinkling

continued

◆ In a large, heavy-bottomed saucepan, bring the water to a boil over medium-high heat. Add the salt and butter, then pour in the polenta in a thin stream, whisking continuously. Reduce the heat to low and continue to cook, whisking nearly constantly, for 30 to 40 minutes. The polenta will have thickened and pulled away slightly from the sides of the pan. Remove from the heat and let stand for 2 or 3 minutes. Whisk in ¼ cup of the goat cheese. The polenta will become lighter in color. Spoon the polenta onto aluminum foil–lined baking sheets or flameproof baking dishes, forming rounds about 3 inches in diameter. You should have 24 to 26 rounds in all. Let stand at room temperature until firm, about 10 minutes. At this point the rounds can be covered and refrigerated for several hours, or as long as overnight.

◆ Preheat a broiler.

◆ Remove the cover, if any, from the polenta rounds, and place them under a broiler about 6 inches from the heat. Broil until thoroughly warmed and slightly dry-looking on the surface, 3 to 4 minutes. Remove from the broiler and, using a spatula, place the rounds on individual serving plates, 3 per serving. Top each with a spoonful of the remaining goat cheese and 3 or 4 peach slices. Serve immediately, with granulated sugar on the side for adding to taste.

Warm Fig and Goat Cheese Dessert

SERVES 4

As the figs soak into the bread, their sweetness will be complemented by the light acidity of the goat cheese. If you use croissants or brioches, the dessert will be sweeter than if made with bread. For an extra fillip, add shreds of candied lemon zest.

2 ½ tablespoons unsalted butter

8 stale baguette slices, or 2 croissants or brioches,
    torn into large pieces

1 egg, beaten

2 tablespoons sugar

⅔ cup milk

8 large, soft ripe figs, any kind

½ cup water

1 teaspoon fresh thyme leaves

1 ounce very fresh goat cheese

1 teaspoon fresh lemon juice

1 teaspoon finely grated lemon zest

◆ Preheat an oven to 375 degrees F.

◆ Using 1 tablespoon of the butter, grease 4 individual ramekins, each about 6 inches in diameter and 2 inches deep.

◆ Divide the bread pieces equally among the prepared ramekins. In a bowl, whisk together the egg, sugar, and milk. Pour the mixture over the bread, dividing it equally. Set aside.

continued

◆ Chop 2 of the figs and put them in a small saucepan with the water and thyme. Bring to a boil and cook until the liquid is reduced by about one-third and a syrup has formed. Remove from the heat and set aside. Cut the remaining figs lengthwise into quarters and strew them equally over the 4 ramekins. Top with the fig syrup, dividing it evenly. With the back of a wooden spoon, press down on the figs. Dot the ramekins with the remaining 1 ½ tablespoons butter.

◆ Bake until the custard has set and the figs are soft, about 20 minutes. Meanwhile, in a bowl, mix together the goat cheese, lemon juice, and half of the lemon zest. Five to 7 minutes before the fig dessert has finished baking, spread each ramekin with an equal amount of the goat cheese mixture. Serve hot or at room temperature, garnished with the remaining lemon zest.

The Potager

RECIPES

[SPRING]
Purée of Artichokes
Artichoke and Fava Barrigoule
Wild Asparagus Salad
Fava Beans and Salt Cod in Green Garlic Cream
Peas and Jambon Cru *with Fettuccine*
Fried Ravioli with Garlic-Spinach Filling
Spring Stew with Lamb and Young Vegetables

[SUMMER]
Tomatoes Provençal
Green Bean and Potato Ragout
Zucchini Fricot
Squash Blossom Rice
Summer Squash, New Potato, and Sweet Pepper Gratin
Summer Vegetables Stuffed with Herbed Bread
Chicken Roasted with Whole Garlic Heads
Le Grand Aïoli

[FALL AND WINTER]
Cabbage Salad with Jambon Cru
Belgian Endive and Mâche Salad
Pumpkin and Green Onion Soup with Gorgonzola
Pumpkin Gratin
Roasted New Potatoes with Rosemary and Sage
Lentils and Carrots with Lardons
New Harvest Chickpeas with Garlic Sausage
Potée of Cabbage, Potatoes, Turnips, Onions, and Sausages

FOR MANY YEARS THE POTAGER, or year-round kitchen garden, was the source of fresh vegetables for every family of Haute Provence. In it they grew virtually everything they needed to supply their kitchens on a daily basis and to store for use later. The stored vegetables were particularly important during the winter months, when they were a necessary supplement to the season's meager cuttings from the garden. Today, vegetables are no less important. In many households they form the major part of the meal—a salad of cucumbers, carrots, tomatoes, or potatoes; a soup with beans, potatoes, pumpkin, or leeks; a gratin of zucchini, potatoes, turnips, or eggplants; a vegetable stew of eggplants and squashes or artichokes and fava beans; beignets and ravioli of squash, fava beans, or even squash blossoms. But today not all the vegetables may come from the *potager.*

One hundred years ago, the location of the *potager* would have been chosen carefully to provide a southern exposure, some form of protection against the mistral, the chilling and destructive north wind, and proximity to water. The wall of the house or an outbuilding could serve as a windbreak, as could plantings of trees, such as peaches and apples, or shrubs, or sometimes just stones stacked to make a wall. Because Haute Provence is essentially a poor area, its *potagers* are not like the elaborate ones found at grand manor houses and chateaus in richer regions, which are laid out in geometric patterns by staffs of gardeners, and kept private by enclosed walls. Instead, the vast majority of the *potagers* in Haute Provence are tended by the family members, often the oldest and the youngest, and although by nature they are aesthetically pleasing, they are not architectural gems.

Many of the houses of the region date back to the seventeenth, eighteenth, and nineteenth centuries, and when I first came to Haute Provence, many still stood empty and decaying, abandoned after World War II. Most have since been purchased and restored. The importance of the *potager* to households is evident; as the properties were inherited or sold, the deeds detailed the land parcels and the buildings that stood on them, including wine *caves,* hay lofts, sheep barns, pigeon towers, water rights, and *potagers.* In the deed to my house, one parcel of land is designated as *"V—un jardin potager avec droit à un puits, un sol de 96 centiares,"* that is, "a kitchen garden with the rights to a well, a surface of 96 centares [1032.96 square feet]." It is located next to a well on a slight rise in the middle of a field that is fully exposed to the sun. The well is now equipped with a pump and a pump house, but the stone and cement basin that were next to the original stone wellhouse remain, along with the hand-turned wheel that was used to lift the water into the basins. It is a *puits profond,* or "deep well," I have been told, that connects with an underground river and so never runs dry. Today our part of the country has "city water" delivered to it through large pipes, routed from the Verdon River, but before 1978, the well near the *potager* was our only water source, and until we had plumbing installed, we hauled what we needed in buckets to the house. Of course, there are many new homes as well, and if these have a *potager,* the site has been carefully chosen, which is why it is not unusual to see the kitchen garden in what Americans would call the front yard.

In the past, the *potager* was a necessity of life, so every farm and almost every village house had one. They were often not contiguous, but could be found on a separate piece of land, frequently near the edge of a *ruisseau,* or a small stream, or near a well.

Since many of the centuries-old villages were built perched on rocky hilltops for protection against invaders, it is entirely common to find both banks of the stream that flows below the village covered with a patchwork of individual *potagers,* sometimes with a fruit tree or two included. It is still not unusual to see a real estate listing for a village house that includes a small separate parcel for a *potager*. Such an arrangement means that in the late morning and early evening, men and women of all ages pedal bicycles or walk at a brisk pace along the small country roads, heading back to the village from their *potagers* with a basketful of fresh vegetables or perhaps only a handful of leeks or onions, anxious to get the harvest to the kitchen.

Today, having a *potager* is no longer a necessity, since market growers from the fertile lands of the Bouches-du-Rhone, the lower Var, and the Luberon make regular appearances at the open markets to supply the vegetables that once came from the *potager*. Regional supermarkets, smaller but similar to those in the United States, are stocked with vegetables, in season and out, but especially with local specialties in season, such as Musquée de Provence pumpkin in winter, fava beans and artichokes in spring, and new harvest garlic in early summer, and the large supermarkets on the outskirts of cities are stocked with vegetables from all over the world.

The cultivation of a *potager* is not lost in the mists of time, however. It remains a strong and viable tradition in Haute Provence, especially in the more remote regions, where the old ways are cherished and the supermarkets are distant. Having a *potager* isn't perceived of as a chore or a burden, but as a pleasure. The garden is tended with passion and patience and is a source of inexpensive vegetables prized for their flavor.

Over the years, driving along the same roads, passing the same farms and country houses, the same backyards of village houses, I have taken great pleasure in observing *potagers* and their caretakers. At the Hôtel du Notre Dame in Quinson, there is a large *potager,* and in the 1970s the grandfather of the extended family who owned and operated the hotel could be seen each morning with a basket, gathering what was needed for the kitchen to prepare the midday meal, and then again in the late afternoon gathering more vegetables for supper. As of 1995, the garden still existed, supplying many of the vegetables for the hotel's kitchen, although the grandfather had been gone for a number of years by then and the garden had passed into other hands.

Although each *potager* is unique, there is a uniformity in the rhythm of their cultivation and tending that is visually measurable. From Rians in the west to Moustiers-Ste.-Marie, and from there to Entrevaux in the east, the February gardens have a feeling of winter. A few large cabbage heads, stalks of cabbages long cut, and the remains of fall's pumpkin vines are still evident, and a compost stack, and maybe one of straw, stand nearby. Gradually, starting toward the end of February, the *potagers* are cleared of any debris, and young leeks, beets, turnips, and fava bean plants begin to emerge. The artichoke plants have been trimmed and cut back, the last of the cabbages harvested, the open ground has been turned, and compost, straw, and manure have been dug in. All is ready to plant. Spring is coming. The same pattern occurs throughout the region, although later at the higher elevations.

By May, spring's work is evident. Artichokes bristle on waist-high plants, and pods filled with fava beans hang nearly to the ground, with masses of black-and-white blossoms set to produce more. Fluffy carrot tops, radishes, lettuces, sprouts from garlic and onion bulbs, and seedlings of summer vegetables rise from the ground.

In high summer, the *potager* is overflowing, boasting tomatoes, eggplants, squashes, green and shelling beans, beets, carrots, and potatoes—all the ingredients needed for the summer dishes of ratatouille, *soupe au pistou,* and the *grand aïoli.* The beginning of fall and winter are present in the garden, even as the midsummer sun sweetens the season's tomatoes. Pumpkin vines with huge uplifted leaves snake along the edges of the garden, sporting green immature balls of Musquée de Provence, the hard-skinned winter squash of the region, and young shoots of fennel, leeks, and onions are lined up next to the seedlings of cabbages.

The sowing and cultivating of the *potager* is only a means to an end, as the real thrill of a *potager* is in the harvest and the eating. I admit to having been spoiled in this fashion. Maurice has grown vegetables on my piece of *potager* land for over forty years—since the time it belonged to the previous owner—and consequently, during sojourns in France, I have all the vegetables I want. Like my neighbors, I saunter out to the garden for ingredients for the midday meal—a little lettuce, perhaps, for a salad, a few carrots and cutting celery for a soup, then back again in the early evening for spinach, perhaps, or more lettuce, if it is winter, and tomatoes, squashes, and peppers in summer and fall.

It was in California that I planted, tended, and harvested my first *potager* garden. We planted it in the front yard of our little wood-frame suburban house, and it was a resounding success. We feasted on spring lettuces and radishes, summer tomatoes, and eggplants—and we had corn, too—and in fall and winter, huge heads of cauliflower and cabbage, plus broccoli and more lettuce. I still have a *potager,* but now it is in the country, surrounded by a green open-wire fence instead of the chicken wire of my first one. It has a perennial planting of artichokes, as well as a high wall of old-fashioned shrub roses and a bed of iris to border it from our north wind, which can be almost as devastating as the mistral. I keep it planted year-round, but while I go on a morning inspection tour, I only pick in the early evening for dinner, because lunch here is usually a quick affair, not the leisurely repast of Haute Provence.

Although the *potager* is primarily for supplying the table's fresh vegetables, if the garden plot is large enough it is also the source of the hard-skinned squashes and pumpkins, onions, and potatoes that are stored through the winter, and for the tomatoes that are made into *coulis* and preserved. If the *potager* is not large enough, tomatoes, chickpeas, and potatoes are grown in a field or purchased in quantity from a local farmer or market grower.

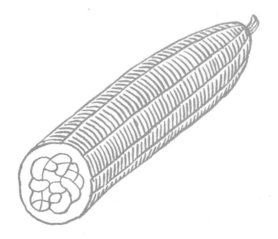

Roasting Peppers

Prepare a wood or a charcoal fire. When the fire is medium-hot, place the peppers on the grill rack. Turn the peppers until the entire surface is scorched black, about 5 minutes. Remove the peppers to a plastic bag, close the bag, and let them sweat for a few minutes. With your fingertips, peel away the skins and remove the stems, seeds, and ribs. If necessary, rinse them, but this will remove some of the smoky flavor. At this point the peppers can be eaten, or used in a dish, whole or cut according to the recipe directions. They may also be packed in a jar, covered with olive oil and vinegar, and the lid tightened and closed. They will keep in the refrigerator for up to two weeks.

Roasting Garlic

Preheat an oven to 300 degrees F. Choose heads that are fresh and hard. They should show no signs of softness or of shriveling. Do not remove the papery skin. Cut off the uppermost tops of the garlic heads and discard them. Rub each head with olive oil, salt, and pepper. Place the heads upright in a baking dish in which they fit snugly. Roast, uncovered, for 20 minutes. Cover loosely with foil and continue roasting until the cloves are soft and easily pierced with the tip of a sharp knife, another 10 to 15 minutes. Remove and let cool. When cooled, the cloves may be separated and used as desired. Roasted garlic cloves may be squeezed on toasts or put into soups or stews, or they may be used whole. Whole, they make tasty morsels in salads, sauces, and stews. In some instances, the cloves are added to a dish with their outer skins intact; other times, the cook removes the skins before adding them.

Tomato Coulis

Commonly called coulis, with everyone understanding that it is made of tomatoes, this sauce is a fundamental ingredient in the cooking of Haute Provence. During the summer, it is kept in corked wine bottles in the refrigerator to be used whenever needed—for pasta sauce, to add to soups, to dress green beans, to spread on pizzas or polenta. As the end of the season draws near, the sauce is made in large batches and canned or frozen to use throughout the rest of the year. It can be made in any quantity, but the key is to use fresh, ripe, flavorful tomatoes.

> 4 pounds ripe tomatoes
> 2 tablespoons extra-virgin olive oil
> 4 cloves garlic, minced
> 2 tablespoons fresh thyme leaves
> Salt (optional)

◆ Peel the tomatoes by putting them in boiling water for 30 seconds, just long enough to loosen their skins, which will slip off. I also find that the skins of very ripe tomatoes often easily peel back with a paring knife without the need to blanch them first.

◆ Put the olive oil in a heavy-bottomed saucepan and place over medium heat. When it is hot, add the garlic and sauté a minute or two. Then add the tomatoes and the thyme and bring to a boil. Reduce the heat to low and simmer, uncovered, until reduced by about one-third and the sauce has thickened, about 20 to 30 minutes. A quicker sauce may be made by leaving the tomatoes unpeeled, although the skins bother some people.

Makes about 4 cups

Spring

Purée of Artichokes

<small>MAKES ABOUT 1 ½ CUPS</small>

*This seasoned purée may be spread on toasts, or served as an accompaniment
to meats and other vegetables. Starchy, mature fava beans, cooked in a broth
and then skinned, can replace the artichokes.*

> 3 medium-sized artichokes
> ⅓ cup grated Parmesan or other dry cheese
> 3 tablespoons extra-virgin olive oil
> 1 teaspoon minced garlic
> ¼ teaspoon salt
> ½ teaspoon freshly ground black pepper

◆ Rinse the artichokes well and place on a steamer rack above boiling water.
Cover and steam until tender, 35 to 40 minutes. Remove from the steamer
and let cool until they can be handled.

◆ Cut off the stem of each artichoke at its base and cut the heads in half
length-wise. Scoop out and discard the furry chokes, leaving the tender
yellow leaves and the solid heart and base exposed. Pull off and discard the
outer, dark green leaves. Cut the tender leaves, heart, and base into chunks.
You should have about 1 cup.

◆ Put the artichokes in a blender with the cheese, olive oil, garlic, salt, and
pepper. Puree until a paste forms. Serve warm or at room temperature.

Artichoke and Fava *Barrigoule*

SERVES 4 TO 6

In late spring, this classic dish of young artichokes and fava beans stewed in olive oil and wild herbs commonly appears on the tables of Haute Provence. The flavor is indescribable. I have lightened it here, however, using chicken broth to replace some of the olive oil. This can be a first course, or a main course served with polenta or fluffy mashed potatoes.

2 to 2½ pounds young, but not tiny, fava beans
2 or 3 lemons, as needed
6 medium-sized artichokes
¼ cup extra-virgin olive oil
1 clove garlic, minced
2 tablespoons minced fresh thyme
⅔ cup chicken or vegetable broth
½ teaspoon salt

◆ Shell the fava beans. Bring a saucepan filled with water to a boil and add the fava beans. Boil for 1 minute, drain, and, when cool enough to handle, slip the skins from the beans. You should have about 1 cup if you have used 2 pounds of unshelled beans. Set aside.

◆ To prepare each artichoke, cut off the stem near the base. Peel back and snap off the tough outer layers of the leaves. Slice off the upper third of the artichoke with a sharp, stainless steel knife. Cut 1 lemon in half and rub the cut surface of the artichoke with the lemon half. Continue to peel back and snap off the layers of leaves until you reach the tender, pale yellow inner leaves. Slice through the uppermost part again, removing any remaining tough leaf tips. Rub with the lemon half. If the choke in the center has developed any prickly tips, scoop it out with the edge of a stainless steel spoon. If the choke is only furry, leave it, as it will be edible once cooked. Fill a large bowl with water. Squeeze 1 or 2 lemons and add 2 tablespoons lemon juice for every 4 cups of water. Cut the artichoke lengthwise into 6 pieces and drop them into the lemon water. When all of the artichokes have been trimmed, drain them and pat dry. *continued*

◆ In a heavy-bottomed saucepan, warm the olive oil over medium heat. When hot, add the garlic and artichokes and sauté until the artichokes turn slightly golden, 4 or 5 minutes. Add the fava beans, thyme, and broth and reduce the heat to low. Cover and simmer until the beans are tender and the bottom of the artichoke pieces are easily pierced with the tines of a fork, 15 to 20 minutes. Serve hot or warm.

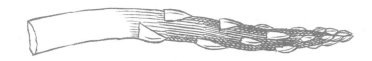

Wild Asparagus Salad

SERVES 2 OR 3

Wild asparagus hunting is one of the great pastimes of spring. The ferns of the asparagus are easy to spot because much of the forest and the hillsides are still brown and their deep green vegetation stands out. Once the fern is located, one follows its prickery branches down to the ground, because the asparagus spears themselves burst through the ground around the base of the fern. They are considerably smaller than those of cultivated asparagus, a large one being the size of a pencil, but with most being no thicker than a piece of sturdy wire. They are cut at the surface of the ground, not broken off in the middle, to encourage further growth.

  2 cups cut-up (1-inch pieces) wild asparagus or
      very small cultivated asparagus
  Classic Vinaigrette (page 74), with shallots added
  2 hard-cooked eggs (optional)

◆ Bring a saucepan filled with salted water to a boil. Plunge the asparagus into the water and boil for 1 minute if wild, 2 minutes if cultivated. Drain and rinse immediately with cold water. The asparagus should remain bright green.

◆ Lay the asparagus on a small platter and drizzle with the vinaigrette. If you like, peel the eggs, cut them in half, and push them, one-half at a time, through the fine wire mesh of a sieve onto the asparagus.

Fava Beans and Salt Cod in Green Garlic Cream

S E R V E S 3 O R 4

Green garlic, like fava beans, is a springtime vegetable, and the delicate flavors of the young garlic and the young favas make a fine match, here paired with salt cod. Poached fresh white fish would be good as well.

    2 to 2½ pounds young to medium-mature fava beans
    2 green garlic bulbs with stalks intact
    ⅔ cup heavy cream
    4 cups water
    2 teaspoons salt
    1 teaspoon freshly ground black pepper
    ¾ pound boneless salt cod, refreshed and poached (pages 224–225),
        kept warm
    6 to 8 baguette slices, freshly toasted and rubbed with garlic

◆ Shell the fava beans. Bring a saucepan filled with water to a boil and add the fava beans. Boil for 1 minute, drain, and, when cool enough to handle, slip the skins from the beans. You should have about 1 cup if you have used 2 pounds of unshelled beans. Set aside.

◆ Cut each garlic stalk into four 1-inch-long pieces, starting from the bulb root end. Discard the leafy green upper ends. Pour the cream into the saucepan, add the green garlic, and let stand until ready to cook. The cream should be heated at the same time as the favas are being cooked.

◆ Put the favas and water in a saucepan with 1 teaspoon of the salt. Place over medium-high heat and bring to a boil. Reduce the heat to low and simmer, uncovered, until the favas are tender, 6 to 12 minutes, depending upon the maturity of the beans. They should be bright green and tender, and neither crunchy nor mushy. Remove from the heat and drain. Return to the saucepan and cover to keep warm.

continued

T H E P O T A G E R

◆ Place the saucepan containing the cream and the garlic over medium-high heat and simmer, uncovered, for 10 minutes. Increase the heat to high, add the remaining 1 teaspoon salt and the pepper, and cook until the cream is reduced by about one-half and has thickened. Scoop out and discard the garlic.

◆ Pour the garlic cream onto a warmed plate, and add the warm fava beans and the warm poached salt cod. Serve immediately with the baguette toasts.

Peas and *Jambon Cru* with Fettuccine

SERVES 3 OR 4

In this delicate dish, butter is used rather than olive oil. Just before serving, the jambon cru *and butter are stirred into the cooked peas, along with a dash of white wine, to make a light sauce for fettuccine.*

    2 pounds young green peas, shelled (about 2 cups)
    4 cups water
    1 teaspoon salt
    10 ounces fresh or dried fettuccine
    3 tablespoons unsalted butter
    6 thin slices *jambon cru* or prosciutto, about 2 ounces total
    1 teaspoon freshly ground black pepper
    ¼ cup dry white wine
    ¼ cup grated Parmesan cheese

◆ Put the peas, water, and salt in a saucepan over medium heat. Bring to a boil, then reduce the heat to low. Cover and simmer the peas for 6 to 10 minutes; the timing will depend upon their maturity. They should be tender, yet remain bright green. Once cooked, drain them and return them to the saucepan. Bring a large pot of salted water to a boil. Add the fettuccine, stir well, and cook until just tender, 2 to 3 minutes for fresh fettuccine or about 8 minutes for dried. Drain and place in a warmed serving bowl.

◆ Just before the pasta is ready, add the butter to the peas and warm over low heat to melt, stirring with a wooden spoon. Add the *jambon cru* or prosciutto, the pepper, and white wine. Raise the heat to high and cook for 1 or 2 minutes, just enough to reduce the liquid a little. Pour over the fettuccine and fold in the sauce, using two spoons to lift and turn the fettuccine. Fold in half of the Parmesan cheese.

◆ Transfer to a warmed platter, garnish with the remaining cheese, and serve immediately.

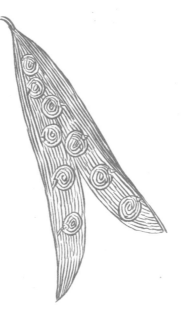

Fried Ravioli with Garlic-Spinach Filling

MAKES ABOUT 20; SERVES 5 OR 6

These ravioli, each as large as the palm of a hand, are sold in the markets of Digne. Some are filled with garlic-laden spinach, others with cheese and potato puree, and still others with seasoned lamb. All are lined up on floured boards and, on request, are dropped into a vat of hot oil, where they sizzle and puff to a golden brown. Removed with tongs and quickly drained, each is then wrapped in a paper napkin and handed over to the happy snacker.

This is my version, but without the deep-frying. Instead, the ravioli are cooked in a skillet in shallow oil. They may also be cooked in boiling water and sprinkled with grated cheese for a nonfried version.

FOR THE FILLING:
3 pounds spinach, carefully rinsed and tough stems removed
3 tablespoons unsalted butter
¼ yellow onion, minced
3 cloves garlic, minced
1 teaspoon salt
1½ teaspoons freshly ground pepper

FOR THE DOUGH:
2 cups all-purpose flour
2 egg yolks
1 tablespoon olive oil
¼ teaspoon salt dissolved in 2 tablespoons warm water
Canola oil or other light oil for frying

To make the filling, bring a large pot of salted water to a boil. Add the spinach and cook until tender but still bright green, 3 to 4 minutes. Drain and rinse under cold running water. With your hands, squeeze the liquid from the spinach until it is as dry as you can make it. Chop finely, using scissors or a sharp knife. Set aside. You should have about 4 cups.

◆ In a skillet, melt the butter over medium heat. When it foams, add the onion and garlic and sauté until translucent, 2 to 3 minutes. Add the spinach, salt, and pepper, and cook, stirring often, until all the liquid has evaporated, about 5 minutes. Remove from the heat and set aside until ready to fill the ravioli.

◆ The dough is easily made in a food processor. First put in the flour, followed by the egg yolks, olive oil, and salted water. Process until a sticky ball forms. Place the dough on a floured work surface and knead until the dough is elastic and will roll out easily, about 7 minutes. Loosely wrap the dough in plastic wrap or aluminum foil and let stand at room temperature for 30 minutes.

◆ Divide the dough into 2 pieces. On a large, well-floured work surface, roll out 1 ball of dough into a rectangle 16 by 20 inches and about ⅛ inch thick. (You can also use a pasta-making machine to roll out the dough. I use an Atlas manual model.) Visualize the sheet of dough as if it were divided into 4-inch squares. Place about 3 tablespoons of the filling in the center of each square, smoothing and spreading it out to within ½ inch of each of the sides. Roll out the remaining dough into a sheet of equal size and lay it over the first. With the edge of your hand, press the upper sheet onto the lower one, forming lines between the filling lumps to seal the edges of the ravioli. With a pastry cutter or a sharp knife, cut along each sealing line, dividing the filled dough into approximately 4-inch squares. Crimp the edges together.

◆ The ravioli are now ready to cook. If, however, you want to wait several hours before cooking them, arrange them in a single layer, not touching, on a flour-dusted cloth or piece of waxed paper. Dust the ravioli well with flour and cover with another cloth or piece of waxed paper.

◆ To cook, pour the oil into a skillet to a depth of ½ inch. Place over medium heat and heat until a drop of water flicked onto the surface of the pan sizzles. Fry the ravioli a few at a time, being careful they do not touch. Cook for about 2 minutes on the first side, and a little less on the second. When golden brown, remove with tongs to paper towels to drain.

◆ Keep the ravioli in a warm oven until all are ready, or serve as they are prepared, a few at a time.

Spring Stew with Lamb and Young Vegetables

SERVES 3 OR 4

Young, tender turnips, peas, fava beans, leeks, asparagus, small new potatoes, and slender carrots—all the vegetables of spring—are incorporated into this delicate stew.

8 baby-sized turnips
1 pound young green peas
2 pounds young, but not tiny, fava beans
12 young asparagus spears
6 young leeks
3 tablespoons unsalted butter
1 pound lamb sirloin or other lean, tender cut, trimmed of
    excess fat and cut into 1-inch cubes
1 tablespoon all-purpose flour
½ teaspoon salt
1 teaspoon freshly ground black pepper
½ cup dry white wine
1½ cups chicken or vegetable broth
12 to 14 small new potatoes, unpeeled
14 to 16 small, young carrots, peeled
2 tablespoons minced fresh chives
1 tablespoon minced fresh flat-leaf parsley

◆ Trim the turnips, leaving about ½-inch of their greens attached. Place the turnips in a steamer rack over boiling water, cover, and steam until they are tender enough to be pierced with the tip of a knife, 8 to 10 minutes. Set aside. Shell the peas; you should have about 1 cup or slightly more.

◆ To shell the fava beans, bring a saucepan filled with water to a boil and add the fava beans. Boil for 1 minute, drain, and when cool enough to handle, slip the skins from the beans. You should have about 1 cup if you have used 2 pounds of unshelled beans. Set aside.

◆ Trim the asparagus by snapping off the woody ends. Steam the peas, fava beans, and asparagus over boiling water until they are tender to the bite, 6 or 7 minutes for the peas and favas and less for the asparagus. Set aside.

◆ Carefully rinse the leeks. Cut the whites and tender greens into 2-inch lengths; you should have about 12 pieces. Mince enough of the remaining tender green tops to fill ¼ cup. Set the leeks and the leek greens aside.

◆ In a large, heavy-bottomed saucepan, melt the butter over medium heat. When it foams, add the lamb and sauté, turning as needed, until the meat is lightly browned on all sides, 5 or 6 minutes total. Sprinkle the flour, salt, and pepper over the lamb and continue to cook, stirring often, until the flour has turned quite brown, 3 or 4 minutes.

◆ Raise the heat to high, pour in the white wine, and, using a wooden spoon, deglaze the pan by scraping up any browned bits stuck to the bottom of the pan. Add about half of the broth and continue to stir until all the bits are scraped up and incorporated into the liquid. Add the remaining broth and the potatoes. Cover with a tightly fitting lid, reduce the heat to medium-low and simmer for 10 minutes.

◆ Stir in the carrots, the leeks, and the ¼ cup leek greens. Cover and cook until the carrots and potatoes are tender when pierced with the tip of a knife, another 8 to 10 minutes. Add the turnips, peas, favas, and asparagus, turning them gently into the simmering stew. Cover and cook for 2 or 3 minutes longer, just long enough for the flavors to incorporate.

◆ If you want a thicker stew, scoop out 1 or 2 potatoes, plus a little broth, puree them together in a blender or a food processor, or mash them with a fork or potato masher, and stir them back in. Taste for salt, adding more if desired, then stir in all but about 1 teaspoon of the chives and parsley. Serve the stew sprinkled with the remaining herbs.

Tomatoes Provençal

SERVES 4

Platters of these appear on everyone's table several times a week during summer, and they are the perfect carriers for the regional flavors of garlic, olive oil, and fresh herbs. They might be served as a first course or as an accompaniment to a main dish, hot from the oven or at room temperature.

6 or 7 medium-sized tomatoes, halved crosswise
3 cloves garlic, minced
2 tablespoons minced fresh thyme
1 tablespoon minced fresh flat-leaf parsley
⅓ cup fine dried bread crumbs
1 ½ teaspoons salt
2 teaspoons freshly ground black pepper
¼ cup extra-virgin olive oil
3 tablespoons grated Parmesan cheese (optional)

♦ Preheat a broiler. Place the tomato halves in a flameproof baking dish just large enough to hold them snugly. Sprinkle each half evenly with the garlic, thyme, parsley, bread crumbs, salt, and pepper, and then drizzle with the olive oil. If desired, top with the Parmesan cheese.

♦ Place the dish under the broiler about 6 to 8 inches from the heat and broil until the tomatoes begin to soften and the topping browns, 8 to 10 minutes. Serve immediately or let cool.

Green Bean and Potato Ragout

[SERVES 4 TO 6]

A mixture of green and yellow snap beans can be used for this ragout. The beans should be rather mature, with some seed development to contribute to the texture of the dish. The more mature the beans the longer the time needed to cook. If you are using bacon, add a little extra pepper to replace the pepperiness derived from the roulade. *This is a good accompaniment to roasts and chops.*

  1 ounce *roulade* (pancetta) or 3 slices bacon, coarsely chopped
  2 tablespoons extra-virgin olive oil
  2 cloves garlic, minced
  ½ yellow onion, minced
  1½ pounds green snap beans, or a mixture of green and yellow, trimmed
  3 to 4 cups water
  1 tablespoon fresh winter savory leaves
  ½ pound small waxy boiling potatoes such as Yukon Gold or
      Red Rose, unpeeled
  Salt
  1 teaspoon freshly ground black pepper

◆ In a heavy-bottomed saucepan, heat the *roulade* in the olive oil over medium heat until it begins to render its fat. Add the garlic and onion, and sauté until translucent, 2 or 3 minutes. Add the beans and cook, stirring, for 2 or 3 minutes. Add the water and winter savory and bring to a boil. Reduce the heat to low, cover, and cook until the beans are tender to the bite but not falling apart, about 15 minutes. Add the potatoes and cook for another 20 to 30 minutes, checking the pan intermittently to see if the vegetables are done. Ideally, the potatoes and the beans should both be meltingly tender, but the potatoes should still hold their shape somewhat, while the beans should be almost falling apart and easily cut with a wooden spoon.

◆ Add salt and pepper to taste. Remove to a serving dish and serve hot.

Zucchini *Fricot*

SERVES 4 TO 6

Fricots are the epitome of fresh garden cooking. I cannot count the times I have eaten this particular dish in Haute Provence at other peoples' houses, or smelled it cooking while visiting, or cooked and served it myself. As rustic a dish as one could want, it is never unwelcome to me. This same treatment can be given to green and shelling beans, eggplants, potatoes, sweet peppers, or any combination of these.

> 3 to 4 tablespoons extra-virgin olive oil
> 4 to 6 cloves garlic, minced
> 1 yellow onion, chopped
> 6 zucchini, chopped or sliced
> 1 tablespoon fresh thyme leaves

◆ In a skillet, warm the olive oil over medium heat. Add the garlic and onion and sauté until translucent, 3 to 4 minutes. Add the zucchini and thyme and continue to sauté over medium heat, stirring, until the zucchini has changed color slightly. Reduce the heat to low and cook, stirring and turning occasionally. When the zucchini is tender and lightly browned in some places, it is ready. The whole cooking process should take no more than about 15 or 20 minutes.

◆ Remove to a serving bowl and serve immediately.

Squash Blossom Rice

Serves 6

Squash blossoms as well as the squashes themselves are used in cooking in Haute Provence. Frequently the blossoms are stuffed with an herbed soft cheese, or with a mixture of minced and seasoned meat, often lamb. The stuffed blossoms are then sautéed or baked and served with a sauce, usually a light tomato sauce Here the preparation is simpler, but still benefits from the striking color and "green" squash flavor of the blossoms.

In the garden, the squash blossoms open wide after dawn, then close by midmorning. It is best to pick them when fully opened, and they are sold that way in the outdoor markets. Should you have a closed blossom, however, it can be opened by plunging it for a minute or two in ice water. Do check inside the blossoms for trapped insects.

> 1 ½ tablespoons unsalted butter
> 1 ½ tablespoons extra-virgin olive oil
> ⅓ cup minced shallot
> 1 ½ cups long-grain white rice
> 10 squash blossoms
> 1 ½ cups water
> 1 ½ cups chicken broth
> 1 teaspoon freshly ground black pepper
> ½ teaspoon salt

◆ In a saucepan, melt the butter with the olive oil over medium heat. When the mixture is foamy, add the shallot and sauté until translucent, 2 or 3 minutes. Add the rice and cook, stirring, until it begins to change color, just a minute or two. Stir in the squash blossoms, and then add the water, chicken broth, pepper, and salt. Raise the heat to high and bring to a boil. Reduce the heat to low, cover, and simmer until the rice is tender, about 20 minutes.

◆ Remove to a warmed serving bowl and serve at once.

Summer Squash, New Potato, and Sweet Pepper Gratin

SERVES 6 TO 8

This is basically a fricot *of summer vegetables, but adding a polenta-based topping gives the dish an unusual texture and presentation. The squash cooks down somewhat, leaving the sweet peppers and potatoes to provide the textured bites.*

2½ tablespoons unsalted butter

2 tablespoons extra-virgin olive oil

½ cup chopped yellow onion

2 cloves garlic, minced

2 green, red, or yellow sweet peppers, cut into ½-inch squares

7 or 8 assorted small summer squashes such as crookneck, pattypan, Ronde de Nice (round zucchini), and zucchini, in any combination, about 2 pounds total, cut into small dice

3 or 4 small new potatoes, about 1 pound total, unpeeled and diced in ½-inch pieces

1 teaspoon salt

1 teaspoon freshly ground black pepper

¼ cup all-purpose flour

½ cup polenta

¼ cup fresh thyme leaves

2 eggs, lightly beaten

1 cup milk

3 tablespoons shredded Gruyère cheese

◆ Preheat an oven to 350 degrees F.

◆ Put 1 tablespoon of the butter and all of the olive oil in a skillet over medium heat. When the butter foams, add the onion, garlic, and sweet peppers, raise the heat to medium-high, and sauté for 4 or 5 minutes. Add the squash and potatoes and sauté for another 7 or 8 minutes, or until the vegetables have released some of their juices and the squash is nearly tender. Sprinkle with ½ teaspoon each of the salt and pepper and remove from the heat. Set aside.

◆ In a large bowl, mix together the flour, polenta, thyme, and the remaining ½ teaspoon each salt and pepper. Stir in the eggs and milk and mix well.

◆ Using ½ tablespoon of the remaining butter, grease a shallow gratin or other type of baking dish. Spoon the vegetable mixture into the dish and top with the polenta mixture; it should fill almost to the rim. Bake until a crust has formed and a knife inserted into the center comes out nearly clean, about 35 to 40 minutes. Dot with the remaining 1 tablespoon butter and sprinkle evenly with the Gruyère cheese. Return to the oven and continue to bake until the crust has browned slightly and the edges are bubbling and crispy, 7 to 10 minutes longer.

◆ Serve hot or at room temperature.

Summer Vegetables Stuffed with Herbed Bread

SERVES 6

When freshly baked bread is bought daily, or even twice daily, as it is in Haute Provence, there are bound to be leftovers, and since the breads are made without preservatives, even day-old bread has lost its freshness. These odd bits of bread don't go to waste, however, because they are used in gratins, in puddings both savory and sweet, and to make stuffings for vegetables.

Zucchini, eggplants, peppers, tomatoes, and onions are all candidates for stuffing. The vegetables are scooped out, leaving a shell. The pulp is minced, and along with onions, garlic and herbs, is added to the bread that has been soaked in milk to soften it, then stuffed into the vegetables and baked.

20 to 25 slices dry bread, preferably from a chewy, country-style loaf, broken into chunks (enough for 8 cups)

5 cups milk or half milk and half water

3 red peppers halved lengthwise

4 long Asian eggplants, halved lengthwise

4 zucchini, each about 4 inches long, halved lengthwise, or 4 Rondes de Nice (round zucchini), halved crosswise

4 medium-sized tomatoes, halved crosswise

3 tablespoons extra-virgin olive oil

6 cloves garlic, minced

1 yellow onion, minced

4 eggs, lightly beaten

¼ cup chopped fresh flat-leaf parsley

¼ cup chopped fresh thyme

¼ cup chopped fresh winter savory

2 teaspoons minced fresh rosemary

½ cup shredded Gruyère cheese

2 teaspoons salt

2 tablespoons freshly ground black pepper

◆ Combine the bread and the milk (or milk and water) in a bowl and let the bread soak while you prepare the vegetables.

◆ Remove and discard the seeds and ribs from the red peppers. Scoop out the centers of the eggplants, leaving a ½-inch-thick shell. Place the pulp in a bowl. Scoop out the zucchini, again leaving a ½-inch-thick shell, and add the pulp to the eggplant. Repeat with the tomatoes, but add only 2 scoops of the pulp to the bowl. Discard the rest or reserve for another use.

◆ Preheat an oven to 350 degrees F. Oil a large baking sheet with 1 tablespoon of the olive oil.

◆ Mince the eggplant, zucchini, and tomato pulp and return it to the bowl. Squeeze the liquid from the bread and add the bread to the bowl, reserving the liquid. Add the garlic, onion, eggs, herbs, cheese, salt, and pepper to the bowl and mix well to make a moist mixture. If it is too dry, add a little of the reserved liquid.

◆ Place the vegetable shells on the prepared baking sheet. Fill each shell to heaping with the stuffing. Drizzle the remaining 2 tablespoons olive oil over the tops. Bake until the vegetable shells are cooked through (pierce with a knife to test), but not collapsing, 30 to 35 minutes.

◆ Serve hot or at room temperature.

Chicken Roasted with Whole Garlic Heads

Serves 4

The garlic heads roast alongside the chicken in its juices; then each serving of chicken is accompanied by a head or two of the sweet, mild garlic.

    6 heads firm garlic
    2 teaspoons olive oil
    1 chicken, 3 to 3½ pounds, trimmed of excess fat
    2 teaspoons salt
    2 teaspoons freshly ground black pepper
    1 tablespoon fresh winter savory leaves or thyme

◆ Preheat an oven to 350 degrees F.

◆ Cut off the uppermost tops of the garlic heads and discard them. Rub the heads with the olive oil. Then rub the chicken and the garlic heads with the salt, pepper, and winter savory or thyme. Place the chicken in a shallow baking dish or roasting pan and surround it with the garlic heads.

◆ Roast, basting the chicken and the garlic heads with the pan juices several times during cooking, until the juices run clear when a chicken thigh is pierced, 1¼ to 1½ hours. Remove the chicken to a platter and let stand for ten minutes before carving into serving pieces. Surround with the garlic heads.

Le Grand Aïoli

SERVES 12 TO 14

This is one of the great summer feasts of Provence. The occasion might be a Sunday midday gathering in the country for friends and family, or a local fête du village, *village festival, such as the one celebrating the Feast of the Assumption on August 15. Throughout the villages one can spot hand-lettered signs posted on the shutters and doors of local bakeries, grocery stores, and city halls advertising* un grand aïoli, *the price of participation, and the* boule *contests that will be held.*

Although I prepare at-home aïoli *parties, nothing quite compares to being part of a village* grand aïoli. *In the morning, long tables covered with white butcher paper are set out beneath the spreading mulberry trees of the town square. Down the center of the table march bottles of local wine. A stand is set up to dispense pastis, and by 11:30, the square begins to fill with men, women, and children. The women are carrying baskets with the necessary plates, silverware, glasses, and napkins, as this is a bring-your-own-table-setting affair. The clank of the* boules *resounds in the background, and the aroma of the golden, garlicky mayonnaise, the* aïoli, *floats on the warm air as bowls are set on the tables.*

By 12:30, everyone is seated, the wine is flowing, and volunteers are bustling about, dropping fistfuls of bread on the table. The village women have been cooking all morning, and now they carry cardboard boxes filled with boiled vegetables to the tables. One by one they file by, dropping onto each waiting plate a carrot or two, a boiled potato, a handful of green beans, a beet, a hard-cooked egg, and a chunk of salt cod. They laugh as they refuse or acquiesce to pleas for more beans or another potato or egg. As the happy revelers dip the first vegetables into the aïoli *massed on their plates, a relative silence settles over the crowd, followed by the rolling sounds of conversation, laughter, and excitement that build until the pastries from the local bakery have been consumed. The crowd begins to drift off for coffee, or to play or watch the* boule *games that have started again, or to take ambling walks.*

Aïoli is used not only for boiled vegetables, eggs, and salt cod, but as a spread for sandwiches or to accompany cold meats such as chicken or pork, as well as other fish. It can be made in small or large quantities, as long as the

continued

proportions are maintained. Classically, of course, aïoli is made with a mortar and pestle. The garlic cloves are first crushed with the pestle; then, still using the pestle, the egg yolks are broken and turned. Finally, the oil is dribbled in. However, the method explained here, using a whisk and bowl, works quite well. The garlic and salt are crushed together in a separate bowl, then added to the finished mayonnaise.

Put out plenty of French bread and wine with your aïoli.

FOR THE AÏOLI:
6 to 10 cloves garlic, minced
Salt
6 egg yolks, at room temperature
3 cups extra-virgin olive oil
Freshly ground black pepper

24 boiling potatoes such as Yellow Finn, White Rose, or Yukon Gold
36 carrots
36 beets
5 to 6 pounds young, tender green beans
24 eggs
12 to 15 pieces salt cod fillet, each about 6 ounces, desalted and
    poached (see page 225)

◆ In a small bowl, pound the garlic cloves and salt together with a pestle, and set aside. In a larger bowl, lightly beat the egg yolks with a whisk. Very, very slowly drizzle in about ½ teaspoon of the olive oil at a time, gently whisking it into the egg yolks. Repeat this until a thick emulsion has formed. This will happen after about 6 teaspoons have been added. Once the emulsion is formed, whisk in about 1 teaspoon of olive oil at a time until all the oil is used. Gently stir in the garlic and salt mixture to make a paste. Season with pepper. You should have about 3 cups. Cover and refrigerate until serving.

◆ Place the potatoes in a large pot and add water to cover with water and 2 teaspoons salt. Bring to a boil, reduce the heat to medium, and cook until the potatoes are easily pierced with the tip of a sharp knife, about 25 minutes. Drain and set aside.

◆ Peel or simply scrub the carrots, then cook them as you did the potatoes. The cooking time will be about 20 minutes. Drain and set aside.

◆ Cut off any leafy tops from the beets, leaving ½ inch of the stem intact. Cook the beets as you did the potatoes, but omit the salt. The cooking time will be longer, about 50 minutes to 1 hour. Drain the beets and set them aside to cool, then slip off the skins. Remember that the beets will stain red any food they touch.

◆ Place the eggs in a large pot and add water to cover. Bring to a boil, reduce the heat to a gentle simmer, and cook for 12 minutes. Drain and immerse in cold water to halt the cooking. Drain again.

◆ To serve, place the vegetables, eggs, and salt cod on individual platters and set on the table along with the *aïoli* divided among several bowls.

Cabbage Salad with *Jambon Cru*

SERVES 3 OR 4 AS A FIRST COURSE OR SIDE DISH

From the pantry comes the jambon cru, *prepared the previous winter, and from the winter garden a fat head of cabbage. The two are cut into shreds, then bound together with olive oil and vinegar. The simplest ingredients and the simplest preparation, but the flavor of the dish is commanding.*

2½ cups shredded cabbage
¼ cup extra-virgin olive oil
3 tablespoons red wine vinegar
1 tablespoon Dijon mustard
½ teaspoon salt
5 very thin slices *jambon cru* or prosciutto, julienned
½ teaspoon freshly ground black pepper

◆ In a mixing bowl, toss together all the ingredients except the black pepper. When well blended, stir in the pepper and transfer to a serving bowl.

Belgian Endive and Mâche Salad

SERVES 4

Belgian endives are planted in spring. Throughout the spring, summer, and into fall they develop their large, thick roots and sprouting masses of dark green, very bitter leaves. Come mid-autumn the tops are cut off to within an inch of the crown, and the roots carefully dug. Then the roots are buried in trenches, or more commonly now, in deep tubs filled with sand and loose soil, and kept outside in all but the most freezing climates. In the dark, beneath the sand, the roots put forth shoots that form heads called chicons. *When they are anywhere from two to eight inches, the roots are dug and the* chicons *are cut from them and taken to the kitchen. The period of growth varies from three to five weeks, but as long as it is cold, they can be kept in the sand for several months. They make excellent raw salads, but may also be braised and served with meats, or used to make a cheese-and-crumb-topped gratin.*

Here, the long slivers of ivory-colored Belgian endive leaves and rounded clusters of bright green mâche (also called lamb's lettuce or corn salad) make a visual as well as gustatory feast. Escarole or frisée might be substituted for the Belgian endive, and watercress or young roquette (arugula) for the mâche.

4 or 5 small heads Belgian endive
1½ ounces Gorgonzola cheese
⅓ cup extra-virgin olive oil
¼ cup balsamic vinegar
1 tablespoon red wine vinegar
½ teaspoon salt
½ teaspoon freshly cracked black pepper
2 ounces *roulade* (pancetta) or thick-cut bacon, cut into strips
    1 inch long and ¼ inch wide (about ¼ cup)
1½ cups mâche
¼ cup chopped toasted walnuts

continued

THE POTAGER

◆ With the tip of a sharp knife, remove the core from each head of Belgian endive. Cut the heads lengthwise into quarters or sixths, depending upon their size. Set aside.

◆ In a small bowl, mash together the cheese and the olive oil with a fork. Add both vinegars, salt, and pepper and stir to make a vinaigrette. Set aside. In a small skillet, cook the *roulade* or bacon until just crisp, 3 to 5 minutes. Using a slotted spoon, remove to paper towels to drain.

◆ Place the Belgian endives in a bowl, and pour the vinaigrette over them. Toss them with two large spoons to coat well with the dressing.

◆ Divide the mâche equally among the 4 salad plates, reserving 4 sprigs for garnish. Divide the dressed Belgian endives evenly among the 4 salad plates. Garnish with the reserved sprigs and the walnuts.

Pumpkin and Green Onion Soup with Gorgonzola

SERVES 4

Stirring in the cheese just before serving adds a velvety texture and an usual zest to this dish. The cheese melts and disappears into the broth to both thicken and flavor it. If desired, a milder cheese may be substituted. The pumpkin should be of a cooking type such as Sugar Pie or Musquée de Provence, as Jack o'Lanterns lack flavor and are usually quite coarse and stringy. Winter squashes such as Butternut and Acorn are also good choices.

3 pounds pumpkin or winter squash (see recipe introduction)
6 tablespoons unsalted butter
1 ¼ cups chicken broth
½ cup half-and-half
⅔ cup minced green onion or leek
½ ounce Gorgonzola cheese

◆ Preheat an oven to 350 degrees F.

◆ Remove any seeds and fibers from the pumpkin or squash and cut into wedges or pieces about 4 inches square. Dot with 2 tablespoons of the butter. Place on a baking sheet and bake until fully tender when pierced with a fork, about 50 minutes. Remove from the oven and set aside until cool enough to handle. Peel off the skin and dice the flesh. You should have about 4 cups.

◆ In a saucepan over medium heat, bring the broth to just below a boil. Remove from the heat. Working in batches, put the pumpkin, the broth, 2 tablespoons of the butter, and the half-and-half in a blender and puree until smooth. Return the mixture to the saucepan and place over medium heat. Add the green onions or leeks and simmer until the soup is hot, 2 or 3 minutes. Add the cheese and the remaining 2 tablespoons butter, and stir just until the cheese and butter melt. Ladle into warmed bowls and serve hot.

Pumpkin Gratin

SERVES 3 OR 4 AS A SIDE DISH

Musquée de Provence is the pumpkin found throughout Haute Provence. Small ones weigh fifteen pounds, and large ones up to forty, but they are distinguished more by their appearance and flavor than by their size. The skin is the color of new copper with a finish of dull green, and the shape is squat and round, deeply and asymmetrically convoluted and lobed. After harvesting in late fall, the pumpkins are taken to the cave, where they will keep until spring. When they are needed in the kitchen, a slice is cut, often only a lobe or two, and the rest is left in storage. In markets throughout the region, they are sold in the same manner, by the slice. The pumpkins are displayed stacked, usually with one already sliced open and a sign indicating the price by the kilogram.

The dense meat is bright orange, and after cooking it has a nutty flavor and a creamy texture. The most comparable squash that we might find in the United States would be a Hubbard, although some market growers are now starting to grow Musquée de Provence here as well.

2 pounds pumpkin or winter squash such as Hubbard or acorn
1½ tablespoons all-purpose flour
2 tablespoons fresh thyme leaves
½ teaspoon salt
1 teaspoon cayenne pepper or other ground dried chili pepper
3 tablespoons unsalted butter
2½ tablespoons extra-virgin olive oil
¼ cup grated Gruyère or Swiss cheese

◆ Preheat an oven to 350 degrees F.

◆ Peel the squash, remove the seeds, and cut it into ½-inch cubes. Place the cubes in a bowl and sprinkle them with the flour, thyme leaves, salt, and ground chili. Coat them by turning and tossing with two spoons. Place half of the butter in a small gratin dish just large enough to hold the cubes snugly in a jumbled single layer. Pour the olive oil into the bottom of the baking dish. Transfer the coated squash to the dish. Cut the remaining butter into small pieces and dot the top of the gratin.

◆ Bake until the squash is somewhat tender, about 45 minutes. Remove from the oven and sprinkle on the cheese. Return to the oven and continue to cook until the squash is thoroughly tender when pierced with the tines of a fork, 10 to 15 minutes. Serve hot.

Roasted Potatoes with Rosemary and Sage

SERVES 3 OR 4

Olive oil helps to crisp the skins of the potatoes as they cook, and rosemary and sage infuse them with flavor. These are excellent served with meats of all kinds, or on their own topped with minced Gruyère or a spoonful of soft or semisoft goat or sheep cheese.

8 medium-sized new potatoes
¼ cup extra-virgin olive oil
2 teaspoons salt
2 teaspoons freshly ground black pepper
6 to 8 fresh rosemary sprigs
6 to 8 fresh sage sprigs

◆ Preheat an oven to 350 degrees F.

◆ Rub the potatoes all over with the olive oil, salt and pepper. Place them in a shallow baking dish just large enough to hold them, and tuck the herb sprigs around them.

◆ Bake until the potato skins are crisp and somewhat browned and the insides of the potatoes are creamy and tender, 1 to 1 ½ hours. The outer skin will have shriveled just a bit. Serve hot.

Lentils and Carrots with Lardons

SERVES 4 AS A MAIN COURSE, OR 6 AS A FIRST COURSE

The sweetness of the carrots combined with the saltiness of the lardons and the nutty flavor of the lentils makes a satisfying combination to serve as a main dish or as a soup course.

4 carrots
2 ounces *roulade* (pancetta) or thick-cut bacon, cut into strips
    1 inch long and ¼ inch wide (about ¼ cup lardons)
1 to 2 tablespoons olive oil
1 yellow onion, chopped
3 cloves garlic, chopped
2 cups French green lentils or brown lentils (see page 76 about lentils)
6 cups water
1 teaspoon salt
2 fresh bay leaves, or 1 dried
3 sprigs fresh thyme
1½ teaspoons freshly ground black pepper
1 tablespoon minced fresh thyme or winter savory

◆ Peel the carrots and cut into ½-inch-thick slices, then cut the larger slices into halves or quarters. You should have about 2 cups. Set aside. In a heavy-bottomed soup pot, heat the *roulade* or bacon pieces over medium-low heat until they begin to release their fat. Add the olive oil and when it is hot, add the onion and garlic. Sauté until translucent, 3 or 4 minutes. Add the carrots and sauté for a minute or two, then add the lentils. Stir well and cook them until they glisten. Add the water, salt, bay, and thyme sprigs, and raise the heat to medium-high. Bring to a boil, reduce the heat to low, cover partially and simmer for 30 minutes. Remove the cover and test the lentils for doneness. They should be soft, but still hold their shape. Continue to cook until the lentils have absorbed most of the liquid, 30 to 40 minutes.

◆ When the lentils are done, add the pepper and minced thyme or winter savory. Taste and adjust the seasonings. Ladle into warmed shallow bowls and serve.

New Harvest Chickpeas with Garlic Sausage

SERVES 6 TO 8

The chickpeas grown in Haute Provence are the size of the tip of a little finger, quite a bit smaller than the ones we see bagged in supermarkets. In late fall, as soon as they are harvested and cleaned, they begin to appear at the open markets and at small, local épiceries packaged in brown paper bags with pois chiche handwritten on the front. They taste nutty and sweet and their texture remains a little bit crunchy, even when fully cooked and well seasoned with bay leaf, thyme, and winter savory. I can eat them by the bowlful, with nothing more than a green salad, fresh bread, and red wine. For a less rustic presentation, include grilled sausages, cut into pieces just before serving. As the chickpeas age, they dry slightly, so those used later in the year or from a previous year's harvest may take considerably longer to cook. I find that locally purchased chickpeas cooked in October take only an hour, while in March they may take a couple hours or more, so it can be fruitful to soak them overnight before cooking them the next day.

  2 cups dried chickpeas
  8 cups water
  2 fresh bay leaves, or 1 dried
  3 fresh thyme sprigs, plus 1 tablespoon minced fresh thyme
  1 teaspoon salt
  1 teaspoon freshly ground black pepper
  6 mild or spicy garlic sausages
  1 tablespoon unsalted butter

◆ Pick over the chickpeas, discarding any tiny stones or other impurities. If the chickpeas are not recently harvested, soak them overnight in water to cover. When ready to cook, drain them, rinse well, and place in a saucepan with the water. Add the bay, thyme sprigs, salt, and pepper and bring to a boil. Reduce the heat to medium-low, half cover the pan and cook until the chickpeas are soft to the bite, 2 to 3 hours. Remove from the heat and drain, reserving the liquid.

◆ Return the liquid to the pan and bring to a boil over high heat. Boil until reduced by half. Meanwhile, prick the sausages with a fork, then place them in a saucepan and add water to cover. Bring to a boil over medium-high heat, reduce the heat to medium low, and simmer for 4 or 5 minutes. Drain. Melt the butter in a large skillet over medium heat. When it is foamy, add the sausages and sauté, turning as needed, until golden brown on all sides. Remove from the heat and cut into 1-inch pieces.

◆ Return the chickpeas to the reduced liquid and add the sausages and their juices. Cook over medium heat until the chickpeas are hot. Ladle into warmed bowls and garnish with the minced thyme.

Potée of Cabbage, Potatoes, Turnips, Onions, and Sausages

Serves 4 to 6

Potée *is a hearty mountain dish that, when made in its most rustic version, contains chunks of* roulade, *salt pork, ham hocks, and sausages. Here I have revised and lightened it, because the flavors, even with most of the meat missing, are a fine mixture, especially to have on a cold winter night with lots of bread for dipping into the broth, mustard for the sausages, and a plate of pickled onions.*

½ pound *roulade* (pancetta), cut into ½-inch-thick cubes,
    or unsliced bacon
1 yellow onion, whole
4 turnips, peeled and quartered
6 boiling potatoes, unpeeled and quartered
4 carrots, peeled and cut into 2-inch lengths
4 or 5 fresh thyme sprigs
2 fresh bay leaves, or 1 dried

continued

6 whole cloves

4 juniper berries

¼ cup chopped fresh flat-leaf parsley

12 black peppercorns

1½ teaspoons salt

1 head green cabbage, cored and cut into wedges

12 mild or spicy, not too fat pork sausages such as Italian

◆ Put the *roulade,* onion, turnips, potatoes, carrots, thyme, bay, cloves, juniper berries, parsley, and peppercorns in a heavy-bottomed soup pot. Add water to cover by two inches and 1½ teaspoons of the salt. Bring to a boil over medium-high heat and skim off the foam that gathers on the surface. Reduce the heat to low and simmer, uncovered, for 15 minutes.

◆ Add the cabbage and then, 10 minutes later, the sausages. Simmer for 30 minutes until the sausages are cooked through and the cabbage has thoroughly wilted into the broth, for a total cooking time of 1 hour.

◆ Using a slotted spoon, remove the *roulade,* sausages, and vegetables and arrange them on a platter. Spoon a little of the cooking broth over them and serve hot.

Sheep, Goats & Pigs

RECIPES

Country-Style Pâté Maison

Caillette

Boudin Noir

Lamb with Rosemary Sauce

Lamb Shanks and White Bean Gratin with Dried Tomatoes

Ragout of Lamb and Fresh Peas

Roasted Chevreau *with Potatoes and Garlic*

Civet of Porcelet

Roast Pork Loin with Red Wine Glaze

Pork Medallions and Green Olives Sauté

IN THE ROUGH, SPARE REGION of Haute Provence, it is inevitable that the grazing animals are sheep and goats. They have survived and flourished on the coarse diet on which they fatten, give birth, and produce milk. In the past these animals were a necessity for the region's inhabitants; the sale of the wool provided income and the meat, milk, and cheese sustenance. Goats accompanied the herds of sheep, and often families would keep several goats for milk and cheese for the household.

The young animals, the lambs and the *chevreaux* (baby goats), were generally sold, and the older animals, those past their bearing prime, were used to make sausages, both salted and fresh. Pigs, easily fattened with grains, roots, chestnuts, and fruits, provided a wintertime feast day with *boudin* and fresh chops when they were slaughtered, but more importantly, they were the main source of meat throughout the year in the form of pâté and air-cured ham and sausages.

In some instances, pigs were allowed to roam the forest, eating on their own, but more typically they were kept in a *porcherie,* a special building for the sow and her young. The sheep and goats were housed in *bergeries.* In villages, the multistoried houses were constructed with large barn doors opening onto the ground level, where the goats and sheep were housed. Each day the animals were taken out to the fields and forests to graze, then returned to the barns, where they might be fed hay or some grain, and if in season, milked. Here, too, the animals gave birth and suckled their young.

After World War I, and again after World War II, a number of farms and *bergeries* were abandoned and left to crumble. The less remote buildings have been purchased and restored, and many *bergeries* converted into houses where zoning laws allowed. Some of the most beautiful buildings in Haute Provence are the old *bergeries,* with long, low, sloping tile roofs set upon two-foot-thick stone walls. Some are still used as *bergeries,* particularly in the less populated mountainous areas, and it is a wonderful experience to be inside one, surrounded by the warmth of the animals and the scent of hay, listening to their soft breathing and the quiet.

In 1605, the practice of *la grande transhumance* was formally instituted in Provence, although evidence exists that it took place in the Middle Ages as well. This was the shepherds' driving of their sheep and goats in the summers from the hot, dry areas of the plateaus and valleys to the lush, green pastures of the high Alps, where *troupeaux* (herds) from elsewhere in Provence joined them.

Until very recently, the trek was made by foot, man and beast together, as it had been done for nearly four hundred years. Then, beginning in the 1970s, trucks were increasingly used to transport the animals, reducing a long week's trip to a few hours, but losing the romance of the journey. Yet the *transhumance* had been such an event for the villages through which the animals passed, and supplied such camaraderie, that now, twenty years later, traveling by foot has resumed, supported by local tourism offices.

The flocks, accompanied by the shepherds and their friends, dogs, and donkeys, are assembled during the last two weeks of June. The donkeys are laden with cooking utensils, blankets, and enough provisions to last for the six to ten days required to complete the trek. With their *troupeaux,* some numbering thousands of heads, others of only three or four hundred, the shepherds set out across the country, following the *drailes,* the *transhumance* paths that were established hundreds of years ago, crisscrossing their way along highways, dirt roads, through villages, and along the edges of farms, orchards, and forests, climbing higher and higher to reach the cool, grass-filled valleys. Their progress is heralded by the sonorous ring of the big bells worn by the lead sheep. It is a grand occasion wherever they pass, so in homes and restaurants bordering the route, people jump up from their tables and stand at doorways to watch the spectacle and to be a part of something historic.

La grande transhumance has undergone few changes since I stood in a restaurant doorway twenty-five years ago and watched hundreds of sheep swelling across the road and onto the sidewalks, pushing their soft bodies next to me as they surged by. I first heard the bells in late June, while I was having dinner with my family at the Hôtel du Notre Dame in Quinson. The twilight sky pulsed with the deep blue-lavender light that seems to be the tint of summer in Haute Provence, and the ripe wheat field below the road made a backdrop of shimmering pale gold behind the passing animals and men. Many shepherds still wear the wide-brimmed black felt hats and the heavy brown or black shepherd's capes that I saw that night, and still carry the hooked staffs, garbed like the Provençal shepherds of old.

In Haute Provence, some cows are kept, but their number is relatively small compared to that of the sheep, and they too may make *la grande transhumance*. More often though, the cows move within a single *départment* rather than crossing over two or more. This is particularly true in the *départment* of the Alpes-de-Haute-Provence, because it includes alpine regions such as Barcelonnette, the Col d'Allos, and Ubaye as well as the lower, hotter and drier areas around Moustiers-Ste.-Marie, Riez, and Banon.

The major slaughterhouses of the region are located in Sisteron, and the lambs of Sisteron are renowned throughout Provence and beyond as being not only especially tender, but also for having flesh that has been perfumed by grazing on aromatic wild herbs. *Agneau de Sisteron* is frequently advertised by stickers or signs on the windows of butcher shops. *Gigots* (legs), cutlets, chops, and pieces of *collier* (neck), are nearly always available, and for Easter, whole lambs may be ordered. French lambs and kids are slaughtered at an earlier age than those in the United States, and they tend, overall, to be especially tender and succulent.

Chevreaux are ordered for Easter as well, and when my husband and I were raising goats and pigs in Haute Provence, in spring my cheese customers would ask if we would be selling any young goats as meat, and if so, how much would they cost and could they order one, knowing, and rightly so, that a *chevreau* bought from us would be less expensive than the ones advertised at the *boucheries*. We sold about half of our kids, keeping most of the females for breeding in fall and for milking the following spring.

We bought our original *troupeau* of goats in 1970, when we left California to live in France. We had told M. Moret, the man from whom we had bought our house, that our intent was to keep goats and to make and sell cheese from their milk. He later told us when he heard there were shepherds in Esparron-du-Verdon who wanted to sell their goats.

We made arrangements to meet at his house the next day and to drive with him to Esparron. Today Esparron is a bustling tourist and second-home mecca, with new villas covering the hillsides and splashy ice cream parlors and pizzerias surrounding a marina full of sailboats and catamarans, but that day it was still a sparsely populated, back-country village. M. Moret parked the car and we walked up one of the narrow cobbled streets. Our French was limited, so we didn't understand why we were stopping in a village instead of going to a farm. Not only was our French limited, but so was our knowledge of goat keeping in Haute Provence. Mme. Dovier, the shepherdess, was willing to sell seven of the twenty-two goats she kept lodged in the barn that was the ground floor of her village house. We understood at last when she opened the big, heavy wooden doors to let us examine the animals for ourselves.

We were thrilled and agreed to her price of fifty francs each. The next day, M. Moret brought them to our little farm and we promptly mastered their names: Café au Lait, Reinette, and Lassie, with the last syllable accented. We were completely unskilled in the metier of shepherding, and our first efforts to control our goats brought laughs and sympathy from the village. We filled tires with cement to create weights, and thus gave each goat an anchor. It didn't work. Next, we tried staking them, attaching them on long ropes to metal stakes driven deeply into the ground. This worked only slightly better.

The following spring, when we moved across the valley to a house that backed up next to the forest, we bought a sheep dog, supposedly trained, and began walking in the forest with the goats for a good part of the day. In the evenings we fed them barley and milked them.

Lassie, who was the oldest, didn't live through the winter. It was our first death and it was very sad. We buried her with ceremony, which was, we later learned, unique in the local annals of goat keeping, as everybody else knew that animals too old to live through another winter were slaughtered and eaten.

We bought our next group of goats several months later from two brothers who were passing the winter with their sheep at La Motte, not far from St.-Julien-le-Montagnier. The old stone farmhouse at La Motte sat perched on the shoulder of the road, overlooking the flat reaches of the valley below. The Audibert brothers were known to us by sight and by reputation, as we had seen them and their housekeeper, as she was called, driving around the villages in their ancient black Citroën, with their berets pulled low over their eyes, or sitting at the cafés, the car parked nearby, smoking and drinking pastis. We knew we were at the right place when we saw the Citroën pulled up under the single mulberry tree at the side of the house.

We walked up the steps to a door that stood partially open and knocked. The door swung farther back and a voice called from the depths, *"Entrez."* Our French had improved, and we understood local customs better, so when one of the brothers, who were sitting at a bare wooden table with a bottle of wine, two glasses, a piece of dry sausage, bread, and a sharp knife, asked if we wanted some—it was about ten-thirty in the morning—we said yes. The other brother came back with chairs and glasses. One didn't just start talking business. Business came only after polite socializing. The room itself was whitewashed, but the walls were yellowed, and even blackened in parts, by years of smoke from the open fireplace, where, from the evidence of still glowing embers and the coffee pot set to the side of the hearth, I surmised the brothers cooked. An east-facing window and the partially open door provided the only light.

After talking about the weather for a while, then telling them where we were from in response to their question, followed by a discussion about

Americans in the area during World War II, the subject of goats was introduced. The Audibert brothers did indeed want to sell their goats, because they weren't going to do the *transhumance* any more. They had decided to settle down in a village house and keep their sheep in a nearby rented *bergerie*. We bought thirteen pregnant goats from them, and brought them back to our little farm in three trips in the back of our *deux-chevaux camionette,* increasing our *troupeau* to twenty-five.

That first Easter we sold some of the kids to be butchered, but we were not intending to eat one ourselves. Our neighbors at that time, M. and Mme. Brumet, were shocked and told us that fresh kid was one of the finest delicacies, and they offered to teach us the traditional method of preparation and to cook the noon meal together after the morning slaughter. We agreed.

After morning coffee on slaughter day, I went into the kitchen with M. Brumet. As I watched him mince green onions and garlic and put them in a skillet with some olive oil, he explained that this would be the first course, a *friture du sang.* I was to hold the skillet with its olive oil, garlic, and green onion and catch the blood, which I did. It coagulated into a crepe, which we cooked on the stove later, turning it the same way. The result was cut into wedges, and although I was apprehensive, as I had been the first time I had eaten blood sausage, I found it to be delicious.

The main course was a sauté of *les abats*—the heart, kidneys, lungs, and liver. It, too, was cooked in olive oil, along with garlic, salt, pepper, and lots of parsley. The rest of the meal consisted of crusty bread from the local bakery, a big green salad and goat cheese—of course—that we had brought, all accompanied with red wine. For dessert we had an apple tart that Mme. Brumet had made with winter's apples, which were nearing their end, and vanilla ice cream from a *glacier* in Aups. After a cup of strong, black coffee, we said our farewells. We gave them one of the *gigots* in thanks, and cooked the other one, well larded with garlic pieces and olive oil, over a grill set in our open fireplace, which, like the Audibert brothers, we used for cooking.

Although older goats, like older sheep, can be eaten, they both require a slightly different treatment because they are not nearly as tender as when young. The flavors of both tend to be stronger, with the strongest taste being in the fat. We had mutton chops far more often during those years than we did lamb chops, and I trimmed away the fat before cooking them. We developed such a strong affinity for the flavor of mutton that we missed it when we returned to California. We bought lamb, but it tasted neither like the lamb nor the mutton we had had in France.

At the time, I was teaching high school in Northern California, and I had a student in the Future Farmers of America who not only raised sheep, but also worked at one of the major sheep slaughterhouses in the upper Central Valley. I arranged to buy a two-year-old sheep of his, and met him at work to pick it up. I begged some thyme from the manager of a spice farm near Dixon, and that summer we regaled ourselves with the taste of our old life in France, feasting on grilled mutton chops with thyme and garden tomatoes. We froze some, too, for winter stews and roasts.

Few of our French neighbors and acquaintances kept their own goats and sheep anymore, so kid and lamb were considered somewhat of a luxury. A pig, however, was still a necessity. Everyone bought a piglet in spring to fatten up and then slaughter in winter. Every bit was used, primarily for making preserved meats such as pâté, *petit salé, jambon cru,* and *saucissons* to provision the family throughout the year. Certain cuts and organs were reserved to eat at the ceremonial midday meal after the morning slaughter. Relatives and neighbors all participated, because not only does it take four strong men to hold the pig for the *mise à mort,* done by cutting the jugular vein, but the process of making *boudin,* pâté, *saucisson, caillettes, rillettes,* and other traditional preparations requires a lot of hands. This was also a social occasion for men and women alike. The men were engaged in the slaughtering, butchering, and salting of the meats, while the women prepared the meats for cooking and processing.

The making of the *jambon cru* and the *roulade* was especially important and required skill because the hams and the fresh bacon were cured by salting and hanging. Both were, and still are, central to the diet, not only as charcuteries but as seasoning elements in *daubes* and ragouts, salads, pastas, and in fruit and vegetable dishes, so their flavors help to characterize the food of the region.

To start, the hams were placed on a bed of rock salt spread on the bottom of a *saloir,* a slope-sided wooden box with a hole in one end, then covered with more salt. The hams were turned every day for twenty days, with new salt being added as needed. At the end of that time, they were rubbed with black pepper, then wrapped loosely in cloth and hung in a cool, aerated *cave* to finish drying. The first slices of the new year's ham were traditionally cut at the beginning of the grape harvest in October, approximately nine months later.

The *roulade,* more familiar to us as its Italian name, *pancetta,* was made at the same time. Laid flat, the belly, or what we call the bacon, was spread with salt, pepper, thyme, ground juniper, and winter savory, then rolled and tightly tied at intervals with twine. It was kept in the *saloir* and turned, but only for five or six days. After that it was wrapped in cloth and hung to cure. Within four to five months, it was ready to use for seasoning or to be cut in slices as part of a charcuterie plate.

Today the custom of buying a piglet and raising it to slaughter size, which had flourished in Haute Provence until the late 1970s, is virtually extinct, practiced only by the older generations, and then generally in the more remote locations. There is no less enthusiasm, however, for all the products that come from the pig.

Many of my neighbors still buy a side or a portion of fresh pork so that they can make their favorite pâtés and their own *jambon cru,* but they simply don't want the responsibility of raising the animal and then having it slaughtered. In *boucheries, épiceries,* and supermarkets, and at *traiteurs,* one always finds the necessities for a charcuterie plate: chunky *pâté de campagne* seasoned with juniper; silky, smooth *pâtés de foie,* plain or spiked with truffles or wild mushrooms; *jambon cuit* and *jambon cru;* and decadently rich *rillettes, caillettes,* and *fromage de tête.* Sandwiches of ham, cooked or salt cured, and of pâté are available at every café, and few things taste better than half a crusty fresh baguette, slit open and spread on both sides with butter and then filled with French ham. This, with a cold *demi-pression*—a beer from the tap—is, to my thinking, one of the best lunches to be had in France. Pork is a common meal, and platters of grilled pork chops are prepared outside in summer, inside in winter, always with herbs. *Rôti de porc,* a tidily tied, rolled pork roast, served cold with mustard and cornichons or hot in its juices surrounded by mashed potatoes, is a mealtime standby in homes and restaurants.

When we were buying our goats, one of the villagers who kept pigs, M. Gos, suggested that we keep pigs as well and sell them as feeder pigs. He explained that there was a large market, and he was getting old and didn't keep as many as he used to, but he also hated disappointing people who had counted on him for years to supply them with their yearly pig or two. The whey, he said, leftover from the cheese making, was excellent food for pigs, mixed with *son,* or "bran." He pointed out to us that our little farm had a *porcherie,* and so we decided to buy a sow and give it a try. We called her Lucretia. She was sweet and familiar when we bought her as a tiny piglet. She always remained familiar, but grew to an enormous size within a short time. Three months after being bred, she delivered a brood of tiny piglets of her own, which in due course we sold to M. Gos's customers.

Country-Style *Pâté Maison*

MAKES ONE 3½ TO 4-POUND PÂTÉ

Each family, each charcutier, and each traiteur makes pâté de campagne in his or her own fashion, none truly identical to the other. The cut, quality, and kind of meat, the freshness and quality of the spices, the proportion of meat to fat, and whether or not the meat and fat were hand chopped or machine ground account for further differences. The following is a very simple version, made only of pork and seasoned only with juniper and garlic, salt and pepper.

Although I suggest hand chopping, which several of my country neighbors do, as opposed to their village cousins who use mechanical grinders, either method will make a fine pâté. The hand chopping gives a more interesting and varied texture, while that of the machine is more uniform. Ask a butcher for the back fat and the caul fat (the lacy sheet of fat that covers the pig's stomach). The meat should be lean, such as pork butt. The proportions are important, so the exact amount of lean meat and of fat will depend upon the weight of the pork liver. Do order a fresh pork liver from the butcher, rather than frozen, as the final texture and flavor of your pâté will be better.

2 pounds fresh pork liver
2 pounds back fat
2 pounds pork butt
1 small head garlic
2 tablespoons coarsely ground black pepper
2 tablespoons juniper berries
¼ cup salt
1 piece caul fat, about 12 by 10 inches, or equivalent amount
    of back fat, sliced ¼ inch thick
Flour and water, to make a paste

◆ Preheat an oven to 325 degrees F.

◆ Finely chop the liver, back fat, and pork butt separately and set them aside. Separate the cloves from the garlic head and mince. Grind the peppercorns and the juniper berries in a spice mill. In a large bowl, using your hands, mix together the meats, fat, garlic, pepper, juniper, and salt until thoroughly blended. (If you are using a grinder, first cut the pieces into chunks before grinding them, but they may be ground together or separately. Mix them well by hand with the seasonings.) Fry a tiny bit of the mixture, then taste and adjust the seasonings, remembering that over time they will become more pronounced as the flavors blend.

◆ Line a pâté terrine or a loaf pan with the sheet of caul fat, allowing it to drape over the sides. If you are using thin slices of back fat, line the inside of the pan with overlapping pieces, reserving enough to cover the top. Now pack the pâté mixture in the pan and cover with the caul fat or back fat. Make a thick paste by mixing together the flour and water, and spread the paste along the edges of the pan. Cover the terrine with its lid. The paste will create a seal during cooking. Alternatively, use a loaf pan and fit it snugly with aluminum foil. Place the pan in a larger baking pan. Pour hot water around the terrine to reach halfway up its sides.

◆ Bake until the juices run clear when pierced with a knife, about 2½ hours.

◆ Remove from the oven and pour off the juices. Replace the lid with a plate and a heavy weight (I use a brick wrapped in aluminum foil). Press the plate down to compact the pâté and cause more juices to flow. Pour these off as well. Let the pâté cool, then refrigerate it, still with the weight in place, for at least 12 hours, but preferably for 24 hours. Then remove the weight and cover the pâté with the lid or with plastic wrap or aluminum foil.

◆ To serve, cut into slices ¼ to ½ inch thick. The pâté will keep in the refrigerator for 10 days.

SHEEP, GOATS & PIGS

Caillette

MAKES 10 CAILLETTES; EACH CAILLETTE SERVES 4

Caillettes are part of the charcuterie ensemble and are traditionally made the day of the slaughter with a portion of the liver, plus the heart, lung, kidneys, and a bit of meat from the shoulder and leg, all cut into cubes along with a little back fat. The mixture is seasoned, shaped into round balls, wrapped in caul fat, and slowly baked. A slice of caillette, *eaten with Dijon mustard and pickles, is a fine beginning to a meal.*

Unfortunately it may be difficult to find some of the ingredients, but a good specialty butcher should be able to obtain them for you, or ask a country butcher who does custom slaughtering. If lungs are not available, increase the pork sholder to 2 pounds

1 pound pork liver
1 pound pork lung
1 pound pork heart
1 pound pork kidney
1½ pounds pork shoulder
¼ pound back fat
8 cloves garlic, minced
2 cups chopped fresh flat-leaf parsley
½ cup fresh thyme leaves
1 tablespoon salt
2 teaspoons freshly ground black pepper
10 pieces caul fat, each about 8 inches square

◆ Preheat an oven to 325 degrees F.

◆ Trim any sinewy strings or veins from the liver, lung, and heart. Trim the fat from the kidney. Cut the liver, lung, heart, kidney, and pork shoulder into ½-inch cubes. Finely chop the back fat. Put the cubes and back fat in a bowl and add the garlic, parsley, thyme, salt, and pepper. Mix together well, then shape into 10 balls each the size of a large orange. Wrap each ball with a piece of the caul fat and set the balls on a baking sheet.

◆ Bake until deeply browned and cooked through, about 2 hours. Remove from the oven, let cool, cover, and refrigerate for up to 10 days or freeze for up to 6 months.

◆ Serve slightly chilled or at room temperature, cut into slices ½ to ¼ inch thick.

Boudin Noir

MAKES ABOUT 40 SAUSAGES

The first time I ate blood sausage was at the home of a French acquaintance not long after moving to Haute Provence. I was horrified when I saw the platter of black sausages appear on the table, after a simple and reassuring first course of grated carrot salad, thin slices of cold ham, and olives. Even considering the circumstances of my being foreign, I knew that it would be unspeakably rude and construed as antisocial or sauvage to refuse to eat the boudin. The gracious hostess, later to become a good friend, explained as she passed the platter that the sausages were a special dish in her family and that they were always eaten with lots of mashed potatoes and applesauce.

I accepted my serving of the fried sausages and their accompaniments, and from the first bite became an aficionado. Boudin noir is one of my favorite French foods, and I order the sausages whenever I see them on a restaurant menu here in California. I have yet to be disappointed. In France, they are easily found in butcher shops and at supermarkets, and when I am there I cook them at least every week or two—and make mashed potatoes and applesauce to go with them, of course.

Many times over the years, especially when we first returned to live in California, we would buy a one-hundred-and-fifty-pound hog and slaughter it ourselves with the help of friends, or a custom butcher, and re-create the festive occasions that we had enjoyed in France at slaughter time. It was the boudin to which I most looked forward, and it was I who held the bucket to collect the blood, stirring it continuously to keep it from coagulating. The night before I had chopped my twenty pounds of onions and hung them in a pillowcase to

continued

drain. On the day of the slaughter, I then mixed these with salt, pepper, cayenne, ground fennel seeds, and quatre-épices, *and slowly cooked them in some of the soft fat, or* saindoux, *gathered from the hog. Using a widemouthed funnel, I stuffed the mixture into sausage casings, made from the intestines that I had washed and cleaned, twisting and tying a sausage every five inches or so. A large kettle of boiling water set on the stove earlier would begin to simmer just in time to start the poaching process, and several lengths of sturdy willow had been cut earlier in the week. Lengths of sausage, first pricked here and there with needles so they wouldn't burst, were tied to the willow lengths, which were then set across the kettle. The suspended sausages poached in the water and, when they were ready, were lifted out on the willow and hung to dry before being gently fried for lunch.*

    10 pounds yellow onions
    3 pounds back fat, coarsely chopped
    1 tablespoon fennel seeds, ground
    2 teaspoons freshly grated nutmeg
    1 teaspoon ground allspice
    ¼ cup freshly ground black pepper
    4 quarts fresh hog's blood
    1 cup heavy cream
    3 tablespoons salt
    32 feet hog casings, well rinsed
    Unsalted butter and extra-virgin olive oil for frying

◆ The night before, coarsely chop the onions and put them in a clean pillow-case or similar bag. Hang up the pillowcase and place a basin beneath it into which the onions can drain. The next day, in a large skillet, cook the onions over medium heat with half of the back fat, the fennel, nutmeg, allspice, and pepper until the onions are translucent and the fat has rendered. Remove from the heat and let cool to room temperature. Grind the onions with their melted fat and the rest of the back fat in a meat grinder. Once ground, stir in the blood and the cream. Mix in the salt.

◆ To stuff the casings, attach one end of a casing to the mouth of a wide funnel. With a ladle or spoon, feed the blood and onion mixture through the funnel into the casing, tying off every 5 inches with kitchen string.

Repeat until all the mixture has been used.

◆ Bring a large pot of water to a boil. Prick each sausage several times with a needle, and add to the pot. Reduce the heat to medium-low and simmer until the juice runs clear when the sausage is pierced with a needle, about 30 minutes. Using tongs, lift the sausages gently out of the water and set aside to drain, preferably hanging them to maximize air circulation.

◆ Once the sausages have cooled, they can be wrapped in plastic wrap or waxed paper and stored in the refrigerator for several days. When ready to cook, melt a little butter and some olive oil in a skillet over medium heat. Add the sausages and reduce the heat to low. Cook until browned on the underside, then turn and continue to cook until browned on the other side and heated through, 7 to 8 minutes total.

Lamb with Rosemary Sauce

SERVES 4

Lamb and mutton chops are common fare in Haute Provence households today, and in local restaurants as well, and they are often dressed up with the addition of a sauce based on regional flavors. Here, rosemary and goat cheese add their unique Southern French accents.

½ teaspoon salt
4 lean lamb chops cut from the leg, sliced about ½ inch thick, or
    lamb shoulder chops of the same thickness, ⅓ to ½ pound each
1 teaspoon freshly ground black pepper
1 teaspoon minced fresh rosemary, plus 5 sprigs
¾ cup dry white wine
½ cup chicken broth
2 ounces fresh goat cheese

continued

◆ Preheat a broiler. In a flameproof skillet large enough to hold the chops in a single layer, heat the salt over high heat. The pan is ready when a drop of water flicked into it sizzles. Add the lamb chops and sear on the first side until browned, 2 or 3 minutes. Turn over the chops, add the pepper, and sear on the other side, about 2 minutes. Add the minced rosemary to the pan and turn the chops, then turn them again. Remove from the heat and slip under a broiler to finish cooking to the desired degree of doneness, about 5 minutes more for rare, 7 minutes for medium, turning as necessary. Remove from the pan and keep warm.

◆ Return the skillet to the stove top over medium-high heat. Add the white wine and deglaze the pan by scraping up any bits clinging to the bottom. Add the chicken broth and 1 sprig of the rosemary. Cook until reduced by one-third, then remove and discard the rosemary. Swirl in the goat cheese to form a thick sauce.

◆ Place the hot chops on a warmed serving platter or individual dishes and spread each with a spoonful of the sauce. Garnish with the remaining rosemary sprigs.

Lamb Shanks and White Bean Gratin
with Dried Tomatoes

Lamb and beans are a classic combination in Haute Provence. The beans might be round, white coco *beans, fresh or dried, but small oval white beans are a good alternative. A tablespoon or two of* coulis *(page 151) or a bit of tomato paste could be used in lieu of the dried tomatoes, but the latter give an added texture and impact to the dish that I like.*

The beans are cooked separately, flavored with bay leaves, winter savory, and eventually the dried tomatoes. Omitting the dried tomatoes, the beans may be served to accompany any meat dish. The shanks are first braised and then the meat is removed and added to the cooked beans. Although the dish may be eaten at this point, the additional topping and baking adds a final flourish to the combined flavors.

For the beans:
1 cup dried *coco,* Great Northern, or other white beans

7 cups water

1 teaspoon salt

2 fresh bay leaves, or 1 dried

4 tablespoons minced fresh winter savory

8 dry-packed unsalted dried tomato halves

For the lamb:
2 lamb shanks, about 1½ pounds total

½ teaspoon salt

½ teaspoon freshly ground black pepper

½ yellow onion, diced

1 carrot, peeled and diced

2 celery stalks, chopped

1 tablespoon minced fresh rosemary

½ cup dry white wine

½ cup chicken broth

continued

FOR THE GRATIN:

2 tablespoons unsalted butter

½ cup coarse dried bread crumbs

¼ teaspoon salt

½ teaspoon freshly ground black pepper

¼ cup minced fresh flat-leaf parsley

◆ Pick over the beans, discarding any tiny stones or other impurities. Put the beans in a saucepan and add the water, salt, bay leaves, and 2 tablespoons of the winter savory. Bring to a boil over medium-high heat. Reduce the heat to low, and simmer until the beans are soft, 2 to 2½ hours. Drain the beans, reserving 1½ cups of the liquid. Set the beans aside in the saucepan.

◆ Pour 1 cup of the hot liquid over the dried tomatoes in a bowl and let stand until the tomatoes are soft, 10 to 15 minutes. In a blender or food processor, puree ½ cup of the beans along with the soaking tomatoes and their broth. Set aside.

◆ While the beans are cooking, prepare the shanks. Preheat an oven to 450 degrees F. Sprinkle the shanks with the salt and pepper and place in a baking dish just large enough to hold them. Bake for 25 to 30 minutes. Turn the shanks over and top with the onion, carrot, celery, the remaining 2 table-spoons winter savory, and the rosemary. Pour the wine and broth over all and cover with a lid or aluminum foil. Reduce the heat to 350 degrees F and cook until the meat is tender and pulls away easily from the bone, 2 to 2½ hours. While the shanks are cooking, remove the cover occasionally and baste with the vegetables and broth, then replace the cover.

◆ Remove the shanks from the oven. Leave the oven set at 350 degrees F. Strain the pan juices, which will be brothlike, through a fine-mesh sieve, and discard the vegetables. Skim off the fat, and reserve 1½ cups of the broth. Remove the meat from the shanks, and add it to the beans, along with the tomato-bean puree and ¾ cup of the reserved broth from the shanks. Place over medium heat and bring to a simmer. Adjust the heat to maintain a simmer and cook uncovered, stirring often, for 20 to 30 minutes. Add more of the reserved bean liquid and broth if the mixture begins to dry out. The resulting mixture should resemble a very thick soup.

◆ To assemble the gratin, grease a 3½- to 4-quart deep gratin dish with ½ tablespoon of the butter. In a bowl, stir together the bread crumbs, salt, pepper, and parsley. Pour the bean mixture into the prepared gratin dish and sprinkle the top evenly with the bread crumb mixture. Cut the remaining 1½ tablespoons butter into small pieces and generously dot them on the surface. Bake, uncovered, until the topping is golden, about 15 minutes. Serve hot directly from the dish.

Ragout of Lamb and Fresh Peas

SERVES 4

Spring, with both lamb and fresh peas in season, is the ideal time to make this simple stew. The flavors of the two elements are balanced, and when served with a complement of steamed rice, pasta, or new potatoes, the ragout makes a complete main dish. Pork may be substituted for the lamb.

    1 tablespoon unsalted butter
    2 tablespoons chopped shallot
    2 pounds boneless lamb, trimmed of fat and cut in 1½-inch cubes
    1 tablespoon all-purpose flour
    1 teaspoon salt
    1 teaspoon freshly ground black pepper
    1 cup chicken broth
    3 or 4 fresh thyme sprigs, tied together
    4½ cups water
    4 pounds green peas, shelled (4 cups)
    2 tablespoons chopped celery leaves

continued

SHEEP, GOATS & PIGS

◆ In a skillet, melt the butter over medium heat. When it foams, add the shallot and sauté until translucent, 2 to 3 minutes. Raise the heat to medium-high, add the lamb, and sauté until lightly browned on all sides. Pour off all but 1 tablespoon of the accumulated juices. Return the skillet to medium-high heat and sprinkle the lamb with the flour, ½ teaspoon of the salt, and the pepper. Stir, coating the meat and browning it; be careful not to burn the flour. Stir in ½ cup of the broth and deglaze the pan, scraping up any bits clinging to the bottom. Slowly stir in the remaining ½ cup broth. Reduce the heat to low, add the thyme bundle and cover. Simmer until the meat is nearly tender, 15 to 20 minutes. Add up to ½ cup water during cooking if needed.

◆ While the meat is simmering, bring the remaining 4 cups water to a boil in a saucepan. Add the peas and the remaining ½ teaspoon salt and cook until nearly tender but still bright green.

◆ The timing will depend upon the age and the size of the peas; they will be ready in 5 to 15 minutes. Drain well.

◆ When the lamb is tender, stir in the peas, along with the celery leaves. Cook, uncovered, for 5 more minutes. Serve immediately.

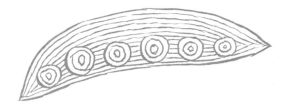

Roasted *Chevreau* with Potatoes and Garlic

SERVES 8 TO 10

This is a classic Easter dish in Haute Provence, although I first had it in early summer. Victorine Freinet, one of my neighbors, came up to my kitchen and showed me exactly what to do. She and her family were invited for Sunday lunch, and I am sure she showed me because she wanted to be sure this special treat was correctly cooked. Pieces of kid, a lean meat, are placed atop a bed of potatoes that have been seasoned and tossed with olive oil and garlic. As the meat roasts atop the potatoes, it lends them its juices, flavoring them as they turn a lovely golden brown. The head, considered to be the greatest delicacy, is split in half and roasted separately on its own bed of potatoes because it requires longer cooking than the other cuts of meat.

½ cup extra-virgin olive oil

12 to 15 potatoes such as Yukon Gold, Rose Fir, or other creamy types, peeled and cut into 1-inch cubes

36 cloves garlic (about 3 heads), peeled but left whole

8 to 10 fresh thyme branches

8 to 10 fresh winter savory sprigs

1 tablespoon salt

2 tablespoons freshly ground black pepper

5 to 6 pounds bone-in young goat meat, cut into serving-sized pieces

◆ Preheat an oven to 400 degrees F.

◆ Pour enough of the olive oil into a 1- to 1½-inch-deep baking sheet or a large, shallow roasting pan to form a thin film. Put the cubed potatoes in a bowl with 24 of the garlic cloves, and half of the thyme, winter savory, salt, and pepper. Turn several times, then add ¼ cup of the olive oil. Spread the potatoes in a layer on the baking sheet and set aside.

continued

◆ Rub the meat with the remaining thyme and winter savory, then add the twigs to the potatoes. Rub the goat with the remaining salt and pepper. Using a sharp knife, cut the remaining 12 cloves of garlic into slivers. Then, with the knife, make slits all over the meat and insert the slivers into them. Arrange the meat on the bed of potatoes. Drizzle the remaining olive oil (a scant ¼ cup) over the meat and onto the potatoes and place in the oven.

◆ Roast for 15 minutes. Reduce the heat to 350 degrees F and continue to roast, turning the potatoes from time to time, until the meat juices run clear when pierced near a bone with the tip of a knife and the potatoes are tender and golden brown, about 1½ hours. Cooking time will be less if the kid is quite young.

◆ Remove the meat to a platter and surround with some of the potatoes. Place the remaining potatoes in a separate bowl and serve alongside.

Civet of Porcelet

SERVES 4

Although civets *are typically stews made with onions and red wine with blood added later, they are also made using white wine and without blood, as here. The* porcelet *refers to pork, and this dish is often offered on country restaurant menus. Near the alpine regions, cream might be stirred in to thicken the sauce, but not elsewhere. Mushrooms might be added, either fresh or dry. All in all, I find it a very practical recipe, adaptable to whatever is in season. As with other stews, the ideal accompaniments are those that are enhanced by the pan sauce, such as root vegetables, rice, or pasta.*

2 pounds boneless pork loin or other tender cut,
    cut into 2-inch squares
4 cups dry white wine
1 carrot, peeled and cut into 1-inch-thick slices
1 yellow onion, cut into quarters lengthwise and stuck with
    6 whole cloves
1 piece dried orange peel, about 3 inches long
10 black peppercorns, bruised with a mallet
2 fresh bay leaves, or 1 dried
1 clove garlic, minced
2 fresh thyme branches
5 fresh flat-leaf parsley sprigs
4 tablespoons extra-virgin olive oil
1 teaspoon salt
¼ cup all-purpose flour
¼ cup crème fraîche or sour cream (optional)

◆ Put the meat in a large bowl and add the wine, carrot, onion, orange peel, peppercorns, bay, garlic, thyme, parsley, and 2 tablespoons of the olive oil. Turn the ingredients to mix well, then cover and refrigerate overnight.

◆ Remove the meat from the marinade and pat it dry. Strain the marinade and discard the vegetables; set the marinade aside. Pour the remaining 2 tablespoons olive oil into a heavy-bottomed saucepan with a lid and place over medium-high heat. Put the pork in the olive oil, and, still over medium-high heat, brown it, cooking it for about 5 minutes and turning it as necessary. Sprinkle the pork with the salt and flour and continue to cook until the flour is browned. Pour in ½ cup of the reserved marinade and deglaze the pan, scraping up any bits clinging to the bottom. Continuing to stir, slowly pour in the remaining marinade. Reduce the heat to low, cover, and simmer until the meat is easily sliced through with a sharp knife, 45 minutes to 1 hour.

◆ Stir in the crème fraîche or sour cream, if using. Serve the pork hot, with its sauce.

SHEEP, GOATS & PIGS

Roast Pork Loin with Red Wine Glaze

[SERVES 6 TO 8]

The drippings from the roasting pork collect in the bottom of the pan and mingle with the red wine. Together they become the basting juices that give the roast its bronzed finish. This is a special Sunday dish, the kind I prepare when I have guests for a long lunch. The roast is sliced and served topped with its reduced juices. I like to serve it with mashed potatoes or mashed and seasoned winter squash, plus lightly buttered fresh spinach or chard.

1 boneless piece of pork loin, about 2½ pounds, tied and with a layer
    of fat on one side
1 teaspoon salt
1½ teaspoons freshly ground black pepper
4 cloves garlic, cut into slivers
4 tablespoons chopped fresh sage
1 tablespoon unsalted butter
¼ cup minced yellow onion
1 tablespoon minced fresh thyme
1¼ cups dry red wine
½ to 1 cup water

◆ Preheat an oven to 400 degrees F. Place a roasting pan fitted with a rack into the oven to heat.

◆ Rub the pork loin all over with the salt and pepper. Using the tip of a sharp knife, make slits all over the loin and insert the garlic slivers into them. Press 2 tablespoons of the sage firmly into the layer of fat.

◆ In a skillet, melt the butter over medium heat. When it foams, increase the heat to medium-high and place the seasoned pork, fat side down, into the skillet. Cook just long enough to brown the fat, 3 to 4 minutes. Remove from the skillet and set aside.

◆ Add the onion, thyme, and the remaining 2 tablespoons sage to the skillet over medium heat and sauté just until the onion is translucent, 2 to 3 minutes. Raise the heat to medium-high and add the wine. Cook for another minute, stirring to dislodge any bits clinging to the bottom. Pour the contents of the skillet into the heated roasting pan, then place the roast on the rack, fat side up.

◆ Roast for 10 minutes. Reduce the heat to 350 degrees F and continue to roast, basting frequently with the pan juices and adding the water as needed to keep the juices liquid, for 45 to 50 minutes. To test for doneness, cut into the meat, or insert an instant-read thermometer into the center of the roast; it should register 140 degrees F for medium well done or 150 degrees F for well done. Remove the meat to a carving board or platter, cover loosely with aluminum foil, and let stand for 10 to 15 minutes before carving.

◆ Meanwhile, place the roasting pan on the stove top over medium-high heat and add ½ cup of the water. Cook, stirring to dislodge any bits clinging to the bottom, until reduced to ¾ cup.

◆ Slice the pork loin into ¼-inch-thick slices and arrange on a warmed platter. Reheat the reduced juices if they have cooled and spoon over the pork. Serve at once.

Pork Medallions and Green Olives Sauté

SERVES 4 TO 6

The olives and bay leaves blend together to season the meat, onions, and juices with a distinctive flavor in this savory dish that takes only moments to prepare. I like to serve it with creamy mashed potatoes on the side to mingle with the savory juices.

1½ tablespoons extra-virgin olive oil
1½ tablespoons unsalted butter
1½ yellow onions, coarsely chopped
2 fresh bay leaves, or 1 dried
24 brine-cured tart green or black olives, pitted
1½ pounds pork tenderloin, cut into ½-inch-thick slices
½ cup water

◆ In a skillet, melt the olive oil with the butter over medium heat. When the butter foams, add the onions and sauté for about 1 minute. Add the bay leaves and the olives and sauté until the onions are translucent, another minute or two.

◆ Raise the heat to medium-high and push the onions and olives to the side of the skillet. Add the pork slices and cook for a minute or two, without turning, until the meat has changed color nearly halfway through. Turn, and cook for another minute or two, just until the pork is cooked through. Add the water and deglaze the pan by scraping up any bits clinging to the bottom, turning the pork in the juices as you do so. Serve immediately.

RECIPES

Brochettes of Small Birds with Juniper

Baked Pheasant with Chestnuts, Cèpes, and Cabbage

Daube of Wild Hare in a Pastry Crust

Daube of Wild Boar

Fish Soup, Mountain Style

Fireplace-Grilled Trout with Olive Oil and Rosemary

Salt Cod Fritters with Tomato Coulis

Crayfish Sauce for Pasta

Crayfish Salad

Salt Cod and Potato Terrine

Anchoïade Roulade

Snails Provençale

LA CHASSE, LA PÊCHE, ET *les champignons*—hunting, fishing, and mushrooms—are the grand passions of those men of Haute Provence who remain steeped in the traditions of their fathers and their fathers' fathers. In the forests and along the fringes of the cultivated fields and vineyards, they stalk all manner of birds, including pheasant, woodcock, dove, and thrush, as well as wild hare and boar. Snails, too, are hunted, but in quite a different fashion. In the mountains, at the beginning edges of the Alps, from the Valley of Jabron and Sisteron in the west to Entrevaux in the east, skilled hunters return with deer and occasionally wild mountain sheep, although the latter are most often found in the more northerly reaches of the alpine areas of Ubaye and Barcelonnette and in the high Alps of Savoy. The game and birds proudly brought home ensure the preparation of traditional regional dishes such as civet of wild boar, toasts spread with spit-roasted thrush, and daubes of wild hare. Families whose men hunt make their own pâtés out of such exotic fare as pheasant, partridge, hare, and boar. Some artisanal *charcutiers* specialize in sausages and pâtés, made with game and birds, selling them in their shops, or from a van parked in the open markets, where their wares are stacked in colorful columns of tins on the counters, hung in loops from the ceiling, and lined in the display windows of their movable shop.

In November and December, the butcher shops of the mountainous regions decorate their holiday windows with garlands of plumed pheasants and trays of neatly arranged plucked *grives* (thrushes). As often as possible, a butcher will display an entire boar, its coat still bristling, outside the door of the shop in the chill winter air, as much a seasonal decoration as the red ribbons and fragrant pine swags that decorate the other businesses. Local restaurants proudly chalk seasonal specialties on their posted daily menus, of which *civet de sanglier* or *daube de marcassin*—young boar—figures high. Hors d'oeuvre plates might include a slice of fresh *pâté de grive* or of *lièvre* (hare).

Come September, when the hunting season opens, men in garb varying from elaborate matching-camouflage ensembles to workman's blues covered with layers of old gray sweaters topped by a hunter's vest can be seen at the cafés. They drink small cups of *café express* laced with sugar, or a glass of pastis or perhaps brandy, and talk about the day's events.

Especially on weekends, one can come upon a half dozen to a dozen men standing along a road, seemingly idly and for no apparent purpose, spaced at thirty-foot intervals, their shotguns hung loosely over their arms. Contrary to appearance, they are only a single portion of a vast circle of intently focused hunters encompassing a portion of *garrigue,* or scrublands, where wild boar are roaming. The *battue,* as the group is called, is hunting prey by advancing forward in an ever-decreasing circle in the hopes that the boar or boars will be trapped within. It is certainly a good excuse for a lengthy promenade through the forest, and the sociability and conviviality of the enterprise is enjoyed by the hunters. Lunches, of course, are packed, replete with fresh baguettes and bottles of wine, since a leisurely midday meal is a necessity, even when one is engaged in the serious business of hunting.

Boars, although often hunted in *battues,* are hunted singly as well, especially by rural men, who are more familiar than the weekend visitors with the patterns of the local animal life. Some shun the idea of hunting in a large group of men and choose instead to be independent.

The number of wild boars in Haute Provence has increased in recent years, so it is not uncommon for them to wander out of the hills and forests into a cornfield or vineyard. Jean-Louis has mounted in his living room the head of one such boar. On hearing an odd noise during hunting season, he grabbed his shotgun from its rest over the fireplace and went out in his felt slippers, silently following the animal as it clumpety-clumped up the narrow paved road until he could get a clean shot. On hearing his shot, the few neighbors came out of their houses to ooh and ahh over the luck that Jean-Louis had had, and to discuss, under the moonlight, how much the boar weighed, its age, and of course, how many daubes could be made from it and whether perhaps a nice roast saddle would be possible, too, since it didn't appear to be too old and therefore tough, and on and on. Jean-Louis fetched his truck while the neighbors stood guard, and together they loaded the boar, which weighed nearly two hundred pounds, into the back of the truck and took it home to hang in the garage.

Early one winter morning, not many miles from where Jean-Louis shot his boar, his wife, Marguerite, hit one with her car on her way to work in Régusse. It was very dark on the slim ribbon of road that winds through the deep woods, and she didn't see the animal that darted in front of the car until it was directly in her headlights. She braked as soon as she saw the mass, but it was too late. Flinging open her car door, interior light left shining, she jumped out to see what had happened. As she stood over the beast, shocked, she was caught in the bright headlights of a car slowing behind her. A man strode out of the dark and demanded to know what she was doing, doors open, lights on, blocking the road. Seeing the dead boar, he warned her not to try to take it home, identified himself as a member of *Forêts et Eaux,* and proceeded to pull the dead animal over to the side of the road. Marguerite continued on to school and immediately telephoned Jean-Louis to tell him what had happened and the exact location, so that he could quickly go get the boar. Upon his arrival, however, a scant ten minutes after Marguerite's call, there was no sign of the animal. Later that morning at the local café, everyone was talking about the boar that Jacques had found on the side of the road, taken home, skinned, and butchered. Jean-Louis laughed, and told them that Jacques had Marguerite's boar, and recounted the story of her early morning encounter with the forestry agent. All agreed he was not at all an agent, but had only wanted time to get a larger vehicle to take the boar home. Later that evening, when Marguerite and Jean-Louis returned from work, they found a big packet of meat, enough for two large daubes, sitting wrapped and tied on their kitchen counter.

Although farm-raised boar meat is available, it is with good reason that wild boar is sought. Its meat tastes of the *garrigue,* a flavor that is distinctively powerful, especially after a classic treatment in red wine. One friend says she always uses a good Chateauneuf du Pape for her marinade: "The wine needs to be full bodied, to stand up to the meat and to match it, for the civet to be as it should." When made into sausages or pâtés, the meat is usually well spiced with juniper and other herbs. In mountain villages in particular, one finds air-cured wild boar from which thin slices are shaved, drizzled with olive oil, sprinkled with black pepper, and then served as an appetizer or layered between lengths of soft, fresh baguette for sandwiches.

One man, now in his eighties, tells of coming from Marseilles to hunt every year. He would stay in a small village near Riez, where he has a little house. His next-door neighbor hunted as well, and they made their own shot from lead and molds. When they had boar, they cooked it on a spit placed in front of the open fire on the low hearth in the neighbor's kitchen.

Although the boar population grew toward the end of the twentieth century, the population of birds and wild hare has decreased in the once-quiet rural areas, which now have widened roads and increased traffic. Hunters must go farther afield to the more wild places. Much of the walking and gun carrying in the upper Haute now is done by men like M. Fretoni, one of my neighbors who is a passionate hunter. Today he rarely sees any game, but glories nevertheless in the routine of the early morning walk across the hills and into the forests, usually alone. He tells me stories of the old days when he was a young man and the woods were full of woodcock, partridge, and pheasant,

and how the people of the area always had game on the table in season. Much of the game served, he recounts, had been *faisandé,* left to hang until it rotted before it was cooked. Although M. Fretoni is not a devotee of the practice, there are those who swear meat aged this way is a magnificent treat. Rules exist for determining exactly how long a particular bird must be hung before cooking. *Becasse,* or "woodcock," is to hang first forty days by its beak, then ten days by its feet, until the beak drips, the signal the delicacy is ready to be plucked, cooked, and spread onto toasts. I share M. Fretoni's view of this process. It is not for me, but I know many people who feel quite the opposite.

Thrushes remain high on M. Fretoni's list of delicacies, and fortunately for him these little birds still abound in the region. The season for hunting them differs depending upon how they are to be hunted. Classified as birds of passage, they may be sought from the opening of the season in September until its close in February, but only from sunrise to sundown. During the day, the birds leave the shelter of the brush and forest and disperse across the vineyards and fields, where they are difficult to shoot, then return to the woods at dusk. During the season, at dawn and dusk, men can be seen poised on the edges of the cultivated fields, waiting for the brief moment when the birds can be counted on to appear.

One method of hunting thrushes is highly specialized and may occur only during the month of March, from dawn to dusk only, and with a limited number of birds per day. This technique used to be a common practice throughout Haute Provence, before hunting regulations became rigid, but today it is rarely practiced and can be considered nearly a lost art.

Small sticks with glue on them are mounted onto long poles that are then thrust into a tree. Patiently the hunter waits for a grive to land on the stick and, when it does, the feet become stuck first, then the wings. The pole is lowered and carried back home, where the bird is freed and gently cleaned. Then it is put into a cage and put in a *cave* or other protected area, where it is kept throughout the season to be used as a live attractant. The cage (or cages, for hunters often have several) is taken into the forest and hung in a tree so the captive can call out to the wild birds. Nearby waits the hunter in his *cabanon,* typically a highly individualistic three-by-five-foot shack of loose construction comprised of old wine boxes, pieces of plywood, and shutters covered with camouflaging tree branches, and in the truly well-outfitted ones, a little wood-burning stove for heat. Thus the hunter is comfortably sheltered as he awaits the *grives.*

It is not unusual to see these odd buildings, or remnants of them, on a walk deep into the forests, or to find them at *brocante* dealers, rescued from dumps and abandoned attics, their delicate cages constructed from small pieces of wood, wired together by hand. To me they are artful testimonials to the ongoing Provençal passion for the small birds they once imprisoned, and to the importance of the *grive* in the ritual of living and eating with the seasons.

When *grives* are made into pâté, the whole bird is used, and when they are grilled or roasted, again it is the whole bird, bones and all, that is spread onto toasted bread, preferably grilled in the same fireplace. The flavor is gamy, yet not overwhelmingly so, and savoring them in a cozy winter kitchen with a fire glowing is, for me, to partake in a past tradition.

Unlike the *grive* and the boar, hare, pheasants, doves, and partridges that are hunted may not be wild at all, but rather raised on a farm, then purchased by a local hunting society to be released in their area not long before the season opens. As might be expected, these do not have a gamy taste, and instead are quite mild and cook more rapidly than their wild cousins.

Snail collecting is an adjunct to hunting game, and gathering them from wet grass and roads after a rainfall is an activity that encompasses the whole family—men and women, old and young. After a rain, it is not unusual to see the roads spotted here and there with bucket-toters in half-bent positions, looking for and gathering snails. At night, the hunt is carried out by flashlight. There are fewer snails now than in the past, just as there is less game, but it is still possible to find the small, flat, round snails called *blanquettes,* and occasionally the larger, cornucopia-shaped ones with pointed, dark brown shells. At one time, when hunting snails and cooking them was not only a pastime, but also as integral a part of the table as olive oil and garlic, everyone had special boxes in their *caves* or outbuildings to keep the snails, where they were fed on a diet of wild thyme and cornmeal to cleanse them for at least two weeks before cooking. In Haute Provence, the word *limace,* which actually means "slug," is used colloquially for snails, but for many years I was convinced that when people referred to eating *limace,* they were indeed eating slugs.

My children loved the whole adventure of collecting snails, and every summer this was an important activity. Our *limacière,* or "snail cage" as we called it, was made of an old grape-picking box covered with a fine wire mesh. We nailed the mesh everywhere, leaving only a little flap loose in order to drop in the new additions as we found them. This we weighted, not very satisfactorily, with a rock. We had many escapees, and on summer mornings and evenings it was part of the daily round of life to check on the snails and the security of their cage. Classically, the different types of snails were kept in separate *limacières,* as they are prone to attack each other, but we kept ours together.

When the time for the summer snail feast arrived, if we had been able to maintain adequate surveillance of our captives, we carefully followed the directions we had been given on the number of washings, the amount of salt and vinegar to add, and the length of the cooking time. The larger snails were plucked from their shells with toothpicks or little forks and eaten with *aïoli.* The small *blanquettes,* of which there were always many more, were cooked in a red sauce, and eaten *à la sucerelle,* that is, the snail was picked up by hand and sucked out, with all but the tip end, which is bitter, being eaten. A more sedate and less adventuresome method for *blanquettes,* although time-consuming, is to pick the little mollusks from their shells once they are cooked, cut off the bitter ends, and then to serve them in a sauce of tomatoes and herbs. Their texture is firm and their flavor pleasantly strong and slightly bitter.

Trout, crayfish, and pike come from the rivers and lakes that carve the landscape of Haute Provence, and fishing, since it is more passive, is even better than is hunting for enjoying the leisurely pleasure of life. The Durance, Verdon, Bléone, and the Asse are the largest rivers, and dams on them have created the lakes of Castillon, Ste. Croix, Esparron, and Quinson. Small rivers and streams trickle through the region; often nearly dry in summer, they become torrents during the winter and spring rains. In trout season one invariably sees tables with chairs set up along the edges of riverbanks, poles stuck into holders, and fishermen napping, caps pulled down, on blankets spread in the shade. Later in the day, the nap over and the afternoon coffee taken, the chairs will be lined up along the banks, filled with the fishermen who are waiting languorously for the late-afternoon hatch of insects that brings the prey to the surface. Women and girls fish, too, which is not generally the case with hunting.

One of my daughter's early gifts from a French fishing friend was a child-sized fishing basket with a selection of flies and hooks. We provided the pole. She happily set out with her little basket slung over her shoulder in true fisher-person fashion, her face full of expectation for the fish she would catch. On her first trip, to the gorges at Quinson, she brought home three small—probably undersized—trout, which she carefully cleaned and then fried and served to us.

At lake and riverside restaurants, such as the Dame d'Argent, on the banks of the Argens River near Sillans-la-Cascade, holding tanks for trout have been built to supply the restaurant's *truite à meunière* or *truite bleu,* but fishermen returning home with a tasty catch are more likely to have them grilled in the fireplace, or pan-fried with a little butter or olive oil. In the landlocked reaches of Haute Provence, anglers longing for the taste of the sea sometimes use their trout to make a reasonable facsimile of *soupe de poisson.* The Mediterranean *soupe de poisson* is made with small rock fish and crabs cooked down—bones, eyes, and all—with potatoes, wild fennel, garlic, water, and tomatoes, and then ground through a food mill to produce an unctuous purée eaten with slices of crusty garlic-rubbed bread and a spicy red pepper sauce. To accomplish this soup mountain-style with trout, and perhaps crayfish, tinned or salt-packed anchovies are added during cooking and these lend the maritime flavor.

Crayfish are another tasty morsel pursued by lovers of good food and fishing, although their numbers are much diminished from the earlier part of the century. This is partly due to the increased use of pesticides and poisonous chemicals in farming that occurred immediately after World War II and again between 1950 and 1990, but which now shows signs of abating due to greater information and stricter controls. The rustic, and so I am told, once much practiced method of catching crayfish was to put a potent-smelling sheep's head in a wire basket and suspend it from a string, dropping it into a deep water hole. There it would stay for perhaps a day, and when pulled up would be crawling with feasting crawfish. A variation on this is to omit the basket, instead wrapping the head with thorny wild berry canes to make it difficult for the crayfish to extricate themselves once the head is pulled from the water. Rancid bacon or lard is also considered good bait. Once caught—and it is not unthinkable to catch fifty or a hundred at a time—crayfish are boiled in water, wine, and herbs, drained, and served by the bowlful. To eat them, the shell is peeled back to free the meaty tail, and if there is a bit of butter, that golden orange cream at the base of the head, it is scooped or sucked out, depending upon one's style and inclination. Like crab butter, it is considered a delicacy. Crayfish are also incorporated into sauces, soups, and salads, where even a small quantity can flavor and elevate a dish.

Anchovies and salt cod have long played important roles in the food of Haute Provence, and early records show that in the 1600s salted fish, spices, and other exotic items were brought by mule to the hinterlands, far from the sea, crossing the hills and climbing the passes to their destinations. Since then, salt cod and anchovies have played such large roles that certain dishes containing them are traditional for feast days and holiday meals. Salt cod is part of the *grand aïoli* and is the raison d'être of *brandade*. It is also an essential ingredient in a traditional Christmas meal, which many households still adhere to, celebrating their Provençal customs within the larger Christian rite.

Vendors still bring salted anchovies to the inland open markets. They stand in barrels side by side with olives and capers, and are scooped up and put into a plastic bag, along with some of the salt in which they are packed, weighed, and sold. The same vendors sell sides and pieces of salt cod, a few displayed hanging from the ribs of their sheltering market umbrellas and the rest stacked up like irregular dinner plates. Anchovies are also available in supermarkets and *épiceries* everywhere, packed in tins with coarse salt, or in semipreserved form in little jars kept in the refrigerator section not far from the cheeses and hams. Anchovies packed in oil are also available, as they are here, but their flavor is often overwhelmed by the oil.

Although anchovies are always available, salt cod is more seasonal, and it is commonly seen only from fall through late spring, so it is considered cold-weather food. After May, it can be difficult to find salt cod at the open markets or elsewhere.

Wherever there is a *boulangerie* or a pizzeria, anchovies are found topping slices of *pissaladière* and pizza. They are pounded together with olive oil and garlic to make *anchoïade,* to accompany raw vegetables or to spread on toasts at aperitif time, and are used to season roast chicken, tomato salad, to add to stale bread to make a flavorful stuffing for vegetables, or to thicken a sauce. Anchovies need only a rinsing if packed in salt (and some traditional dishes call for them unrinsed), but salt cod needs to be soaked in several changes of water before being used. It is difficult to say exactly how long to soak, because it will depend upon how much salt was used and when the salting was done. When using salt cod, though, allow twenty-four hours for soaking and rinsing—refreshing the fish—although it might require as little as an hour or two. Once refreshed, the cod is typically poached, which takes only a few minutes, or it might be steamed or fried.

Refreshing Salt Cod

Rinse the salt cod under running water for 10 minutes, then soak it in cold water to cover in the refrigerator for 4 hours. Cut off a small piece, put it in a saucepan or small skillet with simmering water, and cook for 3 or 4 minutes. Remove and taste for saltiness. It should not be bland, but rather pleasantly salty. Depending upon the piece of salt cod you have, it may be ready to cook, or it may need additional soaking and changes of water for up to 24 hours. Continue to test.

When desalted, the fish is ready to be poached or otherwise cooked.

POACHING SALT COD

Put the soaked cod in a shallow saucepan or skillet and add water to cover. Bring to a simmer, and poach the fish for 3 to 4 minutes, just until it flakes when poked with a fork. Remove from the water and let cool.

Remove any errant skin or bones. If the fish is going to be flaked and combined with other ingredients, excess water should be squeezed out after flaking.

RAISING AND PREPARING SNAILS

Gather snails only in areas that you know to be free of pesticides, herbicides, or other potentially harmful chemicals. Put the snails in a cage or tightly screened box with a 1-inch-thick layer of cornmeal, a dish of water, and, if possible, a layer of fresh thyme branches. Feed them like this for 2 weeks, adding more thyme and cornmeal if necessary. At the end of this time, remove the snails to a large bowl or soup pot and sprinkle them with salt, about 1 cup for 2 pounds of snails. Stir well and leave for 12 to 14 hours, loosely covered with aluminum foil into which holes have been punched. Fill the bowl or container with water, then drain. Fill again with water, this time adding 2 cups distilled white vinegar. Rinse them in as many changes of water as necessary for the water to run clear.

Once the snails are clean, place them in a saucepan with 1 yellow onion, chopped; 1 carrot, peeled and chopped; 1 wild or cultivated fennel stalk, cut into 1-inch lengths; several sprigs each of fresh flat-leaf parsley and thyme; 4 cups dry white wine; 1 teaspoon salt; and 1 teaspoon freshly ground black pepper. Bring to a boil and skim off the foam from the surface. Once the foam has been removed, cover and reduce the heat to low. Simmer until the snails can easily be removed from their shells with a needle, about 2½ hours. Drain, discarding the liquid.

Let the snails cool, then remove them from their shells. Cut off the rear portion from each snail and discard it. Rinse the snails. They are now ready to eat. To reuse the snail shells, rinse them and let them drain.

Brochettes of Small Birds with Juniper

SERVES 4

In Haute Provence, thrushes are the small birds of choice for this simple grill, but squab are used as well. Threaded onto skewers alternately with pieces of day-old bread, the well-seasoned birds soon cook to a tender golden brown over an open fire or coals. Here, quail are substituted because they are more readily available. Creamy polenta and sauteed spinach make good accompaniments.

¼ cup fresh thyme leaves
1 tablespoon freshly ground black pepper
1 teaspoon salt
2 fresh or dried juniper berries, crushed
4 quail, cleaned
4 slices bacon
6 fresh bay leaves, or 4 dried
5 slices day-old baguette or country-style bread
2 cloves garlic

◆ Prepare a charcoal or wood fire, or preheat a broiler.

◆ Make a mixture of the thyme, pepper, salt, and juniper berries, and rub it over the quail, inside and out. Lay each quail on a slice of bacon and wrap the bacon across the middle of the bird. If you are using dried bay leaves, place a leaf inside each cavity. Rub the bread slices on both sides with the garlic. If you are using fresh bay leaves, thread a leaf onto a long, sturdy skewer and follow it with a baguette slice. Thread a quail lengthwise through its body cavity onto the skewer, pressing it against the bread. Repeat with the remaining quail, fresh bay, and bread, ending with the last piece of bread and a bay leaf. The bread holds the birds in place during the frequent turning on the grill and soaks up some of the juices.

◆ When the coals are medium-hot, place the skewer on a lightly oiled grill rack or on a broiler pan. Cook, turning every 3 or 4 minutes, until a thigh can be readily moved and the juices run clear or slightly pink when the thickest part of the thigh is pierced, about 15 minutes.

◆ To serve, slip a piece of juice-soaked bread onto a plate and top with a quail.

Baked Pheasant with Chestnuts, Cèpes, and Cabbage

SERVES 4 OR 5

Here, pheasant is braised in white wine, garlic, and herbs, carved and served on a bed of steamed cabbage and sautéed chestnuts and cèpes. The sweet starch taste of the chestnuts gives substance, as do the meaty mushrooms. Hot braising juices, reduced with additional wine, are poured over all at the moment of serving, bathing the cabbage in pools of flavor. Fluffy, garlicky mashed potatoes are perfect for soaking up the braising juices, while an array of pickles and chutneys adds a spicy note. A green salad of butter lettuce, dressed with a vinaigrette of fruity olive oil, shallots, and red wine vinegar completes the menu.

    2 pheasants with giblets, about 2½ pounds each
    1 teaspoon salt
    1 teaspoon freshly ground black pepper
    4 cloves garlic, minced
    4 celery stalks
    6 fresh thyme sprigs
    3 fresh marjoram or oregano sprigs
    3 cups dry white wine
    1 pound fresh cèpe, shiitake, or portobello mushrooms
    2 pounds chestnuts, roasted and shelled (page 254)
    6 tablespoons unsalted butter
    ½ large head cabbage, sliced ½ inch thick (about 4 cups)
    ¼ cup water

◆ Preheat an oven to 350 degrees F.

◆ Chop the giblets and put them in a saucepan with salted water to cover. Place over medium heat, bring to a steady simmer, cover, and cook until tender, 30 to 40 minutes. Remove from the heat, drain, and set aside.

◆ Rub the pheasants with ¾ teaspoon each of the salt and pepper. Place the birds, breast side up, on a rack in a roasting pan just large enough to hold them, and add the garlic, celery, thyme, marjoram or oregano, and 2 cups of the wine. Cover, place in the oven, and bake until the juice of the pheasant runs clear when pierced with the tip of a knife at the base of the thigh, 1 to 1½ hours.

◆ About 15 minutes before the pheasants are ready, prepare the mushroom-chestnut mixture. Cut the mushrooms (including stems) and the chestnuts into ½-inch pieces. In a skillet, melt 4 tablespoons of the butter over medium heat. Add the mushrooms and sauté, turning them often, until they change color and begin to release their juices, 6 to 7 minutes. Add the remaining 2 tablespoons butter, the chestnuts, and the drained giblets. Reduce the heat to low and cook for 3 or 4 minutes to heat through and blend the flavors. Add the remaining ¼ teaspoon each of salt and pepper. Remove from the heat and keep warm. Place the cabbage on a steamer rack above boiling water, cover the steamer, and steam until wilted and tender, about 5 minutes. Remove from the steamer and keep warm.

◆ Remove the pheasants from the roasting pan. Using a slotted spoon, remove and discard the vegetables from the pan. Carve the breast meat into slices and cut off the legs. Set aside and keep warm. Add the remaining 1 cup of wine and the water to the juices in the pan and place over high heat. Deglaze the pan by scraping up any browned bits clinging to the bottom, and cook until the liquid is reduced to 1 cup.

◆ Make a bed of the cabbage on a warmed platter and top with the mushroom-chestnut mixture (reheated, if necessary). Arrange the sliced pheasant and legs over the top. Pour the hot reduced juices over all and serve immediately.

Daube of Wild Hare in a Pastry Crust

Serves 4 to 6

The flavor of hare is gamier and the texture of its meat denser than that of rabbit, but a delicious version of this dish, which is rustic yet elegant in both presentation and taste, can be made with the latter.

In France, rabbits are sold whole with the kidneys, liver, and heart still attached, but in the United States they are usually sold without their innards, cut up as fryers, except at specialty markets.

The daube can be made a day in advance and it should be, as the flavors improve upon standing. The vegetables can be prepared ahead as well, leaving only the crust and the final assembly. The dish can be served without the crust, although I find that when the crust is broken through, the response around the dinner table to the rising aroma is reward enough for the small amount of extra work. A butter biscuit topping is a possible alternative to the puff pastry.

1 tablespoon extra-virgin olive oil

¼ pound *roulade* (pancetta), cut into ½-inch pieces

1 wild hare or large rabbit, about 3 pounds, cut into serving pieces

2 yellow onions, chopped

2 cloves garlic, minced

½ cup dry red wine

¾ cup red wine vinegar

2 tablespoons fresh thyme leaves

2 fresh bay leaves, or 1 dried

2 whole cloves

1 teaspoon salt

1½ teaspoons freshly ground black pepper

1½ cups water

2 to 3 tablespoons all-purpose flour

2½ tablespoons unsalted butter

4 red or yellow boiling potatoes, such as Yukon Gold, Yellow Finn, or Red Rose, unpeeled and quartered

24 fresh chanterelle, cèpe, or button mushrooms

2 tablespoons minced shallot

2 tablespoons chopped fresh flat-leaf parsley

1 sheet prepared puff pastry, 10 by 12 inches and ¼ inch thick

1 egg white, lightly beaten

◆ In a deep skillet or a saucepan with a tightly fitting lid, combine the olive oil and *roulade*. Place over medium heat and cook for a minute or two. Add the pieces of hare or rabbit and sauté, turning as needed, until lightly golden, about 10 minutes. Add the onions and garlic and continue to cook for a minute or two. Sprinkle with 2 tablespoons of the flour and cook, stirring, for another minute or 2 to brown the flour. Add the wine and vinegar and deglaze the pan by scraping up any bits clinging to the bottom. Stir in the thyme, bay, cloves, ½ teaspoon of the salt, and ¾ teaspoon of the pepper, and 1 cup of water. If you are using wild hare, stop the process now. Let cool, cover, and refrigerate overnight and continue cooking the next day. If you are using rabbit, continue on at this point. Cover the pan and cook over low heat until the meat is tender enough to pull apart with a fork, about 1 hour for the rabbit, depending upon the age and size, and up to 3 hours for the hare. Once the meat is tender, remove it to a plate. To finish the sauce, pour in the remaining half cup of water and bring to a boil. Reduce the heat, combine the remaining 1 tablespoon of the flour and 2 tablespoons of the butter and stir it into the pan, cooking a minute or two until the sauce thickens slightly. Remove from the heat and set aside.

continued

◆ Boil the potatoes in salted water to cover until tender, about 30 minutes. Drain and set aside. Meanwhile, cut any large mushrooms in half and leave small ones whole. Melt the remaining ½ tablespoon of the butter in a skillet over medium heat and add the shallot and mushrooms. Sauté just until they begin to change color, 3 or 4 minutes. Sprinkle the remaining ½ teaspoon salt and ¾ teaspoon pepper and the parsley over the mushrooms, stir briefly, and remove from the heat. Set aside.

◆ Preheat an oven to 400 degrees F.

◆ Select a 3½- to 4-quart baking dish. I especially like to use the glazed French brown ceramic ware. When it emerges from the oven topped with the golden brown crust, it looks as if it was made specifically for the pastry-crust top of the daube. On a lightly floured work surface, roll out the puff pastry into a round 1 inch larger in diameter than the baking dish and about ¼ inch thick. Put the rabbit, potatoes, mushrooms and their juices, and the thickened sauce from the hare or rabbit in the baking dish. Carefully lay the pastry round on top and pinch the edges to seal. Make 3 or 4 diagonal slashes in the top of the crust to allow the steam to escape. These openings will make a pretty design as the pastry puffs and reveals its layers. Brush the top with the egg white (it will make it shiny).

◆ Bake until the crust is golden brown, about 20 minutes. Remove and serve hot, scooping out servings that include some of the crust.

Daube of Wild Boar

SERVES 6

A daube made from wild boar is considered a specialty, and each household and restaurant has its version with slightly varying ingredients for the marinade. The important ingredients, those that do not vary, are a full-bodied wine (in the wealthier households it is a good Rhône wine), bay leaves, thyme, garlic, pepper, salt, and onions. Some people include winter savory and orange peel. Others add a little Cognac, and still others carrots and juniper. In some instances, only wine is used, and in others vinegar and water are added as well. Sometimes the marinade is cooked beforehand, and I highly recommend this, as the kitchen fills with the perfume of the simmering herbs and wine, bringing to life the scent of Haute Provence.

The key to cooking this daube is, I think, as with any wild game, knowing the age of the animal. The meat of a young boar, or marcassin, will require less cooking to become tender than will that of a fully grown boar, several years old. If the wild boar has been raised in captivity, and then loosed for the hunt, the meat will resemble pork. A clue to the age of the animal is the color of the meat, with the younger and consequently more tender meat being light colored, and that of the mature beast darker. In any event, taste the meat as it cooks, and determine the doneness yourself, figuring roughly one and a half to two hours for young or for farm-raised wild boar, and three to four hours for mature animals several years old.

Serve the daube with simple boiled or mashed potatoes, a green salad, and a bottle of good, full-bodied red wine to match the gamy flavor of the meat.

FOR THE MARINADE:
2 tablespoons extra-virgin olive oil
6 cloves garlic, crushed and chopped
1 yellow onion, sliced
4 carrots, peeled and cut into 1-inch-thick slices
4 cups full-bodied red wine
½ cup red wine vinegar

continued

4 cups water

2 fresh bay leaves, or 1 dried

1 teaspoon black peppercorns

6 juniper berries

6 fresh thyme branches, each 6 inches long

3 fresh rosemary branches, each 6 inches long

6 fresh winter savory branches, each 6 inches long

1 teaspoon salt

1 orange zest strip, about 4 inches long and ½ inch wide

4 whole cloves

3½ pounds boneless wild boar meat, such as shoulder,
    cut into 2-inch pieces

2 tablespoons extra-virgin olive oil

5 slices *roulade* (pancetta) or 5 slices thick-cut bacon, cut into pieces
    2 inches long and ½ inch wide

4 cloves garlic, minced

1 yellow onion, chopped

2 tablespoons all-purpose flour

2 fresh bay leaves, or 1 dried

1 orange zest strip, about 4 inches long and 1 inch wide

1 teaspoon salt

1 teaspoon freshly ground black pepper

◆ To make the marinade, in a large saucepan, heat the olive oil over medium heat. Add the garlic and onion and sauté until translucent, 2 to 3 minutes. Add the carrots and sauté another minute or two, or until the carrots change color slightly. Add all the remaining marinade ingredients and bring to a boil. Reduce the heat to low and simmer, uncovered, for 30 minutes.

◆ Remove from the heat and let cool to room temperature.

◆ Place the meat in a nonreactive bowl or pot and pour the cooled marinade over it. There should be enough marinade to cover the meat. Cover the bowl or pot and refrigerate for 24 hours.

◆ To cook, remove the meat from the marinade and dry it thoroughly with paper towels. Set aside. Strain the marinade through a fine-mesh sieve, discarding the herbs and the vegetables and reserving the liquid. In the bottom of a heavy-bottomed pot, warm the olive oil over medium heat. Add the *roulade* or bacon and sauté until it has released some of its fat but has not taken on color. Remove and discard. Add the garlic and onion and sauté for a minute or two. Increase the meat to medium-high, add the meat, and cook, turning as needed, until it has changed color, about 8 to 10 minutes. Sprinkle with the flour, and cook, turning, until the flour has browned, another 3 or 4 minutes, and some of the liquid has been absorbed. Pour in about ½ cup of the strained marinade, deglazing the pan and scraping up any browned bits clinging to the bottom. Pour in the remaining marinade and add the bay leaves, orange zest, salt, and pepper. Bring to a boil and then reduce the heat to very low. Cover and simmer, stirring occasionally, until the meat is tender enough to be cut with a fork, at least 2 hours and as long as 4, depending on the age of the animal.

◆ Remove the meat to a dish and keep it warm. Raise the heat to high and boil the liquid until it is reduced to about 2 cups. Return the meat to the reduced juices and cook over medium heat for 2 or 3 minutes. Serve the meat with a little of its juice.

Fish Soup, Mountain Style

SERVES 4

*Many freshwater fish, like the small rock fish of the Mediterranean, may be too
small or bony to eat easily, but they can still contribute their flavor to a fish
soup. In Haute Provence, carp, perch, small trout, and, when available, crayfish
go into fish soups. The other ingredients are those of the countryside and the
garden: thyme, fennel, potatoes, tomato, bay leaf, garlic, and leeks. They are all
cooked together, then, using a food mill, a flavorful thick soup is extracted and
the bony fish and other components are discarded. The poorest of ingredients
have resulted in an intensely flavorful soup that is then spooned over garlic
toasts. For a taste of the sea, add the anchovies.*

¼ cup extra-virgin olive oil
2 leeks, carefully rinsed and chopped, including tender greens
3 cloves garlic, chopped, plus 3 whole cloves garlic
1 piece wild or 2 pieces cultivated fennel stalk, about 10 inches long,
    chopped, including leaves, or ½ cup chopped fennel bulb
3 potatoes, any kind, unpeeled, cut into pieces
2 to 3 pounds freshwater white fish such as perch, trout, and/or
    carp, cleaned with heads and tails intact
2 or 3 oil-packed or rinsed salted anchovy filets
3 very ripe tomatoes, coarsely chopped
1 fresh thyme branch, or 2 tablespoons fresh thyme leaves
2 fresh bay leaves, or 1 dried
1 piece dried orange zest, about 2 inches long
1 teaspoon salt
1 teaspoon freshly ground black pepper
2 quarts plus ¼ cup water
2 cups dry white wine
12 slices baguette or country-style bread

◆ In a heavy-bottomed soup pot, warm the olive oil over medium heat. Add the leeks, the chopped garlic, and the fennel and sauté for 2 or 3 minutes. Add the potatoes, fish, and anchovies and continue to cook until the fish has colored and started to fall apart, 4 or 5 minutes longer. Stir in the tomatoes, thyme, bay, orange zest, salt, pepper, the 2 quarts water, and the wine. Bring to a boil, reduce the heat to low and simmer, uncovered, for 20 minutes, or until the potatoes are tender.

◆ Remove from the heat and pass the contents of the soup pot through a food mill placed over a clean saucepan, extracting the juices and the essence of the ingredients and forming a puree. Return the pomace trapped in the food mill to the original soup pot and add the ¼ cup water. Cook, stirring, for 3 or 4 minutes, then put the pomace through the food mill into the saucepan again, extracting more juice and essence. Discard the pomace in the food mill.

◆ Place the saucepan over medium heat, and reheat gently, stirring often. Taste and adjust the seasonings. The consistency should be somewhat thick, but not pastelike.

◆ Toast the bread slices and rub them with the remaining whole garlic cloves. To serve, place a slice of toast in each of 4 warmed soup bowls and ladle the hot soup over them. Accompany with the remaining toasts.

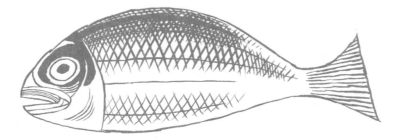

Fireplace-Grilled Trout with Olive Oil and Rosemary

SERVES 2

Although at first the rosemary might seem overly pungent for the delicate flavor of trout, it infuses just a hint of wildness, which creates a pleasing flavor.

  2 whole trout, 1½ pounds each, cleaned with heads and tails intact
  3 tablespoons extra-virgin olive oil
  1½ teaspoons salt
  1½ teaspoons freshly ground black pepper
  6 lemon slices, plus wedges for garnish
  4 fresh rosemary sprigs, each 2 inches long, plus 8 to 10 branches,
      each 8 inches long

◆ Prepare a charcoal or a wood fire.

◆ Rub the trout inside and out with the 3 tablespoons olive oil, then with the salt and pepper. Tuck 3 lemon slices and 2 rosemary sprigs inside each cavity. Place the fish inside a long-handled grilling basket and close the basket tightly. Place the basket over medium-low coals that have been lined with the rosemary branches to form a bed. Grill, turning once, just until the fish is cooked through and the flesh pulls easily from the backbone, 5 to 6 minutes on each side. Remove from the grill and serve immediately with the lemon wedges.

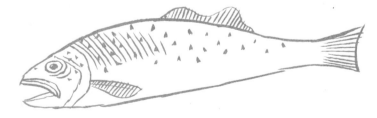

Salt Cod Fritters with Tomato *Coulis*

MAKES 20 FRITTERS; SERVES 6 AS AN APPETIZER OR FIRST COURSE,
OR 4 AS A MAIN COURSE

The light taste of the coulis *adds a distinction to the humble salt cod, and the combination is suitable for serving as an appetizer, a first course, or even a main course.*

> 1 pound boneless salt cod, refreshed and poached (pages 224–225)
> ½ cup minced fresh flat-leaf parsley
> 2 eggs, lightly beaten
> 2 teaspoons freshly ground black pepper
> ¼ cup grated Parmesan cheese
> ½ cup fine dried bread crumbs, preferably homemade
> 2 teaspoons crumbled dried thyme
> Canola oil or other light vegetable oil for frying
> 1 cup Tomato *Coulis* (page 151), heated or at room temperature

♦ Separate the salt cod into small, fine flakes. Put them in a bowl and add the parsley, eggs, pepper, and cheese. Mix together well and shape into balls 1 to 1½ inches in diameter. Flatten the balls between the palms of your hands to make patties about 2 inches in diameter; you should have 20 patties. Set aside on waxed paper.

♦ In a small bowl, stir together the bread crumbs and thyme. Pour oil into a skillet to a depth of ¼ inch and place over medium heat. When the oil is hot, press both sides of each patty in the crumb mixture and place in the pan. Cook only as many at a time as the skillet will hold without crowding. Fry, turning once, until golden, 3 to 4 minutes on each side. Using a slotted spatula, remove to paper towels to drain.

♦ Serve hot or at room temperature with the *coulis*.

Crayfish Sauce for Pasta

SERVES 3 OR 4

*When the fishing has been successful, and the buckets come home loaded with
fresh crayfish, the ideal way to eat them is to boil them simply with salt, peppercorns, and bay leaves. Once they are cooked through and have turned a bright
red, drain them and set them on platters on a table. Set out bowls of melted
butter, bowls for discarded shells, finger bowls, and napkins. When the fishing
has yielded only a dozen or two, use the crayfish in a pasta sauce instead,
but cook them the same way.*

2 quarts water

2 ½ teaspoons salt

1 tablespoon black peppercorns, bruised

4 fresh bay leaves, or 2 dried

2 wild or 3 cultivated fennel stalks, cut into 2-inch lengths

24 crayfish

1 ½ tablespoons unsalted butter

1 tablespoon all purpose flour

¼ cup minced shallot

2 cloves minced garlic

¾ cup dry white wine

½ teaspoon freshly ground black pepper

2 tablespoons minced wild fennel leaves, or 3 tablespoons
    minced cultivated leaves

¾ cup chicken broth

¾ pound fresh fettuccine, or 10 ounces dried

¼ cup grated Parmesan cheese

3 tablespoons minced fresh flat-leaf parsley

◆ Bring the water to a boil in a large pot and add 2 teaspoons of the salt, the peppercorns, bay, and fennel stalks. Boil for 5 minutes, then add the crayfish. Reduce the heat to medium and cook the crayfish until they turn bright red, 6 to 8 minutes. Remove with a slotted spoon, and set aside until cool enough to handle. Strain the boiling liquid through a sieve lined with several layers of cheesecloth, reserving ½ cup. Discard the rest of the liquid along with the contents of the sieve.

◆ To remove the meat from each crayfish, first separate the head from the body. Peel away the upper, loose shells of the tail, then bend back the tail, snapping it. The tail and shell will pull away, and you will be able to extract the meat intact from the tail. Along the back of the tail is a veinlike intestine that should be removed. This is easily done by grasping it at one end and pulling it up. The meat is now ready to use. If the head or the thoracic cavity has yellow roe, or butter as it is sometimes called, scrape it out, as it is very flavorful and adds to the sauce. Set aside the meat and any roe.

◆ Mix together a ½ tablespoon of the butter with the flour and set aside. Melt the remaining 1 tablespoon of butter in a saucepan over medium heat, add the shallots, and garlic, and sauté until translucent, 2 or 3 minutes. Add the wine, the remaining ½ teaspoon salt, the ground pepper, the fennel leaves, and the chicken broth. Raise the heat to high and cook rapidly until reduced to 1 cup. Then stir in the crayfish and any roe and the butter-flour mixture, and continue to cook until the sauce has thickened slightly, just a minute or two. Meanwhile, bring a large pot of salted water to a boil. Add the pasta, stir well, and cook until just tender. Drain well.

◆ Place the pasta in a warmed serving bowl. Stir the Parmesan cheese and parsley into the sauce and pour it over the pasta. Toss and serve immediately.

Crayfish Salad

SERVES 4

Mixed greens are topped with crayfish and their roe, then dressed with a light vinaigrette of olive oil and lemon juice. Serve these salads with toasted croutons and aioli.

4 boiling potatoes such as Yukon Gold, Yellow Finn, or Red Rose

FOR COOKING THE CRAYFISH:
2 quarts water
1 tablespoon black peppercorns, bruised
2 teaspoons salt
4 fresh bay leaves, or 2 dried
2 wild or 3 cultivated fennel stalks, cut into 2-inch lengths
36 live crayfish

¼ cup extra-virgin olive oil
3 to 4 tablespoons fresh lemon juice
½ teaspoon salt
1 teaspoon freshly ground black pepper
2 tablespoons fresh flat-leaf parsley
4 cups mixed young greens such as lettuce, spinach, and
     roquette (arugula)
½ cup *Aïoli* (page 172)

◆ Boil the potatoes in salted water to cover until just tender when tested with the tines of a fork, 30 to 35 minutes. Drain the potatoes and, when cool enough to handle, cut into slices. Set aside.

◆ Meanwhile, to cook the crayfish, bring the water to a boil in a large pot and add the peppercorns, salt, bay leaves, and fennel stalks. Boil for 5 minutes, then add the crayfish. Reduce the heat to medium and cook the crayfish until they turn bright red, 6 to 8 minutes. Drain the crayfish and let cool until they can be handled. Then, to remove the meat from each crayfish, first separate the head from the body. Peel away the upper, loose shells of the tail, then bend back the tail, snapping it, and pull the meat intact from the tail. Grasp the dark veinlike intestine at one end and pull it out. If there is yellow roe visible in the head or the thoracic cavity, scrape it out as well. Set the meat and roe aside.

◆ In a small bowl, mix together the olive oil, lemon juice to taste, salt, pepper, and parsley to form a vinaigrette. Arrange the leaves on individual salad plates. Divide the potatoes and the crayfish and their roe, if any, evenly among them. Pour a little vinaigrette over each salad, garnish with a spoonful of *aïoli* and serve at once.

Salt Cod and Potato Terrine

Serves 4 to 6

Salt cod and potatoes are often combined. In this terrine, layers of thinly sliced boiled potatoes alternate with a spread of salt cod mixed with a béchamel sauce. The layers are topped with buttered seasoned bread crumbs, then baked.

3 pounds boiling potatoes such as Yukon Gold, Red Rose, Red Fir, or White Rose
5 tablespoons unsalted butter
3 tablespoons all-purpose flour
½ teaspoon freshly ground black pepper
½ teaspoon cayenne pepper or other dried ground chili pepper
1 cup milk
1 pound boneless salt cod, refreshed and poached (pages 224–225)
2 teaspoons fresh thyme or winter savory leaves
¾ cup shredded Gruyère cheese
½ cup coarse dried bread crumbs

◆ Boil the potatoes in salted water to cover until just barely tender when tested with the tines of a fork, about 30 minutes. Do not overcook. Drain the potatoes and, when cool enough to handle, cut into thin slices. Set aside.

◆ Preheat an oven to 375 degrees F. Using 1 tablespoon of the butter, grease an oven-to-table standard-sized loaf pan.

◆ To make the sauce, in a heavy-bottomed saucepan, melt 3 tablespoons of the butter over medium heat. When it begins to foam, remove the pan from the heat and whisk in the flour, black pepper, and cayenne pepper until a paste forms. Return the pan to medium heat and gradually whisk in the milk, adding it in a steady stream. Reduce the heat to low and stir until there are no lumps. Then simmer the sauce, stirring occasionally, until it is thick enough to coat the back of a spoon, about 10 minutes. Remove from the heat.

◆ Measure out ½ cup of the sauce and set aside. Tear the salt cod into small flakes and place in a bowl. Add the remaining sauce to the salt cod and mix to make a paste.

◆ To assemble the terrine, make a layer of one-fourth of the potatoes in the loaf pan. Top with one-third of the salt cod mixture, one-third of the thyme or savory, and about one-fourth of the cheese. Repeat the layers twice, then top with the remaining potatoes. Sprinkle the remaining cheese across the top, followed by the bread crumbs and the reserved sauce. Finally dot with the remaining butter.

◆ Bake until the dish is heated through, the sauce is bubbling around the edges, and the top is golden brown, about 30 minutes. (If necessary, slip the pan under a preheated broiler for a minute or two to brown the top.)

◆ Remove from the oven, cover loosely with aluminum foil, and let stand for about 10 minutes to firm up. To serve, cut into slices with a knife, then remove with a spatula to the waiting plates.

Anchoïade Roulade

SERVES 4

Anchoïade, *a mixture of anchovies, olive oil, and garlic, is an archetypal dish not just in Haute Provence, but throughout Provence, where it is served on toasts to accompany aperitifs, used as a dipping sauce for raw vegetables, and is tucked into savory pastries as a filling.*

Here, it is spread on thin slices of beef, which are then rolled, grilled, and served either plain or with a tomato sauce. The flavor is explosive, yet the dish is simple to prepare.

> 10 salted anchovies, filleted and lightly rinsed, or if not available,
>   substitute 20 oil-packed anchovy fillets
> 8 cloves garlic
> ⅓ cup olive oil
> 3 tablespoons chopped fresh parsley
> 8 beef slices such as top sirloin, rumpsteak, or tri-tip, each ¼ inch thick
> 2 teaspoons freshly ground black pepper
> 2 cups Tomato *Coulis* (page 151), heated (optional)

◆ Prepare a charcoal or wood fire. Soak 8 sturdy toothpicks in water to cover. Crush the anchovies and garlic together in a mortar with a pestle, in a bowl with a wooden spoon, or in a small food processor. Gradually mix in the olive oil to make a thick paste. Stir in the parsley.

◆ Drain the toothpicks. Spread a thin layer of the anchovy paste in a 2-inch-wide strip down the center of a beef slice, stopping 1 inch short of each end. Roll up the meat and skewer it in place with a toothpick. Repeat with the remaining paste and beef slices. Sprinkle each roll with a little black pepper.

♦ Place the rolls in a long-handled grilling basket and fasten tightly closed. Place the basket over medium-hot coals and cook, turning once, until the beef is just seared, 3 or 4 minutes on each side, or until cooked to your preference.

♦ Remove to individual plates and serve with hot *coulis* spooned over them, if desired.

Snails Provençale

SERVES 2 OR 3

If you haven't captured and fed your own snails, you can still savor this dish using canned or frozen snails. It is a preparation filled with the flavors of Haute Provence, although it is usually made with the little white snails that are so common there. Serve this as a first course garnished with parsley and accompanied by fresh crusty bread.

   3 tablespoons extra-virgin olive oil
   One 2-inch piece bacon, minced
   1 yellow onion, chopped
   4 cloves garlic, minced
   1 shallot, chopped
   4 tomatoes, peeled, seeded, and chopped (fresh or canned)
   ¼ cup dry white wine
   ¼ cup chicken broth
   2 teaspoons fresh thyme leaves
   1 teaspoon fresh winter savory leaves
   1 teaspoon salt
   1 teaspoon freshly ground black pepper
   1 tablespoon all-purpose flour
   1 can (8 ounces) snails, drained, or 2 pounds live snails,
      cleaned and cooked as described on page 225
   2 tablespoons chopped fresh flat-leaf parsley

continued

◆ In a saucepan warm the olive oil over medium heat. Add the bacon and cook for a minute or two until it softens. Then add the onion, garlic, and shallot and sauté until translucent, 2 to 3 minutes. Add the tomatoes and cook, stirring, for another 2 or 3 minutes. Pour in the wine and broth and add the thyme, winter savory, salt, and pepper. Stir well, reduce the heat to low, and simmer, uncovered, until thickened, about 45 minutes.

◆ In a small bowl, stir the flour into 2 tablespoons of the hot sauce, then whisk the mixture back into the sauce to thicken it. Cook, stirring, for another minute or two.

◆ Add the snails to the sauce and cook for 5 minutes longer to blend the flavors. Serve immediately, garnished with the parsley.

RECIPES

Warm Goat Cheese and Toasted Almond Salad

Purslane and Hazelnut Salad with Lemon Vinaigrette

Escarole and Chestnut Salad with Lardons

Pasta with Walnuts and Gorganzola Cheese

Pumpkin-Filled Ravioli with Walnut Sauce

Ragout of Pork, Chestnuts, and Winter Keeper Apples

Trout with Toasted Almonds

Almond Meringues

Green Almond Ice Cream

Walnut and Sugar Pudding

Sugared Walnuts

Chaussons *Filled with Sweet Chestnut Cream*

Prune Plums Sautéed with Walnuts

Vin de Noix

THE ORCHARDS OF ALMONDS, WALNUTS, hazelnuts, and chestnuts that were cultivated in Haute Provence during the last century and were a viable part of the region's economic life are greatly diminished, and in some areas have disappeared altogether. The Plateau de Valensole was once heavily planted to almonds, but now only a relatively few trees are visible, scattered here and there near the remains of farmhouses. Near Quinson and Régusse, Aups, and Cotignac, small abandoned almond orchards, many of the trees dead and others nearly so, still make a brave springtime show of their scant blossoms. Each year I approach these trees I know so well with trepidation, sure that they, like those of Valensole, will have at last fallen to the saw.

Walnuts are amenable to the lands in the upper regions of Haute Provence, but like the almonds, the commercial orchards that flourished at the beginning of the century have disappeared, and the major area of walnut production today is farther north, in and around Grenoble and to the west near Bordeaux. The area around Moustiers-Ste.-Marie, for example, had substantial orchards as late as the mid-1930s, when they were cut down and the wood sold to German buyers to make gunstocks. In the Valley of Jabron, the trees were cut and the wood sold for furniture. Sisteron, Digne, Annot, and St. André-les-Alpes, the gateway to the passes of the Col d'Allos and the high

Alps, had large walnut plantings earlier in the century as well. Annot had mills for crushing walnuts to extract their oil, which was an important commodity, and the last one closed late in the nineteenth century. Today the large orchards are gone and the small holdings have declined. One finds lone trees here and there, sometimes four or five, with the exception of the Valley of Jabron located in the Lure Mountains running east and west from Sisteron. The walnuts grown in this valley, although greatly reduced in number, are considered to be of an exceptional quality, and *vin de noix* made from them is labeled as a regional specialty. Here, centered around the town of Noyers-sur-Jabron, a few small orchards have been planted, and some families still have enough old trees to harvest and go to market with the nuts. The harvest begins at the end of September with the gathering by hand of some early walnuts, those whose skins have cracked, and whose moisture is about 15 to 20 percent. They have a slightly green taste and a crispy texture that is considered a delicacy, and the ripe yet still soft nuts are spread onto bread with butter to enjoy at aperitif time. The remainder of the crop is left to dry on the trees before being harvested, or is dried before eating.

Chestnuts and hazelnuts are commercially grown outside of Haute Provence on either side. The chestnuts are to the south, in and around the Maure Mountains, in the lower Var, while hazelnuts are grown in the alpine regions. The main production begins about twenty miles northwest of St.-Tropez, in the region surrounding the town of La Garde-Freinet, whose train station is surrounded by huge, hundred-year-old chestnut trees. The mountains above Annot and to the east, near St. Benoit, were terraced at the end of the nineteenth century and planted to chestnuts, acres of them. As World War I and the great flu epidemic of the winter of 1918 took its toll on the population, some of the orchards were abandoned, and then, following World War II, the rest were let go. Hazelnut trees, while not commercially grown in Haute Provence, were part of farmhouse life when growing conditions permitted, as were chestnuts. Consequently these two nuts, as well as the more prevalent almonds and walnuts, are deeply imbedded in the culinary traditions of the area.

Almonds and walnuts figure large in pastry and sauces, and chestnuts in sweets and as a starch in savory dishes such as stews. *Casse-dents,* or "teeth-breakers," biscuits similar to biscotti, are fashioned from a hard pastry and large pieces of almonds, and are still, in traditional homes, made from scratch with local almonds, even though they are available at nearly any *pâtisserie.* Tasting more of nuts than of sugar, *casse-dents* are served with aperitifs, and one dips the rock-hard biscuits into the wine, especially if the aperitif is a sweetish one such as a *vin doux* or sweet vermouth. Combinations of bitter almonds and sweet almonds flavor the creme anglaise that fills apricot-topped pastry shells. Traditionally, ground almonds are used to thicken sauces of basil and olive oil and roasted red peppers, and are often added to *tapenade.* Slices of toasted almonds are the classic topping for *truite aux amandes,* and a crust of warm almonds sits atop fresh goat cheese resting on a bed of butter lettuce circled with thin tomato slices. Walnut sauce is always served with pumpkin-filled ravioli, a winter dish, and walnuts are used in salads, cooked with sweets, and ground for adding to pastry doughs.

Green almonds and green walnuts play special culinary roles in spring, months before the nuts are ready for harvest. The almond trees flower in February and March, and by April the nuts have grown to the size of a thumb and are covered with a soft, furry green hull. Inside the hull, the shell-to-be is also soft and the color of new hay, and under it a white skin covers the just-firm ivory kernel. At this stage, the kernel has a smooth texture and a delicate yet distinct almond flavor, and is considered a great delicacy. At aperitif time, green almonds in their furry hulls are served to be cracked open and eaten with salt. The immature nuts are also shelled and used in fine pastry making. Walnut trees bloom later, in April, when the trees are covered in twirling pollen-spilling catkins. When the feast day of St. Jean comes, on June 24, the green walnuts are large enough to make *vin de noix,* a spicy walnut wine. The nuts are almost their full size, but the shell has not yet developed. The green walnuts are broken open with a mallet, and then put in red wine to macerate. Forty-five days later the walnuts are discarded and sugar and eau-de-vie are added. At one time, *vin de noix* was commercially produced in Haute Provence, but production dwindled away and the wine was made only in family kitchens. Lately, in Forcalquier, on the edge of the Plateau d' Albion, there has been a renaissance of the tradition of making *vins maison,* and a small distillery and aperitif manufacturer has begun making them in quantity once again. At cafés, restaurants, and bars in Haute Provence, *vin de noix* is an increasingly available aperitif, a proud regional product.

Chestnuts bloom in spring, and by midsummer are sporting their coats of bright green stickers. By late fall, the coats have turned to golden brown and have started to split. There are two main types of edible chestnuts (horse or false chestnuts are not edible): *châtaigne* and *marron.* The *châtaigne* is called a wild chestnut and has two or three smallish nuts inside its prickly overcoat. The *marron* has a single large nut. The taste and texture are not noticeably different, and only their size distinguishes one from the other. They are harvested or gathered in late fall, and by November they are being roasted over open braziers in the larger villages and towns and sold wrapped in newspaper cones on market days in Forcalquier, where tables are heaped with fresh chestnuts and walnuts to buy. At home they receive various treatments, from roasting to boiling and pureeing.

ROASTING CHESTNUTS

Chestnuts are roasted for using in a prepared dish or as an occasion for friends and family to gather together to cook and eat the warm, soft nuts. To prevent the nuts from exploding during cooking, cut a cross on the flat side of each nut, piercing through the hard skin. Place them directly on a grill placed over an open fire or in a grilling basket. Some traditions call for them to be *arrosé,* or "sprinkled" with wine (red or white) while they cook, or even with a little eau-de-vie or brandy. When the hard skin around each incision peels back and the skin has darkened, after 15 to 20 minutes, the chestnuts are done and can be peeled and the inner skin discarded, leaving the sweet cooked meat. To roast chestnuts in an oven, preheat the oven to 500 degrees F and place the incised chestnuts on a baking sheet in a single layer. Roast for 15 to 20 minutes. In both cases, the chestnuts are far easier to peel while still warm.

BOILING CHESTNUTS

To boil chestnuts, incise them as above and cover them with lightly salted water. Boil for approximately 2 minutes, or until the skins pop, then, while they are still hot, peel back the hard outer skin and also the papery inner skin. Once the chestnuts are peeled, they may be used for cooking in other recipes, but they are too hard and dry to eat as is. It requires a half hour to 40 minutes for the chestnuts to become soft and ready to eat.

Warm Goat Cheese and Toasted Almond Salad

SERVES 4

A delicate soft, caille doux *cheese is called for here. The almonds form a slight crust on the cheese, and, were it not for the bed of thinly sliced tomatoes and butter lettuce, the cheese and its topping could be considered for dessert. This is my version of this dish, which I had at the Grand Hôtel in Valensole.*

> ¼ cup extra-virgin olive oil
> 1 tablespoon red wine vinegar
> ½ teaspoon salt
> ½ teaspoon freshly ground black pepper
> 2 tablespoons minced shallot
> 3 firm, slightly green, not too juicy tomatoes
> 1 head butter lettuce
> ½ cup thinly sliced almonds
> 4 soft goat cheeses, each 3 to 4 inches in diameter and
>   about ½ inch thick

◆ In a small bowl, stir together the olive oil, vinegar, salt, and pepper to form a vinaigrette. Stir in the shallot.

◆ Cut the tomatoes into very thin slices. If possible, they should be no more than ¹⁄₁₆ inch thick. Separate the lettuce leaves from the head and select the pale, innermost leaves; reserve the others for another use. Tear these tender leaves into large pieces and place in a bowl. Add the vinaigrette and, using two spoons, turn to coat the leaves. Divide the lettuce among individual plates and drizzle with the dressing. Make a bed of several tomato slices in the middle of each bed of lettuce leaves.

◆ Heat a skillet over medium-high heat. When it is hot, put the sliced almonds into it and shake the pan as they toast. The almonds will turn golden in 2 or 3 minutes.

◆ Place a goat cheese atop the tomatoes on each plate, then top the cheeses with the warm almonds. Serve immediately.

Purslane and Hazelnut Salad with Lemon Vinaigrette

SERVES 4

The slight citrus taste of the purslane is heightened by the lemon vinaigrette, while the rich taste of the hazelnuts gives the salad its substance.

¼ cup extra-virgin olive oil
2 to 3 tablespoons fresh lemon juice
½ teaspoon salt
1 teaspoon freshly ground black pepper
2 tablespoons chopped fresh flat-leaf parsley
2 cups purslane leaves or sprigs
2 cups young, tender lettuce leaves
1 cup chopped hazelnuts

◆ In the bottom of a salad bowl, stir together the olive oil, lemon juice to taste, salt, pepper, and parsley to form a vinaigrette. Add the purslane, lettuce leaves, and half of the nuts. Using two spoons, turn the ingredients gently to coat them with the dressing.

◆ Divide the dressed salad evenly among 4 salad plates. Top each with an equal portion of the remaining nuts.

Escarole and Chestnut Salad
with Lardons

Serves 4 or 5

The chestnuts are briefly soaked in a warm vinaigrette before being added to this winter salad that tastes of the mountains.

6 extra-thick slices bacon, cut into 1-inch pieces (lardons)
1 large head escarole
1 shallot, minced
3 tablespoons red wine vinegar
2 tablespoons water
½ teaspoon Dijon mustard
¼ teaspoon salt
1 teaspoon freshly ground black pepper
15 chestnuts, roasted and peeled (page 254), then halved

◆ In a skillet, fry the bacon over medium heat until crisp, 3 to 5 minutes. Remove the bacon with a slotted spoon to paper towels to drain. Reserve 3 tablespoons of the rendered fat and discard the remainder or save for another use.

◆ Tear the pale yellow inner escarole leaves into bite-sized pieces and put them in a salad bowl. Reserve the darker green leaves for another use.

◆ In a saucepan, combine the shallot, reserved bacon fat, vinegar, water, mustard, salt, and pepper in a saucepan. Bring to a simmer over medium heat, stirring to combine the ingredients. Add the chestnuts and simmer for 1 to 2 minutes until heated through.

◆ Pour the hot dressing and the chestnuts over the greens, add the bacon, and toss briefly. Serve immediately, preferably on warmed plates.

Pasta with Walnuts and Gorgonzola Cheese

SERVES 3 OR 4

Here, walnuts are finely chopped and mixed with Gorgonzola, a favorite import in the area, to make a sauce. The creamy texture and salty taste of the cheese are fine complements to the flavor of the walnuts.

> ¾ pound fresh pasta
> ⅓ cup heavy cream
> 2 ounces Gorgonzola cheese, broken into small pieces
> ⅓ cup finely chopped walnuts, plus 4 or 5 walnut halves, coarsely chopped, for garnish
> 1 teaspoon freshly ground black pepper, plus extra to taste
> 2 tablespoons chopped fresh flat-leaf parsley

◆ Bring a large pot of salted water to a boil. Add the pasta, stir well, and cook until just tender.

◆ Just before the pasta is ready, heat the cream in a small saucepan and then stir in the Gorgonzola until it melts. When it has melted, add the finely chopped walnuts and the 1 teaspoon pepper.

◆ Drain the pasta and place on a warmed platter. Pour the sauce immediately over the top, toss briefly, and garnish with the coarsely chopped nuts and the parsley. Sprinkle with pepper and serve at once.

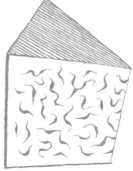

Pumpkin-Filled Ravioli with Walnut Sauce

MAKES ABOUT 60 RAVIOLI; SERVES 4 TO 6

Coarsely chopped walnuts are sautéed with garlic in butter, and then simmered briefly in a little cream to make a rich and savory sauce to contrast with the spiced nutty filling of the ravioli. The pumpkin should have fine-grained, very dense flesh, as one that is watery and coarse will not make a firm filling. If in doubt, choose a winter squash such as butternut or Hubbard. In Haute Provence, the pumpkin is the deeply lobed, meaty Musquée de Provence.

FOR THE FILLING:

1 pumpkin or winter squash such as butternut or Hubbard, 2 to
   2½ pounds, cut in half or quarters and seeded but not peeled
1 egg, lightly beaten
½ cup shredded Gruyère cheese
1 teaspoon salt
½ teaspoon ground cinnamon
½ teaspoon ground cloves
⅛ teaspoon powdered saffron
1 teaspoon freshly ground black pepper

FOR THE DOUGH:

2 cups all-purpose flour
2 egg yolks
1 tablespoon extra-virgin olive oil
¼ teaspoon salt dissolved in about ¼ cup warm water

For the sauce:
1 tablespoon unsalted butter
1 tablespoon minced garlic
2 cups coarsely chopped walnuts
⅓ to ½ cup heavy cream
½ teaspoon freshly ground black pepper

1 tablespoon minced fresh flat-leaf parsley

♦ Preheat an oven to 375 degrees F.

♦ Place the pumpkin or squash, cut side down, on a baking sheet. Bake until the flesh is tender when pierced with the tip of a sharp knife, about 1 hour. Remove from the oven and scoop the meat into a bowl. Mash it with a fork or potato masher. Let cool slightly, then mix in the egg, cheese, salt, cinnamon, cloves, saffron, and pepper and mix well. Set aside.

♦ The dough is easily made in a food processor. First put the flour into the processor, followed by the egg yolks, olive oil, and water. Process until a sticky ball forms. Place the dough on a floured work surface and knead until it is elastic and can be rolled out, about 7 minutes. Loosely wrap the dough in plastic wrap or aluminum foil and let stand at room temperature for 30 minutes. Divide the dough into 2 equal pieces. On a large, well-floured work surface, roll out 1 ball of dough into a rectangle measuring 16 by 20 inches and about ⅛ inch thick. Visualize the sheet of dough as if it was divided into 1½-inch squares. (You can also use a pasta-making machine to roll out the dough. I use an Atlas manual model.) Place a teaspoon of the filling in the center of each square, spreading it to within ½ inch of each of the sides. Roll out the remaining dough into a sheet of equal size and lay it over the first. With the palm of your hand, press down slightly on the mounds of filling. Then, with the edge of your hand, press the upper sheet onto the lower one, forming lines between the filling lumps to seal the edges of the ravioli. With a pastry cutter or a sharp knife, cut along each sealing line, dividing the filled dough into approximately 1½-inch squares. Crimp the edges together.

continued

◆ The ravioli are now ready to cook. If, however, you want to wait several hours before cooking them, arrange them in a single layer, not touching, on a flour-dusted cloth or piece of waxed paper. Dust the tops well with flour and cover with another cloth or a piece of waxed paper.

◆ To cook, bring a large pot of salted water to a boil. Add the ravioli to the boiling water by carefully slipping them off of a spoon. Reduce the heat to low and simmer until the ravioli are tender, about 10 minutes.

◆ While the ravioli are cooking, make the sauce. In a skillet, melt the butter over medium heat. When it foams, add the garlic and sauté for a minute or two, then add the chopped nuts, stirring several times. Add the cream and pepper and simmer for 5 minutes, stirring often.

◆ When the ravioli are ready, drain them and place on a warmed platter. Spoon the hot walnut sauce over them. Sprinkle with the parsley.

Ragout of Pork, Chestnuts, and Winter Keeper Apples

SERVES 6

The sweet, starchy chestnuts, combined with tart apples, bring a fully rounded flavor to this hearty stew. It can be served with steamed greens dressed only with a little lemon, salt, and pepper.

2 tablespoons extra-virgin olive oil
2½ pounds boneless lean pork shoulder or butt, cut into 1½ inch cubes
6 slices bacon, cut into 1-inch pieces
2 yellow onions, chopped
2 shallots, chopped
2 tablespoons all-purpose flour
2 teaspoons salt

1 teaspoon freshly ground black pepper
½ cup dry white wine
2 cups beef broth
2 fresh bay leaves, or 1 dried
2 teaspoons fresh thyme leaves
2 tablespoons chopped fresh flat-leaf parsley
2 pounds chestnuts, boiled and peeled (page 255)
4 tart farm apples such as Granny Smith, peeled, cored,
    and cut into 1½-inch pieces

◆ In a heavy-bottomed saucepan, warm the olive oil over medium-high heat. Add the pork and sauté until browned, about 10 minutes. Using a slotted spoon, remove the pork to a plate, then pour off the accumulated juices and fat from the saucepan.

◆ Add the bacon to the pan and return it to medium heat. Cook for a minute or two, stirring, until the bacon releases some of its fat. Then add the onions and shallots and sauté for a minute or two, or until they are translucent. Sprinkle the flour, salt, and pepper over them, and stir and cook until the flour browns, 2 to 3 minutes. Raise the heat to high, pour in the white wine, and deglaze the pan, stirring up any bits clinging to the bottom. Add the pork without its accumulated juices, the beef broth, bay, thyme, and parsley. Reduce the heat to low, cover, and cook for 30 minutes.

◆ Add the chestnuts, stir gently, re-cover, and cook for 10 minutes. Add the apples, re-cover, and cook until the apples are softened but not dissolving, about 15 minutes longer. Serve hot.

Trout with Toasted Almonds

SERVES 4

Truites aux amandes *is a frequent menu listing in the restaurants of Haute Provence. The plump, fresh-from-the-river fish comes couched in a golden blanket of almonds—a complementary blending of flavors and textures.*

> 1 cup milk
> 1½ teaspoons salt
> 1 teaspoon freshly ground black pepper
> ½ cup all-purpose flour
> 4 whole trout, each about 1½ pounds, cleaned with
>   heads and tails intact
> Canola oil or other light vegetable oil for frying
> ¼ cup unsalted butter
> ½ cup sliced almonds
> 2 lemons, cut into thin slices

◆ Pour the milk into a shallow dish large enough to hold a fish flat. Stir 1 teaspoon of the salt and all the pepper into the milk. Spread the flour on a huge plate. Dip the fish, one at a time, into the milk, then roll them in the flour.

◆ In a large skillet, pour in enough oil to form a film on the bottom of the pan and place over medium heat until nearly smoking. Reduce the heat to medium-low, add the fish, cover, and cook for 1 minute. Reduce the heat to low and cook the fish, covered, for 5 or 6 minutes. Turn over the fish and cook for 4 or 5 minutes longer, covered. The skin should be golden brown and crisp, and the meat should pull away easily from the bone. Transfer to a warmed platter. Meanwhile, in a small skillet, melt the butter over medium heat. When it is foamy, add the almonds, increase the heat to medium-high, and sprinkle with the remaining ½ teaspoon salt. Cook, stirring, until the almonds are golden brown, 2 to 3 minutes, then remove them with a slotted spoon and spread them over the fish, blanketing them. Pour the melted butter over them and serve hot, garnished with the lemon.

Almond Meringues

MAKES ABOUT 50 COOKIES, OR 8 TO 10 SHELLS

Flavored with freshly ground almonds, these meringues can be served as cookies, or formed into shallow shells to hold a filling of ice cream or fresh fruits.

    1 cup almonds
    5 bitter almonds, or 1 teaspoon almond exract
    6 egg whites
    ½ teaspoon salt
    1 ½ teaspoons cream of tartar
    1 ½ cups sugar

◆ In a blender or food mill, grind all the almonds. (If you are using almond extract, reserve it to add later.) They should be fine but not powdery.

◆ Place the egg whites in a large copper or stainless-steel bowl and let them come to room temperature. Preheat an oven to 250 degrees F.

◆ Add the salt and cream of tartar to the egg whites. Using a whisk or a handheld electric mixer, beat until the mixture forms soft peaks. If you are using almond extract, add it now. Alternately add the sugar and the almonds in small portions, about 2 tablespoons at a time, beating well after each addition. As the sugar dissolves, the egg whites will become glossy.

◆ Line a baking sheet with a piece of ungreased brown paper (a piece of a paper grocery bag works well). To make cookies, spoon the egg-white mixture onto the paper by the tablespoonful. To make shells, scoop up about ¾ cup of the egg-white mixture for each shell and pour it into a round on the paper. Then using the back of a spoon, form a well in the center of the round.

◆ Bake the cookies and shells until pale cream–colored and firm, 35 to 40 minutes for the cookies and 1 hour for the shells. Turn off the heat and let the meringues stand in the oven until they are completely cool, at least 2 hours or as long as overnight, if possible. Slip the meringues into a paper bag, fold over the top, and store them in a dry place until ready to use. They will keep for about 1 week.

Green Almond Ice Cream

MAKES ABOUT 1 PINT

In spring, when the kernel is just solid within the still-soft casing that becomes the shell, and the hull is green and fuzzy, almonds can be used for cooking as well as for eating plain. Their flavor is distinctly almond, but delicate, and the texture is slightly crunchy and very smooth, not grainy. To take advantage of these qualities, the nuts are stirred in just before the ice cream is finished, and then served when it is still slightly soft, rather than rock hard. Bitter almonds, gathered the previous fall, infuse the custard with their flavor and fragrance.

> 1 cup heavy cream
> 1 cup milk
> ½ cup sugar
> 2 egg yolks
> 5 bitter almonds, or ½ teaspoon almond extract
> ½ cup shelled green almonds, coarsely chopped
>   (about 3 pounds unshelled)

◆ Combine the cream, milk, and sugar in a saucepan and place over medium heat. Bring to just below a boil, stirring occasionally to dissolve the sugar. Reduce the heat to low.

◆ Put the egg yolks in a bowl and whisk them until blended. Slowly pour about 1 cup of the hot cream mixture into the bowl, whisking continuously. When well blended and smooth, pour the yolk-cream mixture into the saucepan, whisking continuously. Continue to whisk over low heat until the mixture thickens and becomes custardy enough to coat the back of spoon without dripping off, about 10 minutes. Add the bitter almonds or almond extract and let the mixture stand until cooled to room temperature. Remove and discard the bitter almonds, if used.

◆ Pour the custard into an ice cream maker and freeze according to the manufacturer's directions. Shortly before the ice cream is solid—when it is a frozen slush—stir in the chopped green almonds and then continue to freeze a little longer until almost solid. Serve immediately.

Walnut and Sugar Pudding

SERVES 6

This is a voluptuous version of bread pudding, rich and sweet. When served warm as a dessert with a vanilla sauce or ice cream, it makes an elegant finale. Hazelnuts or almonds might be used in place of the walnuts. The coarser, more country style the bread you use, the fluffier and lighter the pudding will be. Conversely, a fine, regular-textured bread will produce a custard-like pudding.

3 ½ tablespoons unsalted butter
4 to 6 cups milk
1 teaspoon vanilla extract
3 eggs, lightly beaten
1 ½ cups sugar
½ teaspoon salt
10 to 12 slices day-old bread (see recipe introduction), each about 1 inch thick
2 cups Sugared Walnuts (page 268)

◆ Using ½ tablespoon of the butter, grease a standard loaf pan or other baking dish. Pour the milk into a large bowl, about 4 cups if you are using a fine-textured bread and 6 cups for a coarser bread. Add the vanilla, eggs, all but 6 tablespoons of the sugar, and the salt. Mix well. Add the bread and let stand until it is thoroughly softened.

◆ Coarsely chop all but 6 of the sugared walnuts. Arrange a layer of bread in the bottom of the prepared pan. Sprinkle it with one-third of the chopped sugared walnuts, then pour about one-fourth of the egg-milk mixture over the walnuts. Repeat twice, pushing the layers down as you go and ending with a layer of bread. Cut 1 tablespoon of the butter into small pieces and dot the top layer of bread. Pour the remaining egg-milk mixture over the top layer. Finely chop the reserved sugared walnuts, combine them with the remaining 6 tablespoons of sugar, and sprinkle the mixture evenly over the top. Cut the remaining 2 tablespoons butter into small pieces and use to dot the surface.

continued

◆ Bake until a knife inserted into the center comes out clean, about 45 minutes. Serve hot or warm, scooped out into bowls.

Sugared Walnuts

Makes 2 cups

Twice-cooking the walnuts in sugar syrup and twice-baking them ensures that they will thoroughly absorb the sugar, and leaves them toasty deep brown on the outside. Single cooking and baking results in a pale sugar coating that flakes off. These walnuts may be served as a dessert with fruit or cheese, or used in baking.

> 2 cups walnut halves
> 1 cup water
> 2 cups sugar

◆ Preheat an oven to 300 degrees F. Line a baking sheet with aluminum foil.

◆ Combine the nuts, water, and sugar in a saucepan and bring to a boil. Boil, stirring, until a clear syrup forms, about 5 minutes. Using a slotted spoon, remove the walnuts to the foil-lined baking sheet, arranging in a single layer, not touching. Bake the walnuts for 1 hour, stirring occasionally to loosen. They will caramelize slightly, and glisten like mahogany.

◆ Remove the baking sheet from the oven and return the walnuts to the sugar syrup. Bring to a boil and boil for 2 to 3 minutes. Cover the baking sheet with a fresh piece of aluminum foil. Remove the nuts from the syrup with the slotted spoon and again arrange them, not touching, on the baking sheet. Return them to the oven and bake until thoroughly dry, 30 to 45 minutes, stirring occasionally to loosen. Remove from the oven and let stand at room temperature until cool.

◆ Store in a tin or jar with a tight-fitting lid and keep in a cool, dry place for up to 6 weeks.

Chaussons Filled With Sweet Chestnut Cream

Makes 12 turnovers

Chaussons *are turnovers, usually made of a flaky puff pastry. They can be filled with applesauce or slices of cooked apples, cooked figs, apricot jam—in short, with anything sweet. Chestnut puree, sweetened with sugar, was one of the special homemade treats of Haute Provence during the early twentieth century. Today, one is more likely to buy it presweetened in cans or tubes, although it is still beloved, especially by children.*

4 cups water
6 tablespoons plus ½ cup sugar
1 piece vanilla bean, 2 inches long
1 pound chestnuts, skinned and peeled (page 255)
¼ cup unsalted butter, at room temperature
2 to 4 tablespoons heavy cream
1 sheet prepared puff pastry, 10 by 12 inches and ¼ inch thick

◆ Place the water, the 6 tablespoons sugar, and the vanilla bean in a saucepan and bring to a boil, stirring, until the sugar has dissolved and a syrup has formed, 4 to 5 minutes. Add the chestnuts and cook, stirring from time to time until soft, about 30 minutes. Using a slotted spoon, remove the chestnuts to a food processor and process until pureed. Add the butter and the remaining ½ cup sugar and process to form a light paste. Stir in enough cream, a tablespoon at a time, to achieve a thick, yet creamy spread. You should have about ¾ cups. Set aside.

◆ Preheat an oven to 400 degrees F.

continued

◆ Roll out the puff pastry into a rectangle measuring 12 by 16 inches and ⅛ inch thick. Cut into 4-inch squares. Fold a square over to make a triangle, and place about 1 tablespoon of the chestnut cream in the center of the imaginary triangle. Moisten all 4 edges of the square, then fold in half to make a triangle. Repeat until all the dough is used. Place the filled triangles on an ungreased baking sheet. Bake until the pastry is puffed and golden brown, about 30 minutes. Do not undercook. Serve warm or at room temperature.

Prune Plums Sautéed with Walnuts

MAKES ABOUT 2½ CUPS; SERVES 4 OR 5

The chopped walnuts absorb both the butter and the sweet juices of the plums as all the ingredients cook together. This mixture can be used as a topping for ice cream, or pound or sponge cake, or to fill crepes.

    6 tablespoons unsalted butter
    2 cups pitted and coarsely chopped prune plums
        (about 2½ pounds before pitting)
    1 cup coarsely chopped walnuts

◆ In a skillet, melt the butter over medium heat. When it is foamy, add the plums and walnuts and sauté, stirring often, until the prunes have cooked down, 4 to 5 minutes. Remove from the heat and serve hot.

Vin de Noix

MAKES ABOUT EIGHT 750-ML BOTTLES

Vin de noix *is made throughout Haute Provence in the homes scattered from Annot to Sisteron, Cotignac, and the Valley of Jabron. It is considered one of the most elegant and long lasting of the* vins maison, *or homemade, fortified aperitif wines. The Restaurant of the Hôtel Deux Lions, a "gastronomique" restaurant, serves homemade* vin de noix *made only from walnuts grown in the Valley of Jabron. The green walnuts, their shells still soft, exude a powerful spicy aroma that is rediscovered in the taste of the infused wine after it has aged.*

By tradition, the walnuts are ready to pick by St. Jean's Day, June 24, and are too developed to pick by Ste. Madeleine's Day, July 22. In warmer climates, the walnuts may be ready earlier. The rule is that they are usable when they can be pierced with a needle.

35 green walnuts
6⅔ bottles (750 ml each) dry red wine such as Zinfandel, Merlot,
    Pinot Noir, or Burgundy
1 quart vodka
4½ cups sugar

◆ Using a wooden mallet or a wooden spoon, strike the walnuts just hard enough to crack open the outer green covering. Put them in a clean, dry widemouthed glass jar or ceramic crock large enough to hold them and the wine. Pour in the wine. Cover the jar or crock, put it in a cool, dark place, and let stand for 40 days. At the end of that time, using a fine-mesh sieve lined with several layers of cheesecloth, strain the wine into a clean, dry crock, jar, or any nonreactive pot large enough to hold it. Discard the walnuts.

◆ Pour the vodka into a nonreactive pot or bowl. Add the sugar and stir until it has dissolved, about 10 minutes.

◆ Wash and sterilize eight 750-ml bottles. Soak 8 new wine corks in boiling water for 2 to 3 minutes to render them supple.

continued

NUTS

◆ Pour the sugar-vodka mixture into the wine and stir well. Using a funnel and a ladle, fill the bottles with the now-fortified wine to within 1 ½ to 2 inches of the tops. Push the corks as tightly as you can into the bottles, to make them airtight.

◆ Label and date the bottles, then store them in a cool, dark place, where they may be kept for several years. Tradition says to wait 1 year before sampling. Once opened, store the bottle, tightly corked, in the refrigerator or in a cool, dark place, where it will keep for up to a year. Serve at cool room temperature, pouring 2 to 3 ounces into each glass.

RECIPES

Figs Grilled with Roulade *and Chicken Livers*

Salt-Seared Duck Thighs with Grapes

Baked Quinces Stuffed with Sausage, Currants, and Walnuts

Apple-Quince Cakes

Fresh Apple Compote

Pain Perdu *with Honey Crust*

Fresh Apricot Clafouti

Dried-Apricot and Fresh-Apple Pastry

Tarte Tatin *of Brandied Pears*

Puff Pastry Fold-Up Fruit Tart

Pear Beignets

Crêpe Packets of Nuts and Dried Fruits with Rum

Peach and Nectarine Gratin

Melon Sorbet

Honey-Quince Ice Cream

Upside-down Vanilla Cream with Strawberries and Raspberries

Nougat Noir

Fig Jam

THE INDIGENOUS SWEETS OF HAUTE Provence, honey and fruits, play an important role in the region's traditions as well as its cuisine. *Nougat noir,* made with honey and almonds, is one of the classic desserts of the Christmas Eve dinner, as are muscat grapes, dried figs, raisins, winter melons, and *pâte de coing,* a candy made from quince. Throughout the year, locally made lavender, *millefleur,* or perhaps *tilleul* or chestnut honey, is the sweetener for infusions made from the herbs and flowers gathered from the fields and forests. Each season brings its special fruit beignets and *clafoutis:* apricots in spring, peaches in summer, figs in fall, apples and pears in winter. In October, during the *vendange,* when the wine grapes are being crushed, figs, quince, and table grapes are made into jams and jellies.

A hundred and more years ago, in the poor kitchens of Haute Provence, honey was the only sweetener; sugar had to be purchased. Consequently, honey was used in all the baking and candy making, was the daily spread for morning and afternoon *tartines,* the topping for cheeses fresh from the mold, was often combined with fruits for desserts, and was stirred into any savory dish that needed a little sweetness.

Until the first part of the twentieth century, many families kept their own beehives, setting them out in spring when the first wildflowers bloomed. Today, however, beekeeping and honey making is more commonly practiced by professional *apiculteurs.* Lavender honey is the most famous honey of the region. In mid- to late June, when the lavender stems elongate and the buds begin to swell, beekeepers position the hives along the margins of the fields. By mid-July, the fields are shimmering rows of purple rising over the hills and sliding into the vales, and the bees are solid in the fields. When the lavender is being cut and bundled to go to the distilleries, the bees are still crawling over the windrows, seeking the pollen. Lavender honey doesn't taste like lavender, but it is reminiscent of its fragrance. When it is freshly made in early fall, it is a pale, amber liquid, but it may crystallize within a month or two because it is one of the honeys that crystallizes early when unpasteurized. As with the other unpasteurized honeys, all of which eventually crystallize, lavender honey is easily liquified by heating the jar in gently simmering water, or the honey itself in a double boiler.

Millefleur, the other well-known honey of the region, is made from the nectar of many of the different flowers, trees, and shrubs that bloom in Haute Provence. Its flavor and complexity varies depending upon the flowers that were blossoming when the particular honey was made. It is a medium gold and stays liquid for longer than lavender honey does. Chestnut honey, available in the mountainous areas near the Alps, has a strong and powerful taste that can vary from year to year. In Riez, the old Roman town at the base of the Plateau de Valensole, there are several honey makers that one can visit in season, and watch the honey being extracted from the combs, cleaned, and poured into jars or paper tubs imprinted with a colorful drawing of a lavender field and a label announcing *miel de lavande.* Road signs marked *Miel du Pays Ici* or *Miel de Lavande Ici* signal artisanal honeys. Like the locally made cheeses and charcuterie, these special products are worth seeking out, not just for their authentic flavors, but also for the adventure that might arise while traveling down the dirt road to the farmhouse.

One such sign points the way to a solitary farmhouse near Contadour. Stopping there one gloriously bright blue afternoon in late fall, on the brink of winter, I found the house snugged up for the months of bitter cold and wind that were to come. Wood was neatly stacked, the fields were cleared of their wheat, and inside the house jars of honey and *crème de marron* were set out in threes and fours on solid wooden tables. Among the honeys were *tilleul,* made from the leaves of the linden tree (which I was told was a good choice for calming the nerves), lavender, chestnut, *millefleur, acacia,* rosemary, and pine. The label of the *crème de marron* announced that only chestnuts, sugar, water, and vanilla had been used in its manufacture. As I was leaving with two jars of honey and one of *crème de marron,* I paused on the rise where the farmhouse stood and looked out across the landscape. It seemed a huge expanse arched on the top of the world, dropping away and across in every direction, near only to the sky. I understood the meaning of Jean Giono's characters when they talk about the vastness, the empty spaces, and the solitude of the hills of Contadour, of Revest, and of the Plateau d' Albion.

Signs are also occasionally posted in the window of a village house or on the open door of a village garage. Knocking and stepping inside, one will typically find a few jars of honey made from the surplus of the hives of a traditional householder.

Most of the fruits of Haute Provence are cultivated, either from a full orchard or simply a tree or two, while melons and berries may come from the *potager* or the fields. Some are wild, like the sour cherries gathered in spring from the trees that grow along mountain ravines, or the tiny alpine strawberries picked in summer in the high-altitude forests. Once cultivated in decent numbers, fig and quince trees now are more commonly found on the sites of abandoned farms, in fragments of forgotten orchards, or as a single tree near a cultivated *potager.* Orchards both large and small produce apples, pears, peaches, cherries, prune plums *(quetches),* and apricots.

The elevation in Haute Provence varies from approximately three hundred feet to nearly four thousand feet, so different varieties of the same tree fruits will be found in the varying climates. Most fruit trees, with the exception of figs, require a minimum number of hours below 40 degrees Fahrenheit to grow and to fruit well the following year.

At the southwestern fringes of Haute Provence, near Manosque, the Golden Delicious apple, which requires six hundred to seven hundred chilling hours, is planted both in home orchards and commercially. It is the dominant apple sold in the small *épiceries* and local supermarkets. In winter, driving through Quinson, Banon, Aups, or Castellane, the displays in front of the little all-purpose stores will have a box of Golden Delicious apples, often small sizes. As winter deepens and then spring promises, the apples become increasingly shriveled. But as shriveled as they become, they never lose their sweet flavor, nor do they become mushy.

Farther north in the high valleys near Sisteron, the Reinette is the more important apple. Large and round, splotched with deep patches of bronze against a dark gold skin, it has a regal appearance. It, like the Golden Delicious, is a long-keeping apple, holding its flavor well into spring, but much less susceptible to wrinkling.

Leaving the town of Valensole and descending the twisting road that follows the Ravin de Vallongue, one arrives in the apple orchards that announce the Durance River, with the entrance to Manosque straight ahead and to the right the highway to Sisteron. This alluvial land at a confluence of rivers has become a major apple center, with over a hundred and fifty producers grouped together growing a dozen different kinds of apples, and shipping them year-round from a gleaming, computerized packing facility. It seems a century removed from the winters when I made trips with Françoise to her *cave* for apples—where the Golden Delicious were spread out on the dirt floor, separated from the potatoes by wooden sticks.

Françoise and Maurice have a small peach orchard and half a dozen cherry trees, as well as a few apple and apricot trees. The apples, apricots, and cherries are for them, their extended family and friends, and their neighbors. The cherry trees were especially wisely chosen, as they ripen sequentially, ensuring the longest possible supply of cherries from mid-May until mid-July. Picking the cherries is an anticipated seasonal diversion for the various children who always seem to be visiting in the vicinity, and they can be relied upon to pick a basketful—and to eat them by the handful. Cereste, not far from Forcalquier, is famous for its cherries, many of which find their way into the notable fruit confits made in neighboring Apt.

Cherries are the favored dessert of early spring, either fresh or baked, pitted or unpitted, made into a *clafouti*. I have come to prefer making cherry *clafouti* with the pits in. The cherries are less mangled, the pits give an extra flavor, and it saves me the time and the messy job of pitting. Some cherries are always reserved to be mixed with sugar and brandy and stored in jars as part of the winter pantry, and these can be used to make wintertime cherry *clafouti*.

The peaches don't ripen until late July, but they continue through mid-September. Although friends and neighbors always get a share, these are destined for the open markets where Maurice and Françoise go four times a week, loading the peaches into wooden boxes and wedging them in their little Renault van. Maurice thins his fruit carefully so that he will have big peaches, to bring the premium prices from summer shoppers. Truly, Maurice's peaches are the largest that I have even seen, and they are intensely sweet. No small wonder that returning shoppers line up at his stall, and then come again in August and September for his melons.

Maurice is a true *melonier*. He always used to save his melon seeds from year to year, effectively selecting his own strains, but as he is increasingly using purchased hybrid seeds, he now saves only some seeds from the open-pollinated varieties such as *l'Américain*. To save the seeds, he lets a very ripe melon become fully mature. He then scoops the seeds into a wire-mesh stainer and sets them in the sun to dry. When the pulp surrounding the seeds is dry, he washes it off, then dries the seeds again in the sun before storing them in old cookie tins. He raises his own seedlings in his small homemade greenhouse. With a handheld mold, he forms soil blocks, and sows a seed into each one. The planted blocks are kept on shelves, to make room for as many as possible. Come May, the carefully nurtured melon plants, now two inches tall, go outside into the prepared ground, which is generally protected with plastic to keep the soil temperature warm, as May can be unpredictable. Some seeds are also sown directly into the ground, and the seeded rows covered with plastic. As soon as the seedling emerges from the soil, an opening is cut into the plastic to let it through. Charentais, cantaloupe, and Jaune Canary are his favorite melons, plus *l'Américain*. Maurice told me last was so named because the seeds came to Provence with the American soldiers during World War II, after their campaign in North Africa. To me, the melons closely resemble in taste and appearance a winter melon whose seeds are sold as Verte de Treste. These are winter keeper melons that are picked in the fall, then stored on straw in a cool place. They can be served on Christmas Eve, as well as eaten throughout the intervening months.

Every day at dawn from mid-July until sometime in late September, when the last of the melons have been harvested, Maurice can be seen in his melon fields, first the upper one near his house, then the lower one on a piece of land in a small valley that he bought several years ago. Both fields together total no more than three acres. Each day the melons are investigated. Any signs of disease? Insect infestation? The Charentais melons need special attention because unlike muskmelons, they do not slip from the vine when they are ripe. Therefore, the exact right moment must be chosen to cut the fruit from the vine. (Oddly enough, the Charentais is the true cantaloupe, whereas the melons Americans call cantaloupes are in fact muskmelons.) A *melonier* knows what to look for on the ripening Charentais. The two leaves closest to the fruit's stem begin to shrivel and dry. The base of the stem shows signs of drying as well, and there is a faint color change from shiny gray-green to gray-green tinged with the color of straw. I know the rules, but it takes me a dozen failures—picking too ripe, not ripe enough, too hard, too soft—to get it right. Once a melon is harvested, the next step is to determine when it will reach its peak of flavor. Today for lunch or tonight for dinner? Or tomorrow for lunch, or better, dinner? These are the questions customers ask Françoise and Maurice, and they always get the correct answers.

As with their other produce, Françoise and Maurice share their melons with gargantuan generosity. When my children were little, each morning I would find on my doorstep a wooden crate with several melons in it, and we were expected to eat them all because the next morning there would be more. We ate valiantly. We ate them for breakfast with our bread and jam, we ate them for lunch wrapped with *jambon cru,* and again at night for dessert.

Strawberries come from Françoise and Maurice's *potager*, but only on a small scale. I can count on a kilo or two from them during May, enough to made a big bowlful, sliced and soaked in red wine with just a little sugar, which is my favorite way to eat them. Sometimes I serve them plain, other times over ice cream or with cake.

Figs, grapes, and quinces, the fruits of fall, have a special role in the traditional life of Haute Provence. Dried or preserved, they were, along with nuts, part of the winter pantry, providing not only important nourishment but significant flavors. A nod to their importance is their place at the Christmas Eve dinner table, which is commonly seven dishes and thirteen desserts. The seven dishes are *maigre*, all without meat, and the desserts are simple ones that reflect the region. Dried figs, raisins, walnuts, and almonds, called *les quatre mendiants*, the "four beggars," are always there, sometimes today with other dried fruits and nuts.

When figs ripen in August and September, they are often served with great presentation as the first course of a meal, along with thin slices of *jambon cru*.

As a dessert, they might be served plain, baked with honey, or made into a *clafouti*. They are also pickled with vinegar, sugar, red wine, and thyme, and a homemade fig jam is a proud addition to any Haute Provence table.

Quinces are odd, lumpy fruits that look like a cross between an apple and a pear, with a knobby end. I didn't understand when it was first explained to me that although they were edible, they had to be cooked. The bite I later took from a fresh fruit was mouth puckering, and I spit it out immediately, incredulous that they could be eaten under any circumstances. Quince trees are beautiful in the landscape, often old, with twisting branches and silvery leaves, and in spring they sport clusters of pale pink blossoms. The fruit has an incredibly rich perfume, which it exudes when stored in a warm place or kept in a bowl in the kitchen. Jelly and jam made from quinces are highly valued and often given as gifts, and quince paste, a kind of candy cut into squares and rolled in granulated sugar, used to be a common treat for children, as well as one of the traditional thirteen desserts on Christmas Eve. In early November, once the quinces have ripened, the small *épiceries* offer freshly made *pâte de coing* for sale. It is displayed in shallow loaf pans and sold by weight, with a one-inch-thick slice tipping the scales at nearly a quarter of a pound. The sugar rolling is done at home, just before serving. During a visit to friends and neighbors during the season, I am sure to be offered homemade *pâte de coing* for dessert or with late-afternoon tea.

Like fig trees, the quince trees are more often abandoned, and few people are planting them anymore. With the revival of interest in all things of the *terroir,* however, quinces are reclaiming their place at the table, even in restaurants, and are now commonly sold in the open markets and sometimes supermarkets. The fruits themselves are not sweet, but the addition of sugar renders them so, and their pale flesh turns a lovely amber-orange during cooking. Quinces may also be used in savory ways, as one would use tart apples or pears.

SUN-DRYING FRUITS

Figs, apricots, sweet cherries, and prune plums are good candidates for drying because they have a high sugar content and their relatively small size means that the moisture needs to move only a short distance from the center to the skin during drying. It is best to start with unblemished fruit that is very ripe and slightly soft. Halve and pit apricots and prune plums. Cherries need only be pitted. Figs and grapes need no special treatment, but the grapes should be left in clusters for ease of handling.

In Haute Provence the fruit is traditionally dried on cane mats or racks, or on trays of wooden slats. Fine-mesh netting is draped over the fruits if there is a problem with insects. A simple frame covered with tightly stretched screen is a good alternative.

Place the fruit in a single layer on the tray and put it in a location where it will receive direct sun and good air circulation. In the evenings remove it to a sheltered place where it will not be exposed to nighttime dew. Drying will take anywhere from 3 to 10 days, depending upon the climate and the size and moisture content of the fruits. Once dry, pack the fruits into clean tins, jars, or plastic bags and store in a cool, dry place or in the freezer. In the old days in Haute Provence, dried figs were put into glazed jars and sprinkled with a splash of eau-de-vie, or in some cases were slit open and stuffed with an almond before being put into the jars. The dried fruits can be served as they are or used to cook in both sweet and savory dishes.

PRESERVING FRUITS IN ALCOHOL

Start with firm, clean, unblemished fruit. Cherries, apricots, and grapes are good choices. Leave the fruits whole. Pack them tightly into a clean, dry, widemouthed preserving jar to within 1 inch of the rim. Make a mixture of sugar and brandy and pour over the fruit to cover. A rule of thumb is 1 cup sugar to 1 cup brandy for each 4 pounds of fruit. This will make about 2 quarts. Cap or tightly cork the jar. Store in a cool, dark place and turn the jar every day for a week until the sugar has dissolved. The fruits are ready to eat after 1 month and will keep for 1 year. Brandied fruits can be served spooned over ice cream, cakes, or meringues, or stirred into the degreased juices from pan-roasted meats to make sauces.

LIQUEFYING CRYSTALLIZED HONEY

Place the jar or pot of honey in a saucepan of simmering water. At least one-third of the jar should be submerged. Simmer until the honey liquefies, 5 to 10 minutes. Alternatively, the honey itself can be poured into the top pan of a double boiler.

Figs Grilled with *Roulade* and Chicken Livers

SERVES 6 TO 8 AS AN HORS D'OEUVRE, OR 4 AS A FIRST COURSE

Sweet figs, chicken livers, and the roulade *of Haute Provence make an excellent hors d'oeuvre or first course, or can be served as a main dish accompanied with polenta or rice and a green salad. Dried figs may be used in place of fresh, as long as they are supple.*

> 16 soft, large, ripe figs, any kind
> 8 chicken livers
> 16 thin slices *roulade* (pancetta), each 6 inches long, or
>   thick bacon slices

◆ Prepare a charcoal or wood fire.

✳ Make a slit in each fig from the stem to the blossom end, but do not cut all the way through. Pat the chicken livers dry with paper towels and cut them in half, discarding any veins. Slip a piece of chicken liver into a slit fig and wrap a piece of *roulade* around the fig. Slip it onto a skewer. Repeat, preparing 4 skewers, each with 4 wrapped figs.

◆ Place the prepared skewers in a long-handled grill basket, close tightly, and place over hot coals. (Alternatively place the skewers directly on the grill rack or in a preheated broiler.) Grill for 4 or 5 minutes, then turn and cook until the *roulade* is lightly browned and the chicken livers are done, 3 or 4 minutes longer. The chicken livers should be a pinkish brown when they are ready.

◆ To serve, slide the figs from the skewers onto individual plates.

Salt-Seared Duck Thighs with Grapes

SERVES 3 OR 4 AS A FIRST COURSE, OR 2 AS A MAIN COURSE

Sweet grapes, such as Thompson Seedless, Concord, or Muscat, marry well with the sturdy flavor of duck. I like to serve these duck thighs sliced atop a fluffy mound of barely braised greens with creamy, Parmesan-topped polenta alongside for a main course, or simply with the greens for a first course. Fresh or dried prune plums or apricots can be used instead of the grapes, as can brandied fruit, and chicken thighs adapt well to this simple treatment.

½ teaspoon salt
2 duck thighs
½ cup Riesling or other fruity white wine, or as needed
2 tablespoons fresh lemon juice
1 tablespoon yellow minced onion
1 tablespoon finely grated fresh ginger
2 tablespoons brown sugar
2 cups sweet grapes (see recipe introduction), stems removed

continued

HONEY & FRUITS

◆ Sprinkle the salt in the bottom of a nonstick skillet just large enough to hold the duck thighs in a single layer. Heat the salt over high heat. When the pan is very hot, add the duck thighs and sear, turning once, until the skin is crisp and browned, 2 to 3 minutes on each side. Remove the duck thighs to a plate, reduce the heat to low, and add ½ cup wine and the lemon juice to the skillet, deglazing the pan by stirring up any bits clinging to the bottom.

◆ Add the onion and return the duck thighs to the skillet. Cover tightly and cook over low heat for 12 to 15 minutes for rare meat, 4 to 5 minutes longer for medium, or as desired. Check occasionally to see if more liquid is needed, and add a little more wine or water if the pan is drying out.

◆ While the duck is cooking, in a small bowl, stir together the ginger and sugar. About 3 to 4 minutes before you anticipate the duck will be ready, tuck all but ½ cup of the grapes around the duck thighs. Sprinkle with the ginger-sugar mixture and replace the cover. After 2 minutes, turn over the duck thighs, re-cover, and cook for another minute or two until the grapes are soft and the sugar has dissolved into the juices to form a sauce.

◆ Serve the duck thighs whole or sliced on warmed individual plates. Spoon the pan juices and grapes over them and garnish with the reserved grapes.

Baked Quinces Stuffed with Sausage, Currants, and Walnuts

SERVES 4

As with apples, firm-fleshed quinces can be cored, filled with a savory stuffing, and then baked.

 4 medium-sized quince
 2 tablespoons sugar
 1 pound bulk pork or chicken sausage
 ¼ cup chopped walnuts
 1 tablespoon minced fresh sage
 ¼ cup dried currants or raisins

◆ Preheat an oven to 350 degrees F.

◆ Cut a thin slice off the top of each quince and scoop out the seeds and most of the flesh, leaving a ¾-inch-thick shell. Be careful, as quinces break easily. Even if one does break, it is still usable, however, because the filled quinces are packed tightly against one another in the baking dish. Discard the seeds and mince enough of the flesh to measure ½ cup. Reserve the remaining flesh for another use. Sprinkle the inside of each quince with sugar. In a bowl, combine the minced quince, sausage, walnuts, sage, and currants or raisins and mix well.

◆ Put the quince shells in a baking dish that is just large enough to hold them snugly. Fill each one with one-fourth of the sausage mixture, heaping it about 1 inch above the rim of the fruit. Pour water into the baking dish to a depth of ½ inch and place in the oven. Bake until the stuffing is cooked and browned and the skin of the quince can be easily pierced with a fork, about 40 minutes. Serve hot.

Apple-Quince Cakes

MAKES 12 TO 14 CAKES; SERVES 3 OR 4 AS A SIDE DISH

These small, light cakes, more savory than sweet, are an ideal accompaniment to game, roasted meats, daubes, and other rich dishes.

    1 Golden Delicious apple
    1 quince
    1 egg
    ¼ cup all-purpose flour
    ⅛ teaspoon salt
    ¼ teaspoon freshly ground black pepper
    2 tablespoons unsalted butter

◆ Peel and core the apple and the quince. Grate them on the large holes of a hand-held grater into a bowl. Stir in the egg, flour, salt, and pepper.

◆ In a large skillet, melt the butter over medium heat. When it foams, drop in a bit of the batter. If it sizzles and begins to cook immediately, the pan is ready. Drop heaping tablespoonfuls of batter into the pan, allowing 1 inch between the cakes. Cook each cake until it is golden on the underside and holds together, about 1 minute. Turn over the cakes and cook until golden on the second side, about 1 minute longer. Remove to a warmed platter and keep warm until all the cakes are made. Serve hot.

Fresh Apple Compote

MAKES ABOUT 2 QUARTS; SERVES 8

An easy, yet flavorful way to preserve an abundance of apples fresh from the tree for a few days is to poach them in a simple wine-based syrup and store them in the refrigerator. I use them both as a sweet, served with ladyfingers or ice cream, for example, and as an accompaniment to a wide range of savories, from grains and legumes to roast pork and grilled sausages. The sweet, warm apples also go well with cooked spinach or chard that has been seasoned with olive oil, garlic, and a little dried red chili pepper.

This same syrup can also be used for poaching other fruits such as peaches, nectarines, apricots, and pears. For figs, however, use a light red wine.

> 2 cups dry white wine
> 1 cup water
> ½ to ¾ cup sugar
> 1 piece dried orange peel, 3 inches long
> 2 whole cloves
> 4 to 4½ pounds apples, peeled, cored, and cut into thin slices

◆ Combine the wine, water, sugar, orange peel, and cloves in a saucepan and place over medium-high heat. Bring to a boil, stirring to dissolve the sugar. Boil until a light syrup forms, about 5 minutes. Reduce the heat so the syrup simmers gently and slip the apples into the pan. Poach the fruit until just tender when pierced, 3 to 4 minutes, then turn off the heat. Transfer the contents of the saucepan to a heatproof glass or enamel bowl. Let cool, then cover and refrigerate for up to a week. They may then be reheated, served at room temperature, or chilled.

Pain Perdu with Honey Crust

SERVES 3 OR 4

Leftover slices of sturdy country bread or refined, flaky croissants work equally well because the dish is defined by the honey. It can be dressed up with brandied fruit or ice cream.

2 eggs
4 large, thick slices day-old country-style bread, or
    2 day-old croissants, halved lengthwise
3 tablespoons unsalted butter
4 tablespoons liquid honey such as *millefleur,* lavender, or clover

◆ In a bowl, beat the eggs until blended. Dip the bread slices or croissant halves in the eggs, coating them fully. In a large skillet, melt the butter over medium heat. Drizzle 2 tablespoons of the honey over one side of each of the bread slices or croissant halves and place them, honey side down, in the hot butter. Fry for just a minute or two to brown. Meanwhile, brush the remaining 2 tablespoons honey on the tops. As soon as the undersides are nicely browned, turn over the pieces and fry them on the other side for 1 or 2 minutes. Serve hot.

Fresh Apricot *Clafouti*

SERVES 6 TO 8

Each June I have to make at least two of these French-style puffy puddings, one with apricots, one with sour cherries. In summer I use nectarines, plums, and figs, and in winter, brandied fruits. It is a simple, wonderfully versatile dessert.

1 ½ teaspoons unsalted butter
1 cup milk
¼ cup heavy cream
¼ cup granulated sugar, firmly packed, or brown sugar
3 eggs
1 tablespoon almond extract
1 teaspoon salt
⅔ cup all-purpose flour, sifted
18 apricots, halved and pitted (about 4 cups)
Confectioners' sugar for sprinkling

◆ Preheat an oven to 350 degrees F. Using the butter, grease a baking dish about 10 inches in diameter and 1 ½ inches deep.

◆ In a bowl, combine the milk, cream, granulated or brown sugar, eggs, almond extract, salt, and flour. Using an electric mixer, beat on medium speed until the mixture is frothy, about 5 minutes.

◆ Pour enough of the batter into the prepared dish to form a layer about ¼ inch deep. Put the dish in the preheated oven for 2 minutes, then remove it from the oven. Place the apricot halves, face down, evenly over the batter, which is now slightly set. Pour the remaining batter over the apricots.

◆ Return the dish to the oven and bake until puffed and brown and a knife inserted in the center comes out clean, 30 to 35 minutes. Serve warm from the oven, plain or sprinkled with confectioners' sugar.

Dried-Apricot and Fresh-Apple Pastry

SERVES 6

Tart yet sweet, the dried apricots melt into the softening apples, creating an irresistible combination concealed beneath a pastry top.

1½ teaspoons unsalted butter
3 or 4 cooking apples such as Golden Delicious or Granny Smith,
    peeled, cored, and coarsely chopped
1 cup finely chopped dried apricots
1 tablespoon fresh lemon juice
1 cup firmly packed brown sugar
½ cup granulated sugar
1 tablespoon cornstarch
1 teaspoon ground cinnamon
½ teaspoon freshly grated nutmeg
½ teaspoon ground allspice

FOR THE TOPPING:
2 cups all-purpose flour
4 teaspoons baking powder
½ teaspoon salt
1 teaspoon granulated sugar
¼ cup unsalted butter, chilled and cut into pieces, plus
    1 tablespoon melted butter
¾ cup milk

◆ Preheat an oven to 400 degrees F. Using the butter, grease a 2-quart baking dish, 2 to 2½ inches deep.

✳ In a large bowl, combine the apples, apricots, and lemon juice. In a small bowl, stir together both sugars, the cornstarch, and all the spices. Add the sugar mixture to the apples and apricots and turn the fruits to coat them evenly. Place the mixture in the prepared baking dish and set aside.

◆ To make the topping, in a bowl, sift together the flour, baking powder, salt, and sugar. Using your fingertips, quickly work the ¼ cup chilled butter into the flour mixture until pea-sized particles form. Do not overwork. Add the milk a little at a time, stirring with a wooden spoon until the dough holds together. Lightly form the dough into a ball and place on a floured work surface. Roll out the dough ½ inch thick onto a sheet large enough to cover the baking dish. Carefully transfer the pastry to the baking dish, covering the apple mixture and rolling or tucking the edges as necessary. Leave a gap or two on the sides or cut a slash or two on the surface to allow the steam to escape during baking.

◆ Brush the surface of the pastry with the melted butter. Bake until the top is toasty and golden, the apples are soft, and the juices are bubbling, about 45 minutes. Serve warm or at room temperature scooped from the dish.

Tarte Tatin of Brandied Pears

SERVES 6 TO 8

Half of the pears are marinated in a brown mixture of sugar and brandy, and the other half are plain. The whole is topped with a thick, butter-rich crust whose edges become crispy with the caramelizing juices. The leftover marinade, which has taken on a pear flavor, is then warmed and poured over the tart slices at serving time. The same treatment can be used with apples or poached quinces.

4 firm, ripe pears such as Bosc, Anjou, or Red Bartlett (about 2 pounds)
½ cup brandy
½ cup firmly packed brown sugar
2 cups all-purpose flour
1 teaspoon salt
3 tablespoons margarine, chilled
½ pound unsalted butter, chilled
6 tablespoons ice water
½ cup granulated sugar

◆ Peel 2 of the pears. Cut them in half lengthwise and remove the cores. Cut each half lengthwise into 4 or 5 slices. Combine the brandy and the brown sugar in a bowl, stir to dissolve the sugar, and then add the pear slices. Cover and let stand for at least 6 hours or for up to 18 hours, turning occasionally.

◆ In a bowl, stir together the flour and salt. Cut the margarine and all but 1 tablespoon of the butter into ½-inch chunks and add them to the flour mixture. Using a pastry blender or 2 knives, cut in the butter until pea-sized particles form. Add the ice water 1 tablespoon at a time, turning the dough lightly with a fork and then with your fingertips. This will help to keep the pastry light and flaky. Do not overwork the dough, or it will become tough. Gather the dough into a ball—it will be a little crumbly—wrap in plastic wrap, and refrigerate for 15 minutes.

◆ While the pastry is chilling, peel the remaining 2 pears as you did the first 2 pears, but do not add to the brandy mixture.

• Preheat an oven to 375 degrees F. Using ½ tablespoon of the remaining butter, grease a pie dish 9 to 10 inches in diameter and 2 to 2½ inches deep, preferably of glass so you can observe the syrup forming in the bottom.

• Sprinkle the bottom of the prepared pie dish with ¼ cup of the granulated sugar. Using a slotted spoon, remove the pear slices from the brandy mixture, reserving the brandy mixture, and arrange them in the bottom of the dish, interspersing them with the just-sliced pears. They will make a single, tightly packed layer. Cut the remaining ½ tablespoon butter into small pieces and use to dot the pears. Sprinkle with the remaining ¼ granulated sugar and spoon 2 tablespoons of the brandy mixture over all.

• Remove the dough from the refrigerator, unwrap, and place on a floured work surface. Roll out into a round about the same diameter as the pie dish and a scant ¼ inch thick. Carefully transfer the pastry round to the pie dish and gently drop it over the pears. Tuck the edges of the pastry down to the bottom of the dish. Any excess dough will form a rim, standing slightly above the edges of the dish. Prick the top with the tines of a fork.

• Bake until the crust is lightly golden and a thickened, golden syrup has formed in the bottom of the dish, about 1 hour.

• Remove from the oven and let stand for 5 minutes. Slip a knife or spatula between the pie dish and the edge of the crust to loosen it, if necessary. Invert a serving platter on top of the pie dish and, holding the platter and the baking dish together firmly with pot holders, flip them. Lift off the pie dish. If a few slices of pear stick to the dish, gently remove them and place them on the tart.

• Strain the reserved brandy mixture through a sieve into a small saucepan, discarding any bits of fruit. Place over medium heat and bring to a simmer. Cook until reduced by one-fourth, 4 to 5 minutes.

• Serve the tart warm, and drizzle each slice with the brandy syrup.

Puff Pastry Fold-Up Fruit Tart

SERVES 6 TO 8

Slices of fruit, tossed with sugar and dotted with butter, are placed on a circle of puff pastry, and the rim of the dough is folded up around the edge of the filling to create a free-form pastry shell. Chopped nuts can be added as well.

3 cups sliced fruits such as pears, nectarines, peaches, plums
    or whole blackberries, mulberries, seedless grapes, or
    pitted cherries
¼ cup sugar
1 tablespoon all-purpose flour
2 tablespoons fresh lemon juice
1 sheet prepared puff pastry dough, 10 by 16 inches and ¼
    inch thick, thawed if frozen
1 tablespoon unsalted butter, cut into small pieces

◆ In a bowl, combine the fruits, sugar, and flour and toss to mix. Add the lemon juice and stir to combine. On a floured work surface roll out the puff pastry into a round 15 inches in diameter and about ¼ inch thick. Place the pastry on an ungreased baking sheet and spoon the fruit into the center, leaving about 2 inches uncovered around the perimeter. The fruit will be stacked high, but it will reduce in volume as it cooks. Fold the uncovered edges of the pastry up to cover as much of the fruit as possible, pinching and tucking the dough as necessary. Dot the top of the fruit with the butter pieces.

◆ Bake until the pastry is puffed and golden brown, about 30 minutes. Do not undercook. Serve hot, cut into wedges.

Pear Beignets

MAKES ABOUT 24 BEIGNETS; SERVES 6

Fruit beignets are often served to children as a late-afternoon snack. Bits of fresh or dried fruits come piping hot to the table, enrobed in a crispy golden crust and sprinkled with sugar. I remember Françoise making these not only with fruit, but also with long clusters of white acacia blossoms (Robinia, false acacia, which is not the American acacia), as well as with zucchini blossoms.

If you use ice water or cold beer in place of the milk, this same batter will work beautifully for making vegetable beignets. Artichoke hearts, sweet pepper strips, asparagus tips, and eggplant rounds are all good choices.

1 ¾ cups all-purpose flour
¼ cup cornstarch
½ teaspoon salt
1 tablespoon baking powder
2 cups milk
Canola oil or other light vegetable oil for deep-frying
2 cups peeled, cored, and coarsely chopped pears (about ½ inch cubes)
Granulated sugar for sprinkling

◆ In a bowl, stir together the flour, cornstarch, salt, and baking powder. Beat in the milk just until a batter forms.

◆ Pour oil into a deep-fat fryer or a deep skillet to a depth of 1 inch and heat to 350 degrees F, or until a tiny bit of batter dropped into the oil sizzles and begins to cook immediately. Add the pear pieces to the batter. Then, working in batches, scoop out the pear mixture by heaping tablespoonfuls and drop into the hot oil; do not crowd the pan. Cook just until golden on the first side, then turn and cook on the other side, 3 to 4 minutes total. Using a slotted spoon, remove to paper towels to drain briefly. Serve the beignets hot, sprinkled with sugar.

Crêpe Packets of Nuts and Dried Fruits with Rum

MAKES ABOUT 16 FILLED CREPES; SERVES 8

This is my version of a dessert once served to me at a friend's house the week before Christmas in Haute Provence. Festive and flavorful, it is reflective of the region's winter pantry.

FOR THE CRÊPE BATTER:
4 eggs
1¾ cups milk
3 tablespoons light rum
1⅔ cups all-purpose flour
½ teaspoon salt
4 tablespoons sugar

FOR THE FILLING:
¼ cup pitted prunes, chopped
¼ cup dried apricots, chopped
¼ cup raisins
¼ cup toasted almonds, chopped
¼ cup toasted hazelnuts, chopped
2 tablespoons fig or apricot jam
Juice of ½ orange
2 tablespoons grated orange zest
1 tablespoon hot water

¼ cup unsalted butter
¼ cup sugar
3 tablespoons light rum (optional)

◆ To make the batter, in a bowl, whisk together the eggs, milk, and rum until blended. Whisk in the flour a little at a time, and then whisk in the salt and sugar to make a thin, lump-free batter. Alternatively, process in a blender for 2 or 3 minutes. You should have about 4½ cups batter. Cover the batter and refrigerate for 2 hours. If, after this period, the batter seems too thick — it should be the consistency of thick cream — thin it by beating in a little milk.

◆ To make the filling, in a bowl, stir together the prunes, apricots, raisins, almonds, and hazelnuts. Add the jam, the orange juice and zest, and the hot water and stir to blend all the ingredients together.

◆ Preheat an oven to 400 degrees F.

◆ Heat a 12-inch skillet, preferably nonstick, over medium heat. Flick a drop of water into the pan; if it sizzles and spatters, the pan is ready. Drop 1 teaspoon of the butter into the pan. Once it melts, tilt the pan so the butter evenly coats the bottom. Pour a scant ¼ cup batter into the pan, quickly tilting and swirling the pan to coat the bottom. Pour off any excess and return to the heat, shaking the pan to even out the batter. In a very short time the batter will begin to form bubbles on the surface, to dry at the edges, and to pull away from the pan. Using a spatula, turn over the crêpe and cook it for just a moment on the other side. Remove to a plate and keep warm. Repeat, adding 1 teaspoon butter to the pan for each crêpe, until all the batter has been used. Stack the crêpes as they are cooled.

◆ To fill, place a heaping tablespoon of the filling in the center of each warm crêpe, then fold in the sides, overlapping them to make an oblong packet about 2 inches by 4 inches. Place the folded packets snugly in a baking dish. Dot them with the remaining butter and sprinkle them with the sugar. Bake until heated through and the sugar has melted, 10 to 15 minutes. Serve immediately, drizzled with more rum if desired.

Peach and Nectarine Gratin

SERVES 6 TO 8

A scant amount of batter is just enough to bind this confection together, and the crumbled sugar, butter, and walnut topping makes a crunchy crust over the fruits. Other fruits such as pears, apples, or prune plums may be substituted.

    4 tablespoons unsalted butter
    6 tablespoons sugar
    2 peaches, peeled, pitted, and quartered
    2 nectarines, peeled, pitted, and quartered
    1 egg
    ¼ cup milk
    ¼ cup all-purpose flour
    ⅛ teaspoon salt
    ¼ cup coarsely chopped walnuts or almonds
    ½ teaspoon dried lavender flowers (optional)

◆ Preheat an oven to 425 degrees F. Using 2 tablespoons of the butter, heavily grease a 9-inch pie dish, then sprinkle 2 tablespoons of the sugar over the bottom.

◆ Place all the quartered fruits, cut side down, in the pie dish. In a bowl, whisk together the egg, milk, flour, and salt until there are no lumps. Pour the batter evenly over the fruit, letting it drizzle down through the pieces to the bottom of the dish.

◆ In a small bowl, stir together the remaining 4 tablespoons sugar, the nuts, and the lavender, if using. Sprinkle evenly over the fruit. Cut the remaining 2 tablespoons butter into small pieces and use to dot the top.

◆ Bake until the topping is crisp, the fruit is tender when pierced with the tip of a knife, and the batter has puffed and cooked through, about 15 minutes. Serve hot or warm.

Melon Sorbet

MAKES ABOUT 1 QUART; SERVES 6

The distinct varietal taste of the melon is maintained in this sorbet, but it is heightened by a little lemon juice. Each bite is an icy explosion of pure melon. Try making three different sorbets and serving a scoop of each, or serve a single sorbet with a slice of the melon from which it was made as garnish.

    2 cups sugar
    1 cup water
    4 cups peeled, seeded, and coarsely chopped melon such as
        cantaloupe, honeydew, or Charentais
    Juice of ½ lemon (about 1 tablespoon)
    Raspberries, blackberries, or melon slice for garnish (optional)

◆ Combine the sugar and the water in a small saucepan over medium heat. Bring to a simmer and cook, stirring often, until the sugar has dissolved and a thin syrup has formed, about 5 minutes. Remove from the heat and set aside to cool.

◆ When the syrup is cool, combine it with the chopped melon and the lemon juice in a food processor or blender and process until coarsely pureed. Transfer to an ice cream maker and freeze according to the manufacturer's directions.

◆ To serve, scoop onto chilled plates or into bowls and garnish with berries or a slice of fresh melon, if desired. The sorbet can be stored in the freezer for up to 2 weeks.

Honey-Quince Ice Cream

MAKES ABOUT 1 QUART

The glorious rose-amber color the quinces impart to the ice cream is reason alone to make it. The flavor, though, outshines even the extraordinary color. The honey gives a deep sweetness, and the quince lends its exotic, vaguely citrus flavor.

    4 or 5 large quinces
    4 cups granulated sugar
    2 cups water
    1 vanilla bean, split lengthwise
    2 tablespoons fresh lemon juice
    2 cups heavy cream
    2 cups milk
    ½ cup light liquid honey such as *millefleur,* acacia, or clover
    ½ cup firmly packed brown sugar
    ¼ teaspoon salt
    4 egg yolks
    1 teaspoon freshly grated nutmeg
    ¼ teaspoon ground cloves

◆ Peel and core the quinces. Cut the fruits into large chunks and set aside. Combine the granulated sugar, water, vanilla bean, and lemon juice in a non-reactive saucepan large enough to hold the quince eventually. Bring to a boil over medium-high heat and continue to boil, stirring often, until a light to medium-thick syrup forms, about 10 minutes. Reduce the heat to low and add the quinces. Poach the fruits until just barely tender when pierced with the tines of a fork, about 15 minutes. The cooking time will vary depending upon the fruits' maturity.

❋ Using a slotted spoon, remove the quince pieces from the syrup, draining them well over the pan. Discard the syrup or reserve it for another use. Set aside ½ cup of the quince pieces. Puree the remainder in a blender. Transfer to a bowl. You should have about 4 cups puree.

◆ In a heavy-bottomed saucepan, combine the cream, milk, honey, brown sugar, and salt. Bring to just below a boil over medium-high heat, stirring often until the sugar has dissolved. Meanwhile, in a bowl, whisk together the egg yolks until they are lemon colored. Slowly whisk about 1 cup of the hot milk mixture into the yolks. Now, whisk the hot yolk mixture into the hot milk mixture, and continue to cook, stirring constantly, until the mixture thickens enough to coat the back of a spoon, about 10 minutes. Remove from the heat and let cool to lukewarm.

◆ Whisk about 1 cup of the cooked milk-egg mixture into the quince purée. Finally, whisk this mixture into the remaining milk-egg mixture, and then whisk in the nutmeg and cloves.

◆ Transfer to an ice cream maker and freeze according to the manufacturer's directions. To serve, scoop into bowls. Chop the reserved quince and scatter over the top.

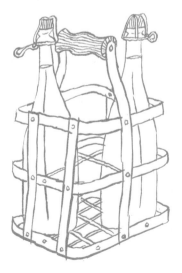

Upside-down Vanilla Cream with Strawberries and Raspberries

SERVES 4

The delicate custard, lightly flavored with a few berries, dissolves in your mouth, and the puree of fruit that dresses the custard tastes tart and refreshing.

> 1 tablespoon unsalted butter
> ½ cup sugar
> 1½ cups milk
> 2 eggs
> ½ cup raspberries
> ¼ cup strawberries, hulled and coarsely chopped
> Boiling water, as needed
> 1 tablespoon water

♦ Preheat an oven to 350 degrees F. Select four ¾-cup ramekins or custard cups and grease them with the butter. Sprinkle each prepared dish with about 1 teaspoon sugar to coat the bottom and sides evenly, then shake out any excess sugar. Set aside.

♦ Pour the milk into a small saucepan and place over medium heat just until it is steaming. Meanwhile, in a bowl, combine the eggs and 4 tablespoons of the sugar. Beat with a wire whisk or rotary beater until the mixture is pale yellow and thick enough to fall in ribbons from a spoon, about 10 minutes. Gradually pour the hot milk into the egg mixture, whisking continuously to incorporate it. Strain the mixture through a fine-mesh sieve into a clean bowl. Combine the raspberries and strawberries in a bowl, toss to mix, and remove ¼ cup to use for making the sauce. Add the remaining berries to the custard. Divide the custard evenly among the prepared ramekins or cups. Place them in a baking dish and pour boiling water into the dish to reach halfway up the sides of the custard dishes. Place in the oven and bake until a knife inserted into the center of a custard comes out clean, 40 to 45 minutes.

◆ Remove the ramekins or cups from the water bath and set aside to cool completely. (If you would like to unmold them and serve them warm, place them in a bath of cold water to which a few ice cubes have been added and let stand for 5 to 10 minutes, then unmold as directed below.)

◆ To unmold, slide a knife between the edge of the custard and the dish to loosen it. Invert an individual plate on top of each custard and, holding both the plate and the custard dish firmly, invert them. The custard will drop gently onto the plate. Lift off the custard dish.

◆ To prepare the sauce, mash or puree the reserved berries with the remaining 2 tablespoons sugar and the water.

◆ Spoon a little sauce around each custard and serve.

Nougat Noir

MAKES ABOUT 18 PIECES

This favorite holiday candy, was, until only recently, homemade throughout the kitchens of Haute Provence, using the region's local honey and almonds. One of the traditional thirteen desserts for Christmas Eve, it still appears on the table the night of December 24, but is more often purchased than homemade. It is not difficult to make, as it is simply a mixture of honey and nuts. The almonds become toasted during the cooking, and are bound together with the honey, which has become chewy. The trick is to spread it into the waiting mold at just the right moment, when it is cooked neither too little nor too long. Use light honey, as the dark honeys may change flavor when cooked over high heat.

½ teaspoon unsalted butter
½ pound light honey (¾ cup)
½ pound shelled, unskinned almonds (1¾ cups)

◆ Prepare a mold, such as an aluminum ice-cube tray, with the interior removed, by greasing it with the butter and then lining it with parchment paper.

◆ In a heavy-bottomed pot, heat the honey over medium-high heat, stirring until it boils. Add all the almonds, and keep stirring. Reduce the heat to medium and continue to stir. The mixture will thicken, the almonds will cook, and the honey will change from golden to dark caramel brown. It is essential to keep stirring in order to prevent the almonds from burning. When it reads 250 degrees F on a candy thermometer and is brown, it is time to pour it into the prepared mold. Spread it evenly across the surface and top with a piece of parchment paper. Put a weight, such as a brick, on top and let the candy cool.

◆ When thoroughly cold, unmold the nougat, peel off the parchment, and cut into 1-inch squares. It should be firm, yet cuttable. Store in an airtight tin. The candies will keep for about 2 weeks.

Fig Jam

MAKES ABOUT 1 ½ PINTS

In the past, when fig orchards flanked the hillsides of Haute Provence, fig jam was common fare in the local households. Today, there are far fewer trees and many of them are wild. Fig jam is now considered a special treat, rather than a homely staple. It is extremely easy to make, and each fig variety will render a jam of a different flavor and color. Some figs have undertones of citrus, others of strawberries or of spices. Skin color ranges from bright yellow-green to shades of brown and deepest purple, while the flesh might be amber, rose-pink, or garnet.

2 pounds soft, ripe figs, any kind
½ cup water
2 tablespoons fresh lemon juice
1 tablespoon minced lemon zest
2 cups sugar

◆ Coarsely chop the figs and combine them with the water in a saucepan. Place over medium heat and bring to a simmer. Cook until the figs have dissolved somewhat to make a thick sauce, 10 to 15 minutes. Add the lemon juice and zest and sugar and increase the heat to medium-high. Cook, stirring, until a candy thermometer inserted into the mixture registers 220 degrees F, another 10 to 15 minutes. The jam is ready when it will coat a horizontally held spoon and fall from the lower edge of it in a single sheet or stream, no longer forming individual drips.

◆ Have ready hot, sterilized canning jars, either with screw-top rings and fitted lids with hinges, or glass lids with rubber rings (European style). Ladle the jam into the jars and cap tightly. Let cool and then verify for a seal. If using screw-ring types, the lids should be concave. On glass-lidded jars, the seal has taken if you cannot readily lift open the glass lid when the wire hinge has been released. If the seals are not good, store in the refrigerator for up to 6 months. If the seals are good, store in a cool, dark place. Once opened, they will keep in the refrigerator for up to 4 weeks.

Bibliography

Aliquot, Hervé. *Les Alpes de Haute Provence*. Avignon: Aubanel, 1976.

Amouretti, Marie-Claire, and Georges Comet. *L'Olivier en Provence*. Aix-en-Provence: Edisud, 1979.

Benoit, Fernand. *La Provence et le Comtat Venaissin*. Paris: Gallimard, 1949.

Blanc, Gabriel-Henri. *Autrefois . . . la table*. Cotignac: Gabriell-Henri Blanc, 1994.

Brennan, Georgeanne. *Potager: Fresh Garden Cooking in the French Style*. San Francisco: Chronicle Books, 1992.

———. *Aperitif: Recipes for Simple Pleasures in the French Style*. San Francisco: Chronicle Books, 1997.

Damon, Jean-Louis. *La Cuisine au pays d'Annot et ses environs*. Nice: Serre Editeur, 1995.

Domenge, Georges. *Cuisine de tradition du Var et des Alpes du Sud*. Aix-en-Provence: Edisud, 1993.

Escallier, Christine and Danielle Musset. *Pétrir, frire, mijoter: Les Cuisines des Alpes du Sud*. Salagon: Les Alpes de Lumière, 1991.

Guitteny, Marc. *Herbes et plantes de Provence*. La Bernerie, France: Editions Marc Guitteny, 1993.

Meunier, Christiane. *Lavandes et lavandins*. Aix-en-Provence: Edisud, 1985.

Musset, Danielle. *Lavandes et plantes aromatiques: Un Itinéraire de découverte en Haute Provence*. Salagon, France: Les Alpes de Lumière, 1989.

———, et al. "Revenons à nos moutons . . ." *Histoire et actualité de la transhumance en Provence*. Salagon, France: Les Alpes de Lumière, 1987.

Nazet, Marion. *Cuisine et fêtes en Provence*. Aix-en-Provence: Edisud, 1992.

Ollivier-Elliott, Patrick. *Terres de Sault d'Albion et de Banon*. Aix-en-Provence: Edisud, 1996.

Olney, Richard. *Provence the Beautiful Cookbook*. San Francisco: Collins, 1993.

Reboul, J.-B. *La Cuisinière provençale*. Vingt-troisième Edition. Marseille: Tacussel, 1985.

Rocchia, Jean-Marie. *Des Truffes en général et de la Rabasse en particulier*. Avignon: Editions A. Barthélemy, 1992.

Sabatier, Robert, and Becker, Georges. *Le Gratin des champignons*. Editions Jacques Glénat et Roland Sabatier, 1986.

Index

What's on the Disc

The companion CD-ROM contains software developed by the authors, plus an assortment of third-party tools and product demos. The disc is designed to be explored using a browser program. Using the browser, you can view information concerning products and companies, and install programs with a single click of the mouse. To install the browser, here's what to do.

Windows 3.1 Installation Instructions

1. Insert the CD-ROM disc into your CD-ROM drive.
2. From File Manager or Program Manager, choose Run from the File menu.
3. Type <drive>\setup and press Enter (<drive> corresponds to the drive letter of your CD-ROM). For example, if your CD-ROM is drive D:, type D:\SETUP and press Enter.
4. Installation creates a Program Manager group named Teach Yourself VB DB. To browse the CD-ROM, double-click on the Guide to the CD-ROM icon inside this Program Manager group.

Windows 95 Installation Instructions

1. Insert the CD-ROM disc into your CD-ROM drive. If the AutoPlay feature of your Windows 95 system is enabled, the setup program will start automatically.
2. If the setup program does not start automatically, double-click on the My Computer icon.
3. Double-click on the icon representing your CD-ROM drive.
4. Double-click on the icon titled Setup.exe to run the installation program. Follow the on-screen instructions that appear. When the setup ends, the Guide to the CD-ROM starts up so that you can begin browsing immediately.

Following installation, you can restart the Guide to the CD-ROM program by pressing the Start button, selecting Programs, and selecting Teach Yourself VB DB and Guide to the CD-ROM.

Note: The browser program requires at least 256 colors. For best results, set your monitor to display between 256 and 64,000 colors. A screen resolution of 640×480 pixels is also recommended. If necessary, adjust your monitor settings before using the CD-ROM.

Table of Equivalents

The exact equivalents in the following tables have been rounded for convenience.

LIQUID AND DRY MEASURES

U.S.	METRIC
¼ teaspoon	1.25 milliliters
½ teaspoon	2.5 milliliters
1 teaspoon	5 milliliters
1 tablespoon (3 teaspoons)	15 milliliters
1 fluid ounce (2 tablespoons)	30 milliliters
¼ cup	60 milliliters
⅓ cup	80 milliliters
1 cup	120 milliliters
1 pint (2 cups)	480 milliliters
1 quart (4 cups, 32 ounces)	960 milliliters
1 gallon (4 quarts)	3.84 liters
1 ounce *(by weight)*	28 grams
¼ pound (4 ounces)	114 grams
1 pound	454 grams
2.2 pounds	1 kilogram

LENGTH MEASURES

U.S.	METRIC
⅛ inch	3 millimeters
¼ inch	6 millimeters
½ inch	12 millimeters
1 in	2.5 centimeters

OVEN TEMPERATURES

FAHRENHEIT	CELSIUS	GAS
250	120	½
275	140	1
300	150	2
325	160	3
350	180	4
375	190	5
400	200	6
425	220	7
450	230	8
475	240	9
500	260	10

Nyons
JABRON
Noyers
Montagne
de Lure
DURANCE
Sault
Redortiers
Banon
Plateau
d'Albion
Forcalquier
Manosque
Valensole
Esparron
Gorges
de Verdon
HAUTE PR